FISHING FOR

Barrie Rickards with part of a morning's catch of 27 tench and three bream totalling 162lb, one of the best single-session, one-man catches in tench-fishing history.

# FISHING FOR BIG TENCH

By

Barrie Rickards, Ray Webb
& Martin Gay

**Camden Publishing Co. Ltd.**
323 Upper Street, Islington,
London N1 2XQ, England

First published in Great Britain by
ROD AND GUN PUBLISHING LTD.,

© 1976 *By* BARRIE RICKARDS and RAY WEBB

Reprinted 1979

1986 Enlarged & Revised Edition
Published by The Camden Publishing Co. Ltd.
323 Upper Street, London N1 2XQ
© 1986 by BARRIE RICKARDS, RAY WEBB AND MARTIN GAY

ALL RIGHTS RESERVED. NO PART OF THIS PUBLICATION MAY BE REPRODUCED, STORED IN A RETRIEVAL SYSTEM, OR TRANSMITTED IN ANY FORM OR BY ANY MEANS, ELECTRONIC, MECHANICAL, PHOTOCOPYING, RECORDING OR OTHERWISE WITHOUT PRIOR PERMISSION OF THE COPYRIGHT OWNER.

ISBN 0 900249 11 0

PRINTED AND BOUND IN GREAT BRITAIN BY
NENE LITHO AND WOOLNOUGH BOOKBINDING,
BOTH OF IRTHLINGBOROUGH, NORTHANTS.

This new edition contains a total of four new chapters, new photographs, and is thoroughly revised throughout, including addition of notes at the end of chapters, where judged necessary. Photographs and line drawings have been renumbered as figures 1-n; and all cross references have been corrected accordingly.

# Preface and Acknowledgements to the First Edition

NATURALLY the preface to a book is the last part that you write, and as I pen this (November 13th, 1975) the weekly angling newspapers have just announced the acceptance by the British Record (rod caught) Fish Committee of a new record tench of 10lb 1oz, thus exceeding Mr Salisbury's Hemingford Grey fish by exactly 1lb. It is amazing how many giant fish weigh exactly 1oz over some magical poundage figure! Apparently the net in which the tench was weighed has still to be checked by the Committee's secretary, Peter Tombleson, but if the weight is shown to be correct then tench angling has its first-ever, authentic, double-figure fish and we can all rejoice in the reflected glory of Mr Lewis Brown, the captor. This great tench was caught in a Peterborough brick pit, and may well be the last claim to be accepted without production of the body of the fish: I hope it turns out to be a ten-pounder for it validates some of the comments I make in this book, and will enable the reader to ignore with glee some of the other comments I make! It seems a fine moment for a book on big tench to appear in print, and I'm sure Derek Swift, John Gibbons and Alan Vare, the enthusiastic, mad bunch from *Rod and Gun Publishing*, will not be long in getting it on to the bookshelves.

Of course, Ray and I could not have written this book without a great deal of help from other tench anglers. We should like to thank several anglers for their most generous contributions in the form of chapters or parts of chapters: David Mawer, Fred Carter, Terry Coulson, Revd Alston, Peter Wheat, and Eric Hodgson. Not only would the book have been seriously depleted without these contributions, but Ray and I would have risked over-exposure and the reader becoming bored with us. The same applies to the photographs: we received an overwhelming response to our appeal for interesting tench pictures, and only the modern stringencies on publications have prevented the publishers from using all the pictures received. I think the readers will agree, however, that they have done a magnificent job in publishing far more photographs than do most angling books. For the photographs used and supplied we thank the following most warmly: Fred Carter, Steve Crawshaw, Martin Gay, Eric Hodgson, Len Head, Ed Foottit, Dave Mawer, Bob Church, Robin Haywood, and Peter Jackson. In addition we would single out Steve Crawshaw, who really did pull the stops out for us, and the Tenchfishers who gave unstintingly of information to a couple of anglers who are not, if we are honest about it, quite in their league as tench fishers. We would also particularly like to thank Christine Rickards who did the typing, and David Bursill who prepared the prints from the authors' negatives. It has given Ray and I great pleasure writing the book and we hope you derive as much pleasure and success from reading it. At a late stage it was decided to add further text-figures, and these are labelled A-H. However, cross-reference is clear and the reader should not be confused in any way.

*Barrie Rickards*
*4 Willow Crescent*
*Milton*
*Nr. Cambridge*
*November 13th, 1975*

# Preface to the Second Edition

It is almost a decade since I penned the preface to the first edition and a great deal has happened. The tench record has been broken again by fish of 10lb 1oz 4dr. and 12lb 8oz 11dr. from Wilstone Reservoir near Tring in Hertfordshire. In fact this is only a few drams more than the 1975 record holder but several other near misses have been recorded including some that were certainly just above the record at the time of capture. Yet to think on records only is to look at the tip of the iceberg. The truth is that during the last decade tench fishing has taken off as never before in recorded history. Anyone who digests our first edition will be aware that a tench of 6lb was regarded as quite outstanding and a seven pound fish as bordering on the unbelievable. It is correct that Ray still holds the Irish record with that splendid fish of 7lb 13¼oz, but on this side of the Irish Sea seven pound fish have been caught in many parts of the country with fair numbers of eight pounders and several in excess of nine pounds. The reasons for the relative lack of big Irish tench, especially considering its pre-eminent position to 1975, are puzzling and obscure – perhaps fishing pressure from tourists has dropped during recent troubled times, or possibly the tench of 1975 were at a growth ceiling. Whatever the plight of the Irish, tench fishing here has been dream-like. When will it all end? I'll try to answer that question shortly, but meantime cannot resist quoting my prophetic words from the Introduction to the first edition: "We may be about to see a considerable revival in tench fishing . . ."

It has been claimed that tackle improvements and new techniques are the cause of the superb results of the last decade. There have without question been fundamental advances in both facets and these we shall consider in the new chapters of this edition, myself dealing with techniques and tackle and Martin Gay considering new baits, amongst other matters. But to my mind there is clear evidence that such matters are not the *cause* of the good tench fishing. Good tench are the cause and they are big because they have grown so on a widespread scale. Spectacular though the captures of 7lb plus fish have been, they tend to obscure the fact that over the whole nation the average size of tench has risen; and in waters which produced fish to 3½lb in 1975, 5½ pounders are now being caught. Such fish do not hit the headlines today but the fact that waters all over the country are producing bigger fish than they have hitherto yielded proves that, for some reason, tench are growing bigger.

Why should tench have grown so much better during the last decade? I believe that the answer is to be found in considering the northern hemisphere distribution of the species. Within the U.K. the tench is close to its northern limits of tolerance. This is not simply a matter that the further north one goes the more acid the waters become, but largely a matter of temperature. In northern maritime lands the tench does not go much further north than 55°, and never as big fish. In continental climes, with very hot summers, it persists a little further north but again declines in size. In short, the tench is vulnerable to temperature changes and in particular to the dangers of winterkill in the shallow lakes of these islands, which have in addition problems of anaerobic environments developing beneath thick ice cover.

Now, prolonged ice cover is something of a rarity in this country but in 1947 lakes were locked in the grip of thick ice for several months and thousands of tench, especially, died. Prior to 1947 some quite big tench were being caught, of six and, rarely, seven pounds. After that freeze-up a slow recovery took place and, just prior to the 1963 freeze-up, a few big fish were again showing, some sixteen years being enough to allow a recovery of the tench populations and a growing on of the older fish. 1963 saw heavy mortalities of tench beneath the ice, the extent of it only becoming apparent of course as the ice thawed and stinking corpses were found.

Since then there has been no real freeze-up lasting more than three weeks: I estimate that it needs at least eight weeks to effect thorough winterkill with a minimum of survivors. So the tench have had 22 years to recover and grow on, and it is no surprise to me that around 1980, 17 years after 1963, the full extent of the tench "boom" became obvious to everyone. It could yet go on for a while, dependent only on the timing of the next freeze and the strength of the backup stocks to the current older, giant fish.

By coincidence anglers in this country were ready for the boom with vastly improved tackle and techniques and quite stupendous catches were taken. First and foremost of these anglers was the new contributor to this book, Martin Gay, a friend of mine for many years. For several seasons he caught, to his pair of modern rods, more giant tench than all other serious tench anglers put together. The special reasons for this are outlined by him in chapters 3 and 9, but paramount in the saga are the very skilled uses of modern baits and modern ideas, and the equally skilled use of new techniques.

Finally let me return to that prophetic Introduction to the first edition: "There are things to come for me, I'm sure, since I've never had a 6lb fish, in spite of all the five-pounders. I hope to crack that one . . . with a seven pounder". Well, I had some six pounders and a seven pounder, and I cannot realistically ask for anything more! And if you ask me to be prophetic now I cannot be so: I *hope* for a few more winters without a winterkill, though our chances decrease! If the temperature stays high we could yet see a sprinkling of eleven and twelve pound fish . . .

Barrie Rickards

# Contents

| | | |
|---|---|---|
| | Preface and Acknowledgements | 7 |
| | Preface to the 2nd edition | 9 |
| 1 | Introduction | 15 |
| 2 | Giant Tench | 20 |
| 3 | Supergiants | 39 |
| 4 | Basic Tackle | 47 |
| 5 | New Tackle & Techniques | 70 |
| 6 | Food of Tench | 78 |
| 7 | Tench Swims | 92 |
| 8 | Analysis of a new water | 105 |
| 9 | Analysis of the finest tench water in history | 115 |
| 10 | Where and when to fish | 129 |
| 11 | Winter Tench | 139 |
| 12 | Irish Tench | 143 |
| 13 | Weather and water conditions | 158 |
| 14 | Playing Tench | 166 |
| 15 | A Tench Trip | 173 |
| 16 | The Tenchfishers | 178 |
| 17 | Biology of the Tench | 183 |
| 18 | Modern Research | 192 |
| 19 | Tench Fishing – The Future | 203 |
| | References | 207 |

CHAPTER 1

# Introduction

THE time was 4 a.m., the place the banks of the River Shannon at Lanesborough in County Longford, Ireland, and the action was quickly forthcoming, for with the first cast of the day I was into a fish that was obviously a good one, even in the light of a somewhat murky dawn. Successfully netted after a brief tussle, the tench, for such it turned out to be, was quickly unhooked, placed in a bag of precisely 1oz weight and hooked on to the spring balance to record a weight that was way beyond my expectations, for I'd estimated it somewhere around the 6½lb mark. Without announcing my reading I asked Mitcham angler Frank Ordoyno, fishing the next peg downstream, to check-weigh on his balance, and on doing so he immediately proclaimed a new Irish record of 7lb 13oz as near as he could make it. In an instant the dozen or more anglers out along the bank gathered round to admire the capture and a set of scales with tripod and weighing basket was produced, capable of recording to the dram, the needle stopping this time just ¼oz over the previously announced figure. Proven beyond all doubt at this stage we still had to weigh-in on tested and approved business scales in the town, no easy matter at this early hour and it was only after rousing Lanesborough Development Official Bill Brennan out of bed that we finally gained access to a set of Avery scales that confirmed the new record at 7lb 13¼oz, just 1¼oz heavier than the previous best.

Extremely elated by such an outstanding capture, I resumed fishing around 6.15 a.m. and persevered for a further five hours or more, but for once my mind wasn't on the job, my thoughts continually turning to the various highlights and breakthroughs of a tench fishing career that stretched back a full 25 years or more, a quarter of a century of thought, study, experiment and persistent effort.

It was way back in my early schooldays in Sheffield that I first witnessed the action curve of a rod bent double by the pull of this consistently hard-fighting species, a far-off day when three young enthusiasts cycled over to Harthill to fish the middle reservoir, only to find several of the regular local men occupying the swims we had set our hearts on. Settling down as near as possible, our best efforts produced one minute pike of around 6oz taken on maggot, between the three of us for a full morning's fishing; but around mid-afternoon a lively breeze sprang up accompanied by the first glimpse of sunshine for the day and straightway one of the local men's rods was bent over to an alarming degree. Regular gudgeon catchers with the occasional small roach thrown in at that stage, we advised the unfortunate fellow to 'bang the butt end of your rod mister', a ruse that we had often employed successfully when hooked on a snag ourselves, to be met with silent contempt as the angler continued to exert the maximum pressure his 6x hook length would permit, for this was in the days before monofilament line, when plaited silk measured in O's and gut yard bottoms in X's were still in vogue. It was some considerable time before we realised that the 'snag' was moving, slowly and irresistably taking line out against the check of the centre pin reel, and after a prolonged battle our comments were decisively terminated by the breathtaking sight of a tremendous boil on the surface as an olive-flanked fish headed back down into the depths. Half a dozen times or more the performance was repeated before the fish was finally lifted and held on the surface to be drawn to the waiting net and hauled ashore. At somewhere around the 3lb mark, the size and beauty of this first-ever tench in our extremely youthful eyes made such an impact that all three of us were immediately struck with tench fever, a condition that in my case at any rate, shows no signs of abating even to this very day; the smooth rounded lines of form, powerful fins and bright red eye commanding my admiration as strongly as ever.

Back home at the end of the day enquiries were made amongst neighbouring anglers about this newly discovered species, which local waters contained them, appropriate tackle, baits and groundbait, etc. and a start was made, though initial progress was so slight as to be virtually non-existent. Eventually, however, I did succeed in landing a very welcome tench of $2\frac{1}{2}$lb, this one also coming from Harthill Reservoir and my feet were firmly planted on the first rung of the ladder that was to take me to a series of outstanding catches culminating in 1971 with the 7lb $13\frac{1}{4}$oz Irish record.

For Barrie, although he achieved equivalent status with the zander, the breaking of a National Tench Record is yet to come! Actually, he always felt his progress with tench to be terribly slow with more headaches than elation, and for long periods he felt he wasn't getting anywhere at all. Rather like walking in a vat of treacle; although this may reflect his penchant for fishing small, muddy, farm ponds. By and large these are not the places for big tench, say over 4lb, and the usual average weight is 1lb-3lb. But let him tell his history himself:—

Like Ray it was seeing somebody else get a tench that gave me the bug. Twenty-two years ago I approached a tiny farm pond at Snaith in the West Riding with a view to fishing for anything that came along. It was pretty early, about 5 a.m. and I was shattered when I breasted the rise behind the pond to see a mist-shrouded figure crouched in 'my' swim and clutching a big box of Puffed Wheat. Of course, *I* thought he was having his breakfast, but it turned out he was fishing for tench using a single grain of wheat about a couple of inches from a sizeable shot, with a small porcupine quill float set about 6in over depth. Although this constituted a lift rig (see later!) he didn't label it for me, and I remember the bites were decisive enough with barely a lift of the float before it sank out of sight. I could hardly contain myself (standing on a rickety platform of branches) as his rod really bent as he strove to keep the fish out of the weed beds. That fish, when netted, went only about 1lb, and it was rather a dark brown fish on its back, but its red eye commanded attention, and its thick, yet petal-like fins waved in indignation. He got several fish that morning, and in subsequent weeks I took up to five or six fish up to nearly 3lb at each sitting, as well as some good perch over the 1lb mark, and a 10lb pike.

That Tench Pond, for as such it became known, was only 25 yards in diameter, circular, and with 2 feet of weedy water above 3 feet of black mud. I learnt a lot by catching plenty of tench, but the idea of small farm ponds became firmly implanted in my mind as far as tench go, and the notion took a lot of shifting despite a 3lb-plus fish from the nearby Cowick clays pits in a swim 10 feet deep. I did manage to graduate to Carlton Towers which was a *large* shallow, muddy, water! and there the average weight of my fish went up to nearly 3lb and it was unusual to get them much under 2lb. It was at this water, incidently, that Ray and I first met when tench fishing as I think we explained in some detail in 'Fishing for Big Pike'.

I began to realize eventually (for fishing conclusions dawn slowly with me), that bigger, deeper waters yielded bigger, deeper tench.

And the matter was finally driven home to me when I saw tench certainly in excess of 6lb spawning in a deep brick pit in the East Riding of Yorkshire, at Newport. Naturally I began to look around a bit and fished a variety of waters including gravel pits in Yorkshire and Cambridgeshire. In the last county I was totally sucked in by stories of big tench at Landbeach Lakes and spent several summers catching enormous numbers of tench up to 3lb 14oz, before I appreciated that the weekly stories of 4lb and 5lb fish were figments of the local imagination, or worse. . . . I did eventually get a 4lb-plus fish from the small lake, where the average size was greater at 3lb than in the larger lake (1lb 14oz). From then on things began to improve, and I had four-pounders at Southill Lake in Bedfordshire, surely the most consistently good tench lake in history.

Apart from this appreciation of the *type* of water likely to yield bigger fish, I had one major snag to overcome, namely that in June each year I was hopelessly bogged down, at first *taking* examinations, then *giving* them! Because of this I missed the cream of some good tench fishing, and still do as a matter of fact, and the most disappointing of all was to miss Garnafailagh's heyday. Ray and a few others 'discovered' this water, but all I could do was to get there in early May *before* the tench came on, or in July when they were going off! In July 1968 I again arrived at Garnafailagh too late, with the exception that this time it wasn't: for some reason, possibly connected with a heat wave, the tench had been 'off' for weeks, and I arrived to fish a swim that Ray, John Weston and Dave Cumpstone had kept going with bait and groundbait but without much in the way of results. You can imagine how I felt, not only was I 'late' but the weather turned rather squally, with some hot sun, but a lot of wind and rain too. And yet that is what did the trick, for the first morning I took 27 tench and three bream for a weight of 162lb, and finished the week with 55 tench averaging 5lb 2oz, with six at $5\frac{3}{4}$lb. I'd had five-pounders before, but this catch was really a pinacle of years of tenching and I'm sure it will remain so for me, whatever I catch in the future. It is probably the second best catch in tench angling history, being bettered by Eric Hodgson's astonishing 83 fish catch. Both catches are described in detail in Chapter 3, for they are certainly worth looking at in detail. There are things to come for me, I'm sure, since I've never had a 6lb fish, in spite of all the five-pounders. I hope I crack that one in the same way that Eric Hodgson did – with a seven-pounder.

Such then were two of the highlights of our tench-fishing careers, demonstrating in as dramatic a fashion as could ever be hoped for, the value of a painstaking, thorough approach to the problems encountered, no stones being left unturned in our efforts to get to grips with the really outsize specimens. Pressing on regardless of set-backs and disappointments the success finally achieved was sufficient to establish our names in the tench fishing scene along with anglers like Murgett, the Taylor Brothers, Salisbury and the Revd Alston, although thinking about it, perhaps we don't quite measure up to those stalwarts! The Revd Alston actually stocked the water from which his record tench came: that surely takes some beating. The Taylor Brothers really set the angling world alight with tench talk when everything was swinging into the big carp boom, and the approach and techniques they evolved have lasted until the present day as a kind of backbone to tench fishing activities. We may be about to see a considerable revival in tench fishing, relative to carp that is, and we sincerely hope we'll be in there amongst the big ones with both tenchfishers and Tenchfishers.

CHAPTER 2

# Giant Tench
*Barrie Rickards*

TENCH are just about the best-loved British freshwater fish: all anglers have a soft spot for them. Yet during the last twenty years or so, although that enthusiastic band, the Tenchfishers, has kept going a deep interest in them, tench have tended to be overshadowed by the bigger carp and the terrific expansion of carp fishing. Even Richard Walker, who led with others the revolution in carp fishing, preferred to fish for tench by way of relaxation after struggles with carp hunting! Before carp became such an 'in' fish, before many waters were stocked with fast-growing common carp, the tench was probably the best chance most anglers had of doing battle with a lusty fighter on balmy summer days. Nowadays big carp are very widespread, grow bigger than tench, usually fight superbly, and have ousted the tench amongst those who look for these attributes in a fish. But anglers love tench just as much as before, and the band of fanatics grows.

The God many tenchers worship is the 10lb fish. Twenty years ago most keen tench anglers were saying that the ten-pounder was just around the corner: its coming was nigh. It never came. The British Record was held for a while by the Revd E. C. Alston with a 7lb fish from Ring Mere in Norfolk; the same weight as Mr Stacey's (1882) Weston-Super-Mare fish, and later by a fish of 8½lb from a Leicestershire canal, a fish returned alive to the water. In 1963 Mr J. Salisbury took the present tench record of 9lb 1oz from some famous tench lakes at Hemingford Grey in Huntingdonshire. That's getting pretty close to the magical 10lb, and it may well be that the chances of a ten-pounder are greater today than ever before, not only because the tackle is generally better, but because an increasing number of 7lb-plus fish have been taken in recent years. Another nine-pounder is on record, caught in June 1970 by Peter Pilley of the Isis Specimen Group. At capture this weighed 9lb 1½oz, that is ½oz over Salisbury's record fish, but weighed again a considerable time later its weight had fallen to 8¾lb due to the loss of at least 1 pint of spawn. It seems a great pity to me that this fish was not accepted as the new record, for the clock balance used was presumably accurate and checked, and the capture was witnessed. The fish, pictured on the front page of 'Angling Times' for June 25th, was clearly a tremendous fish, and to me, at least, the weight of a fish is its weight *at capture*, not several hours later. I know a little of what Pete Pilley must have felt, for I once missed the zander record by something similar happening.

In the past a 7lb fish was almost heralded by trumpets, quite rightly so, and the fuss continued for years after Frank Murgett, the roach pole expert, took one of 7¾lb in 1952 from Blenheim Palace Lake. Since 1960 nearly 30 tench over 7lb have been reported, with no less than 12 of 8lb or over. One other nine-pounder is on record, that caught by Mr G. Young from a Berkshire pond in October 1964. There have been other reported big tench, and quite a few rumoured, but they have been unsatisfactory for varying reasons.

Fish in excess of 10lb *have* been caught, but in each case they have proved to be sick, dropsical fish, abnormally fat, and with an abnormal water content. They didn't look very nice and were not accepted as records. One was taken weighing 11lb from Wraysbury, Middlesex, and another of 12½lb from the River Kennet in 1951.

The Thornville Royal tench, a vermillion-bellied fish (see Chapter 17) that weighed 11lb 9¼oz, wasn't caught on rod and line but found trapped amongst roots when a pond was drained. The finders concluded that it had taken on the shape of its small prison, for it was unusually fat and unusually shaped. As Richard Walker says in 'Still Water Angling' the only odd thing is 'how a fish having the length and girth of a 30lb carp could weigh so little!' The engraving published by Denys Watkins-Pitchford ('BB', 1955) shows a bloated and dropsical-looking fish, so it is perhaps as well that it did not fall to rod and line: indeed, if it really *was* trapped, during life, amongst the roots, then that possibility never existed.

Ten-pounders undoubtedly exist. The Revd Alston saw them in the reed beds in Ring Mere (since dried up) at the time he took his record, and Richard Walker has played (and lost) them amongst water-lily roots criss-crossing unusually for several feet above the bottom. It almost looks as if giant tench haunt entangled areas.

Perusing the specimen tench list produced by Bob Church (1974), apart from the fact that most of the fish came from the southern part of the country they are remarkably widespread. I have already mentioned Frank Murgett's fish, and another of note is that of 7½lb taken by that tench fishing fanatic Eric Hodgson, whose achievements I discuss in the next chapter. This fish was taken in Yorkshire and is, in fact, just about the most northerly of all the big ones. Eric's fish was a climax to a lifetime of catching big tench. Bob Church doesn't include the Irish fish, of course, but for this information the annual Report of the Irish Specimen Fish Committee is invaluable. There you will find (see pp. 144-5), in the 1971 list that Ray holds the Irish record with a fish of 7lb 13¼oz: in addition he has had fish of 7lb 0¼oz and two at 7lb 1½oz, surely a fantastic achievement, for Irish tench fishing is every bit as difficult as British tench fishing.

Comparable British results have been achieved by Len Head of the Tenchfishers' Club, for not only did he have tench of 7lb 9oz and 7lb 10oz to his credit prior to 1975, but in the June of that year he had fish of 7lb 1oz and 8lb 2oz in one session, followed by a fish of 7lb 13oz a week or so later: truly a momentous record.

So the annals of tench fishing are every bit as full as those of carp fishing, with the distinct possibility that the best, in terms of giant fish, is yet to come. I hope that once again anglers will turn towards these big tench, and really *search* for them. It is almost certainly a case of *finding* a small population of very big fish, rather than trying to work out a technique that will sort out the giants from the average fish. I have a feeling also that the really immense tench feed in the middle of the day, since a surprising number of the 7lb-plus fish were taken then rather than at the classic early-morning period. The Revd Edward Alston's record tench was one such fish, and he has very kindly sent us his account of its capture and some related matter which I think the reader will enjoy:—

'The story is not much and does not take long to tell. It was all part of the experiments I made at Ring Mere at that time: the mere used to dry up about every twenty years, and remain dry for about a year. This, of course, meant that it was full of food for fish when it filled up again. In those days I did not kill the fish I caught, unless I wanted to eat them, but I stocked other places with them. I caught a bunch of rudd, roach and tench at Stamford Water and put them in Ring Mere which had just filled up after being dry and so was just right to take fish.

'I think it was as soon as the next year that I got evidence that the experiment was going well, as a boy I knew called Alan Hunt, who is still alive, caught a 3¼lb rudd. I went there straight away and had a wonderful catch of rudd with several fish of 4lb. The biggest of 4½lb

1. Superbly conditioned 5lb-plus fish taken by Peter Jackson.

3. Len Head with a superb tench of 7lb 10oz caught in 1974.

2. A brace of very big tench caught on sweetcorn.

and 4¼lb I had mounted by Griggs. I also noted the tench which seemed very large, and I came on another day and tried to catch them. I hooked them but they went straight into the weeds and I lost them. I did get the 7lb fish I now have mounted. It was not the biggest of them, nor was it a very fair fish as it had a complaint some tench do seem to get, and was full of a watery kind of spawn, a condition that I think is common to tench: I think they recover from it in a natural way. But it did weigh 7lb so I had it mounted. It was caught on a worm, groundbait was bran and bread, in the afternoon of a fine day.

'Of the other fish I put in, strangely the roach did not make much size. The odd pike I put in went to 12lb. They then must have started to extract water from the ground and Ring Mere started to dry up again. When low I went in with a landing net and saved what I could. The only large fish that I got were some very thin, large tench which each weighed about 6lb. They were so thin the tops of their backs were very sharp. I put them into other waters and one of them was caught by a keeper's wife in West Mere later on in the summer. It weighed about 7–8lb.

'My tench still exist in Thetford Heath as I put some in the small ponds around which did not dry up. I am told they are still being caught there. It is very strange that after years of being dry due to water abstraction that Ring Mere is now filling up again. What a chance for the people round there if they will only make use of it.

'I think I told you that I stocked the pond at Emmanuel (Barrie's College!). I happened to go there a short time ago and it is now almost just a puddle. In my time it took up most of that green and was quite a good place for a pike or two as it was full of small fish: it is a pity the pike took the Dean's ducks! I fear that I was unpopular at that time, and badly thought of; but I was right, it was just the place for pike for a bit. We had a nice fishing club, its headquarters at Caius College, where we used to have fishy dinners. John Elam was one of our leading members: I never saw better spinning than I saw with that club and all with Nottingham reels, balanced right. Anything can be done with them. Elam was a great expert also with trout on the Mayfly which was common then.

'I got no pike fishing in this last winter. I am now 80 and I feel the cold much; also they say I am too old to drive a car, which is nonsense as I am certain that I can drive better than any instructor or examiner.

'I enclose the interesting account of the strange creature [Chapter 12] for which I thank you. These things go back in the history of Ireland. In fact one could go on forever about these things. I wish I could hear your account.*

May all good things attend you,

Edward C. Alston.'

*(\*A reference to the outline of the 'monster' story in 'Fishing for Big Pike', which Barrie and Hugh Reynolds have steadfastly refused to enlarge upon.)*

I shall let the reader judge for himself whether 'The story is not much . . .', to quote the Revd Alston, but I know what I think about it. Tench fishing is *made* of this love and depth of feeling.

## OUTSTANDING CATCHES OF TENCH

Tench fishing is one branch of angling where the fisherman can hope to take a *bag* of fish: not just ordinary fish like roach and bream, but *tench* where every fish caught is plump, clean, healthy and gives a tremendous scrap. There's nothing quite like lifting a hefty netful of tench to just below the water surface, seeing the lake erupt, and shielding yourself from the resultant spray which goes for yards and yards. The disturbance created by a dozen fat bronze tench averaging 3–4lb has to be seen to be believed. A fifty-pound bag of bream is about 45lb bream and 5lb slime, the nets are covered in it, and weighing and returning fish to the water can be a wee bit messy. Tench are clean and nice to handle in comparison, and they have that look in their little red eyes. . . .

My own efforts at amassing a bag of tench have not always met with success, and whilst when I really have the tenching bug I can more or less be sure of one to four tench at a sitting I've had comparatively few bags of more than 10 fish at a sitting. For much of the time I've never really clicked with tench and I should think the number of times I've topped 10 fish at a sitting is about twenty. The most I've had in one session is 27, of which more later. And, quite frankly, I think that's about the measure of reality of the situation: an evening's tenching might get you one or two fish on a water you know; an early-morning session might get you up to half a dozen. Talking around amongst tench fanatics I find 10 fish a bag is really good going. So perhaps I've expected too much of life. . . .

But big, say enormous, bags of tench *are* taken, and having been involved in one or two myself I can say that there is no sight in angling like a huge bag of *big* tench. Let's begin with an astonishing catch. If you look up the Sheffield 'Angling Telegraph' for June 1970 you will find an account of a catch made on Ireland's Lough Patrick by Colin Dyson, Dennis Lemmon and Peter Farmery, that will make you gasp. They had 190½lb in a single boat-fishing session starting in the early morning and going well into the day. And yet they had to work for their fish, using a great deal of skill with lines between 3 and 4lb breaking strain, to take their bag of tench which averaged over 3lb each: the best was 4lb 9oz. In conjunction with fine lines they used a sliding float and tackle so arranged that the baits dropped into small 11-foot deep holes in a swim that was mostly about eight feet deep. At first the fish were localised in the holes; but later in the day moved out and were taken more generally throughout the swim. Maggots, as so often in tenching, were the best baits, and larger baits produced fewer, less frequent, and no bigger fish. They must have had about 60 tench, and remembering how tench fight, and bearing in mind the fish they lost in the anchor ropes, those anglers must have been totally worn out at the end of the session.

That's the best Irish group bag of tench I've ever heard of. The Irish Tourist Board were quoted in the same newspaper as saying 'the biggest tench catch we've ever heard of'. It depends what you mean by biggest, but they *had* heard of a bigger catch (*per angler* or *per hour*) for in the year 1968, also fishing in Ireland on Killinure Lough, I had 27 tench (and three bream) for a weight of 162lb: 23 of the tench scaled over 5lb, and the average weight (all fish weighed and recorded) was 5lb 4oz exactly. The fish were taken in 5½ hours fishing from 3.30 a.m. to 9 a.m. when I went in to breakfast. Two days later I had, in the same period of fishing 23 tench and some bream and rudd totalling 165lb: in four mornings I had 55 tench with an *average* weight of over 5lb, and six weighing 5¾lb exactly. I've never had a 6lb tench, and seven at 5¾lb remain my best tench.

Those are the bare bones of a fantastic catch or two that I was *lucky* enough to make, but there are lessons enough in the detail of those tenching days, so let me recount them as I told it to Peter Wheat in 1970 for his 'Anglers' Year Book':

'It is interesting to find that some of the best summer tench swims have one characteristic in common with the autumn to early summer pike "hot-spots" – namely the common reed, growing in deepish water for some distance behind the swim. In addition, they usually have thick bullrush beds immediately before the 8–12 ft deep open water of the lough. Whilst the lough may eventually deepen to over 50 feet out from the shore, the 8–12ft zone has, for preference, an abundance of water-lily and in particular underwater cabbage patches.

'My own success with tench in these swims had been fairly good and constant, but never spectacular until one week in July 1968, which I spent fishing a side lough of Lough Ree in County Westmeath. The chosen swim – chosen because of previous successes there – was located on the northern shore of a large, deep lough, situated in an exposed position at the western end of perhaps a quarter of a mile of rush and reed margin, indented by many minor bays and curves. The water on the landward side of these reed fringes was several feet deep for a short distance before sloping up to very shallow water and a rocky shore.

'Immediately in front of the thick bullrushes backing the swim, the water was 7ft deep dropping off to 10ft at a rod's length from the margin, and to 12ft at about 8 yards distance. The bottom consisted of fairly clean mud and a certain amount of *Chara* sand. Weed growth was rich and included soft weeds and water-lily which reached the surface above cabbages in 11ft of water. The water was clear and the bottom with its beautiful jungle of weeds, quite visible at 8–9ft down. On the evening prior to the start of fishing I had stirred up this bottom with long oars and spread groundbait and hook items (worms and flake) in a carpet from the bullrushes to a distance of some 15ft.

'The following morning found me staggering through Fred Carter's wet woods at Coosan Lough at 3.15 a.m., a quite unearthly hour to be out and about. Down to the boathouse I went, and into the boat where my gear was already made up ready for fishing. A few minutes later I was groaning the big, heavy craft across the lough and into the next one, waking up slowly in the chilly cold of a dirty dawn. Then on through a narrow channel and out into the vastness of Lough Ree, windswept and forbidding. With the wind behind me, I approached the swim within 30 minutes, shipped the oars and glided gently for the last 50 yards until the bows stabbed deeply into the bullrushes. A turn or two of rope on a stake in the rushes, a pause for the stern to swing round with the wind, and a bow rope knotted to a fistful of stems completed the securing.

'Both rods were fitted with 5lb monofil and single swanshots set some 12in above size 10 hooks. It was just breaking light as the two flake baits hit the water. I sat back in the boat with a shiver; I was not optimistic, partly because the south wind was spraying water over the side of the boat, and partly because results over the past two weeks in the swim had not been particularly good. But Dave Cumpstone had worked hard at the swim and had, a few days earlier, started to get it going. It may well be that this was the critical factor in the success that was to follow.

'A twitch on the silver paper indicator, and I was at last wide awake, watching as it moved almost 3ft in a slow run typical to bream. I hit the fish hard and it yielded quickly, but then as realisation dawned it started to fight back as Irish bream do; diving to the bottom from near the surface in 8-9ft of water, churning the sediment, and tending to run out into the lough rather than into the lily and bullrush. This one was still thrashing madly when I heaved it over the big landing net. Weighed straight away it pulled 6lb 9oz.

'I forced a large keepnet into the bullrushes behind me, carefully slid the bream in, and turned back just in time to see the bite on the other rod which I hit as the rod tip started to pull round. Another hectic battle, chaos in the bottom of the boat, and a superb bream of 6lb 8oz was duly weighed and recorded. I had one more bite in that first 20 minutes, on lobworm. Yet another bream, this time at 6lb 4oz. Three six-pounders in three casts is all a man could reasonably expect. My guardian angel had clearly cast a happy spell and then gone off and forgotten about me. The spell was to continue for the next four hours.

'After the bream a short pause of half an hour and then quite suddenly I was connecting a bite and feeling the tremendous power of a hard-battling tench which mowed down many of the lilies in the swim. This one went 4lb 8oz and was to prove the smallest in a four-day catch of 55 tench. With daylight now firmly established I changed over to float gear, a porcupine quill on each outfit; one set so that the lobworm bait would be quickly on the bottom, and the other set slow sinking to reach a depth of 10ft. The wind calmed slightly; tackle control became easier, and bites came regularly. All the bites were on lobworm, mostly on the slow-sink tackle, and by morning, when surprisingly the sun filtered through, I was playing my sixth tench. One other weighed 4lb 12oz, and four between 5lb and 5lb 12oz – the largest equalling my best-ever tench.

'My elation was fast fading now I realised I was getting desperately

5. *Above* John Weston with a 6lb 2oz fish taken whilst boat fishing on Garnafailagh.

4. *Left*—Eric Hodgson with a 7lb 8oz fish, for a while the Yorkshire record, and one of the biggest tench ever taken in the north.

6. 7lb 7½oz and Martin Gay's first seven pound tench.

short of the really giant lobworms the fish were interested in. As I toyed with the idea of returning to the boathouse for more I heard, in the distance, David Cumpstone's boat returning from a night on the River Shannon. He glided up to pass the time of day, and, on hearing the news, dug out a great tin of lobworms, approached from the reeds at the rear, tossed me the tin, and retired to a suitable distance to watch the proceedings.

'The saga continued, like some dream from which one must shortly awaken. The sun shone hot and continuous; the waves died down, but the tench fed steadily on. I missed few bites and lost not a single fish. Several of the tench reached 5lb 12oz, most were well over 5lb, and all gave an incredible account of themselves. At the final tally I'd caught 27 tench and three bream weighing 162lb. Twenty-three of the tench scaled over 5lb with an average of 5lb 4oz exactly.

'For the rest of the week I fished less intently, and with a growing realisation that a 6lb fish would elude me. I had one further great haul of fish – 23 tench and a number of bream and good rudd totalling 165lb. By the end of the four mornings in the swim I had taken 55 tench with an average of over 5lb. By then other anglers had joined in and were making good catches also. It was enjoyable to sit back, relax and watch others take specimen fish.'

I have deliberately mentioned these Irish catches first for two reasons: 1. Many anglers mistakenly think such fantastic catches can only be made in Ireland, and I intend, next, to correct them; 2. It gives me a chance to air my own, single, contribution to the list of tremendous tench catches! Of course, the techniques involved are highly informative too!

But the most incredible of all tench sessions was that pulled off by Eric Hodgson, for many years stalwart and mainstay of the National Association of Specimen Groups. Fishing a Yorkshire lake in June 1969 he began before dawn, about 3.30 a.m. and fished for 12 hours, packing up at about tea-time. In that time he landed an astounding 83 tench for a total weight of 336lb, 25 of the fish were over 5lb, and the average weight over 4lb. Obviously this catch completely eclipses my own efforts, and those of Colin Dyson and friends, both in terms of numbers and weights of tench caught. And they came from a *northern* lake, which merely makes the catch the more remarkable. I'd like to let Eric tell the tale in his own way; and the capture of his $7\frac{1}{2}$lb fish:—

'Experienced tench anglers will know that the first six or seven weeks of the season offer the greatest chance of taking a large bag of fish. Now and again during this crucial period weather conditions coincide to offer the angler his optimum chances of success, and it was just such a coincidence which came my way on June 19th, 1969 when the region where I fish for my tench was enjoying a superb spell of weather with the mid-day temperature into the 70s. Already we had enjoyed these high temperatures for several days and the steady barometer condition which goes with such an anticyclonic spell had created what I consider to be the ideal conditions for early-season tench fishing. The water temperature had climbed up to 67°F and large shoals of tench could be seen moving into the shallows to take advantage of the warm conditions to shed their spawn. Two days before a fishing companion and I had already taken a large bag of superb tench consisting of 36 fish ranging in weight from $1\frac{3}{4}$lb to $6\frac{1}{2}$lb all in excellent condition and all were returned safely to the water.

'It wasn't surprising, therefore, that when I returned to the water on Monday morning very early, I selected the same swim I had fished the previous Saturday.

Having mixed a large tub of groundbait I remember sitting down and studying the swim and wondering if my performance of two days ago could be repeated. The tactics I employed then were obviously correct and I had no intention of changing them today, so without more ado I commenced heavy dragging in a 30-foot radius from my spot; and having satisfied myself that the area had been given a good stir I then introduced three full buckets of medium groundbait, heavily laced with maggot and chopped worm. I concentrated the bait in two main areas some three yards apart as it was my intention to fish two rods using the laying-on float method and this was about the right distance apart at the range I was fishing to observe both floats simultaneously.

'By now time was getting on and it was already fully daylight and an air of expectancy crept over me as I fixed my mesh screen in front of me and set my rod-rests, the outer ones about four inches higher than the inner ones so as not to allow one rod to interfere with striking of the other. Two 11ft 6in Avon-type rods were equipped with five-pound breaking strain line, six-inch porcupine quill floats suitably shotted to expose about half an inch of the float above the water and size 12 eyed hooks tied direct.

'For the first hour one or two small perch and a well conditioned $2\frac{1}{4}$lb eel were taken but at 5.45 large quantities of small bubbles began to rise, a clear indication that a shoal of fish was starting to feed. I continued to loose feed in maggots and the worm. The water had cleared by this time revealing the two areas of groundbait and as I observed these dark shadows could be seen passing over them. Could this be the preamble of another Bonanza I thought? My float was performing every movement imaginable but going down, confirmation in fact of the fish activity down there, and already the areas of groundbait had been reduced and, as I asked myself why they hadn't picked up my bait, my right-hand float shot away after one or two tentative dips. Quickly I led the fish out of the baited area so as not to disturb the swim too much; after a few characteristic thrusts and runs I netted my first fish of the day and with my usual care I removed the hook and proceeded to weigh her – she was in spawn excellent fish of 5lb 7oz, and as I slipped her into my keepnet already positioned in the water, the ratchet on the reel of my other rod began to scream. I struck quickly and was into another good fish. This one I played out to the left of my swim under a willow bush. Finally she tired and was netted cleanly and quietly and turned out to be another five-pounder, only a little smaller than my first fish. Both rods were again baited and recast, within seconds the left-hand float was away again and I was clearly into a much smaller fish, this time of 2lb 1oz. Three fish in less than 10 minutes! At this stage I decided to fish one rod until the feeding spate settled back to make two-rod fishing more manageable.

'Fish after fish came to the net and by ten o'clock I had taken 52 fish, the best one going 5lb 13oz, but by now all the bubbles had ceased, in fact all activity had disappeared and a feeling of deflation crept over me, thinking as I did that whilst I had taken the largest bag of fish in my life I was aware of thinking throughout the feeding spate during the morning that it could go on until midday with conditions being what they were. Then like a fool I realised what had happened in my excitement – I had failed the golden rule: when they are going, keep them going with a little but often loose feed. I hadn't groundbaited for almost an hour; I hurriedly mixed up another batch of groundbait, redragged my swim, and baited up once again, putting down long tracer lines of groundbait and maggots leading from two large adjacent weed beds back to my swim and, like magic, within ten minutes I was back in business.

'Sport was much slower and it was clear I had allowed one or two of the shoals to move too far away to be drawn back to my swim. So if

I had now to fish hard for them I would, and out came my second rod again but this time fished the two much closer together, no more than a couple of feet apart. I began to ring the changes with baits and presentation and fished both rods with the over-shotted method: the six-inch quill was changed for a four inch and most of the shot was moved up to mid-water so that the float only showed the ghost of nothing above the surface. In fact the points of the floats just pierced the surface with one number six shot just resting on the bottom only two inches from the hook. This method is extremely sensitive, for the moment the fish sucks in the bait the shot on the bottom is lifted off the bottom and since the float cannot sustain the extra weight it sinks instantly. Intermittently I continued to take fish until 2.30 in the afternoon but by this time I was very tired, very dirty and extremely hungry.

'My tally of fish for the day was 83 for a total weight of 336lb with 25 fish over 5lb. I was prepared to fish on through the evening but I would have needed to travel seven miles to buy bait and food. I wrongly decided to call it a day and return home. On reflection this was a mistake in that in the following years the pond sustained the disease UDN which reduced fish stocks considerably and it is doubtful if I will ever have a chance again of such a catch of fish on this or any other water. Moreover, I will kick myself for allowing a break in the feeding spate mid-morning due to failing to keep the swim fed in a vitally crucial period and I'm sure had I not made this silly mistake a bag of 400lb would have been possible; a lesson I'll never forget.'

That catch of Eric's makes pretty tremendous reading, and amongst his other good catches was one which included one of the biggest tench ever caught in the north of the country, a $7\frac{1}{2}$-pounder. Eric again:—

'From time to time, more by premonition than sound angling science, I have returned to that same swim to be rewarded with good fish. So it was two years ago when on a tench-fishing holiday with my good friend and fishing companion Dr Coulson, about the middle of the week the barometer started to rise steeply, as did the air and water temperatures. I registered the water temperature on the Saturday at 52°F and sport correspondingly slow, deep-water fishing being the more profitable.

'By Tuesday night of the following week the water temperature had risen to the low 60s. Early on the Wednesday morning I moved my tackle back to my favourite swim near the shallows. The previous winter had been rather long if somewhat on the mild side, but, as often happens with this kind of winter, we experienced a very cold snap in late March and early May which resulted in life within the pond being severely retarded. Normally by early June large banks of amphibious bistort and common pond weed can be seen in great banks all over the shallows whilst the bottom is usually covered with quilwort and *Elodia*. Not so this year, the pond bottom was almost clear and the water was so clear that the bottom seven feet down could be clearly observed.

'I began my Wednesday morning session by dragging my swim with my heavy drag and baiting with a mixture of medium groundbait, maggots, and red worm. By six o'clock I had netted six or seven good tench up to $5\frac{1}{4}$lb and since my gamble seemed to be paying off I invited Dr Coulson, who had not yet moved his tackle back to the shallows, to come and join me in my swim. The swim was reorganised to accommodate the two of us and by seven o'clock we had settled down again to continue our morning session; by now the water had completely cleared after my earlier dragging and my groundbait and maggots could be clearly seen spread over the swim bottom. As the sun climbed into the sky the air and water temperatures continued to rise and prospects clearly were improving. Careful observations over our mesh screen erected before us revealed very large tench indeed making sorties over the baited area in twos and threes but not remaining too long before returning to the scant weed cover at the edge of the dragged swim area.

'Then two large female fish entered the swim from the left-hand side and commenced feeding as they moved towards my baited hook. At first I thought they had ignored my two maggots on my no. 16 hook but suddenly my float shot away. I struck and I was into the larger of the two fish and whilst the preceding minutes had created considerable tension and excitement I played my fish very confidently. She made a long run towards a nearby weed bed; I increased side-strain by thumb pressure on the rim of my centre pin and the angle of the rod, and as she neared the weeds I clamped down solidly, relaxed the rod quickly and retensioned almost at once. This action if done quickly enough has the effect of disorientating the fish which hopefully will swim off on a different tack. The trick worked and my fish swam to the right and towards me making it necessary for me to recover line very quickly. I brought the fish under

8. Typical eruption of a bag of big tench as Ray, and John Weston, heave to get it aboard. Note the boat's thole pins . . .

9. . . . and aboard it comes.

Ray Webb with the Irish Record
nch described in the text.

full pressure again some four yards out which caused it to roll revealing for the first time the full depth of the fish. For the first time I was aware that my fish was bigger than anything I had taken before and decided to play it out completely, but just then she turned again towards the bank where my good friend was waiting, landing net already in the water. The fish was taken cleanly and swiftly from the water. Both Dr Coulson and I looked admiringly for a few seconds at the fish and I remember I broke the silence by saying "this will go six, Terry!" and in his usual professional manner merely nodded his agreement. Quickly I slipped my weighing net under this beautiful fish and carefully weighed it. As the pointer bounced down to seven and a half pounds I really couldn't believe my eyes and asked Dr Coulson to confirm the weight: "it's $7\frac{1}{2}$lb, Eric". I quickly but carefully slid this fine fish into my keepnet. I then sat down recounting almost disbelievingly what had happened. After a few minutes I rebaited my hook, recast and settled down to the pleasurable business of catching tench.

'About midday Dr Coulson struck a bite almost at the same time as I did and immediately we were aware that we had both hooked the same fish. The fish had taken Terry's bait and swum into my line; I had duly struck and foul-hooked the fish. A very powerful fish it turned out to be and at once it made off towards the centre of the pond taking line off both reels. My hook had gone in near the tail of the fish and very quickly my hook pulled out when increasing pressure had to be applied. Seconds later Terry's line broke leaving us both speechless for a while. My view is that this fish was exceptional even for this water; in fact had we been able to land it I'm certain we would be admiring a new British record but Terry confines his comments to saying it was a good fish.

'By the end of this session we had taken a good bag of fish including a number of good five-pounders.

'Weather conditions had started to change and with it our chances of further fish diminished although several good fish were taken during the remainder of the week but none as big as those on Wednesday morning.'

I have singled out these enormous catches for special mention partly because 100lb bags of tench averaging 3lb or so are not all that uncommon, and it would be rather pointless listing all of them here. But it does lead us on to a related subject, that of consistency in results. Eric Hodgson is probably just about the most successful tench angler in history, having taken at the time of writing (April 1975) no less than 253 tench over 5lb weight (compared to my 65 for example) and literally *hundreds* of fish over 4lb weight. And his best is that dreamy 7½-pounder. The techniques I shall outline later on in the book.

Another group of major contributors, and better known to most because of their extensive penmanship and numerous exploits, are the Taylor brothers, particularly Fred J. Taylor himself. When Fred wrote 'Angling in Earnest' in 1962 he'd had 36 five-pounders and 360 tench over four pounds. Although Wotton Lakes, from whence many of these tench came, was reputed to slow up a little in later years, I'm sure he had many more. On one occasion the Taylor brothers-three took 45 tench (15 each) all over 4lb, and including three five-pounders. And that wasn't their best bag from the lakes! On another occasion, fishing from dawn until midday, the three of them took 79 tench of which only nine were less than 4lb, several over 5lb; all on big lobworms. If we assume an average weight of rather less than 4½lb it gives a weight of more than 350lb for three anglers! The techniques evolved by these anglers have been most important to the enjoyment of tench anglers everywhere, and I shall attempt to summarize them in later sections of the book dealing with groundbaiting and with the lift method.

Frank Guttfield, the Hitchin angler, also hit the headlines with some consistency in the period following the Taylor brothers' acme. He used to fish a lake, amongst others, in proximity to the legendary John Simpson, and in 1966 both had had over 50 five-pounders. In that year John Simpson caught his first six-pounder, witnessed by Ray, and a few months later Frank also had *his* first six-pounder. Nice things often happen in tench fishing.

In more recent times the catches of John Cadd, well-known Oxford angler, are well qualified for any list of all-time greats. He is featured in the 'Angling Times' of June 28th, 1973 after three sessions which produced: 34 fish weighing 100lb (i.e. averaging about 3lb); 44 fish for 110lb (average less than 3lb) and 109 fish for 250lb. Altogether 187 fish for 450lb, which for sheer *numbers* of tench must be one of the best catches in history. John displayed a great deal of skill, setting his relatively light float tackle so that the flake bait lay *on* the thick bottom weed and did not sink into it. June 1973 also saw tremendous catches by Bob Church and Peter Chillingsworth who appear on the front page of 'Angling Times' for June 21st in what is surely one of the nicest pictures ever seen of tench anglers after a session: they shared a one-session catch of 240lb, which included rudd and bream. But how fine those tench look, matching only the expressions on the faces of the two anglers.

I have left mention of one Ray Webb until last, with much the same feeling as one who leaves the choicest piece of a plateful of food until last. Ray has taken enormous numbers of tench over the years, including many good bags of fish, from all over Britain and Ireland, but his main aim has always been *big* tench rather than amassed netfuls. Probably this is why he took four seven-pounders mentioned in the last chapter, and probably also why he has had 15 six-pounders, many five-pounders and a great many four-pounders. He has always been fond of pioneering new methods and new waters and, as with the others mentioned in this chapter (myself excluded), consistency has been the keynote of his fishing. Amongst his best catches he particularly rates the considerable numbers of four- and five-pounders taken at Coosan Lough and in Killinure. I remember him doing a film for somebody once, and there he was, playing a five-pounder from one boat (into which he'd had to step to please the camera man) when he got a take on his second rod in the other boat. He immediately leapt from one boat to the other, still playing his tench, struck with his left hand the second rod, and subsequently played both fish into one net. Both went well over 5lb weight, and all was recorded faithfully, if jerkily, by the enthusiastic camera crew. Having paused for thought he reckons his catch of 120lb of mixed tench and bream was his best one: nine of the fish were tench and the best five went 6lb 4¾oz (2); 6lb 8oz; 6lb 14oz and 7lb 1½oz. The next day he took fish of 6lb 5oz (2) and 6lb 6oz! The experience which goes to make up Ray Webb is, we hope, distilled and condensed into the later parts of this book.

CHAPTER 3

# Supergiants
*Martin Gay*

In the 10 years or so since the book was first written, and as Barrie has already outlined, there has been quite a remarkable upward trend in the specimen size of tench caught in England (for reasons which as yet escape us a similar phenomenon has failed to materialize in Eire; but perhaps it is simply late coming?). A few years back Des Taylor, past secretary of the National Association of Specialist Anglers, wrote in the angling press about the notion that 7lb plus tench were coming from waters all over England was in fact incorrect, and that this false impression was being given by a few anglers reporting misleading locations, to put others off the scent. Des's argument was that in reality one water in Surrey, one in Norfolk, Kent and in Oxfordshire were, in fact, accounting for almost all the really big tench caught.

Now, I sympathise with Des, and there was certainly some truth in his notion, but overriding his complaint was his urge for anglers not to report misleading catches. Such is the pressure on the modern specimen fishery that many anglers feel the need to do all they can to put off others, in the fear (sometimes most apparent!) of hordes of anglers descending on their quiet backwaters and shattering the peace.

However, Des was, I respectfully suggest, a little off the mark in his belief that only very few waters were growing big tench – there being no doubt at all that numerous pits, lakes, and reservoirs in particular, were throwing up really big tench. Some fisheries have in the last few years yielded tench of 8lb and 9lb in many cases bigger than in their history and previous heyday maybe 20 or 30 years ago. And this trend is not uncommon. What has happened in several cases is that a water, perhaps many decades mature, had been at one time producing bags of tench of 4lb and 5lb with the occasional monster 6 pounder. Inevitably the fishing declined, the tench having "gone back" and the anglers' interest went to new waters and new tench.

Whether or not a fishery without anglers allows the tench to grow unhindered is open to interpretation (there being ample evidence to

39

suggest that fish can actually benefit from an angling presence), but with the angling pressure now off the water, at some time during the early 1970s there appeared a resurgence of growth amongst tench, which this time round grew even faster than in any time in recorded angling history, resulting in the biggest tench ever. One water in Bedfordshire for instance, in the early 1980's produced at least two tench over 9lb!

Rather interestingly, newer and maturing gravel pits with no previous tench fishing history, and therefore no previous growth cycle, have also, since 1975, been producing tench of a size to match any previously in Britain. Clearly then, these particular tench are young and capable of fast growth – there being no question of them being of "a good strain".

Lakes, meres and particularly gravel pits have undoubtedly produced the greatest number of big tench in this latest "boom" but some reservoirs, particularly the Tring group, have not been left behind. It was Wilstone reservoir that gave two double figure tench in 1982, in addition to numbers between 7lb and 9lb.

But why has this last decade seen what is unquestionably the finest spate of specimen tench in history, with more people catching 6lb plus fish than would ever have dreamed the like just a few seasons back? Barrie puts forward the theory that it may the period between successive "winterkills" that has enabled the tench (and bream, let's not forget what has happened with this latter species too!) to live longer and therefore grow larger. Personally I cannot fault this idea, and indeed, whereas the interpretation may be different it actually agrees with my own ideas. Taking Barrie's theory to its logical conclusion it could mean that given sufficient time there is really little reason why tench shouldn't actually grow to 15lb, assuming that is, that they live for 20 years or more. On the basis that the last major "winterkill" was in 1963 and that it took 3 or 4 years for the stocks to "get back on their feet" it has taken around 13 years for some tench to growth from 0lb to 7½lb (average), but I would add that two of those pounds were added over the last 3 years of that time span, suggesting that we could still see an 11lb or 12lb tench before the next inevitable (?) bad winter.

We now have to discuss what is perhaps the most controversial aspect of this whole matter – exactly the cause of some quite dramatic weight increases in waters widespread throughout the country. Barrie's theory suggests that tench are in fact naturally slow growing

0. Martin Gay with a 7lb 6½oz tench, caught n sweetcorn, late afternoon over a shallow reedy ar.

11. Four six pound fish at a sitting. In the past a six pound fish was unusual in a lifetime's fishing (see first edition).

. 3 big tench, taken in July on HNV baits weighing 6lb, 7lb 3½oz and 7lb 4oz.

fish, putting on, at best 8oz per year. In other words they need 12 to 14 years to grow to 6lb and upwards, but at the same time are long-lived fish that given sufficient time will continue to grow for maybe 18 or 20 years. Recent evidence from carp anglers (Kevin Clifford and Len Arbery 1984 and previously) has for all intents and purposes proven that carp do in fact only grow (that is increase in *length*) for the first 12-14 years of life, thereafter "freewheeling" at that final length but increasing, or decreasing, in weight according to seasonal fluctuations in food – including anglers' baits.

It may well be that tench can grow for more years than carp (but if such evidence exists I do not know of it) thereby achieving greater relative weights than carp (that is weight over years of age). But in the absence of such proof we have a comparable situation which grows tench to 6lb in 12 years, or a length of about 22 inches, and only after that do the weights continue to increase up to 8lb or exceptionally 9lb. Particularly fast growing, young fish which reach 24 inches in 12 years can then, having stopped growing in length, increase in weight in the remaining years of life to perhaps a record size of 10lb plus. A 24 inch tench at 8½lb without spawn is a potential 10 pounder in June and prior to spawning, in the majority of waters – the problem is that comparatively few fisheries can grow 8lb plus tench without spawn, and conversely tench in some waters carry a lot more spawn than others, so a shorter and lighter, tench could actually weigh more by virtue of the additional spawn. But which is the *better* fish?

There is however, only *one* factor which actually allows, or causes, fish to grow and that is the availability of food. Other things like water quality, volume of the fishery etc. all, of course, matter, but all of these factors in turn result in the production, or otherwise, of food. A lake which grows big tench is a lake rich in food, there can be no argument about that. If in addition to masses of readily available food the tench live long and grow for many years then you have the makings of a potential record-breaking water.

But why then have so many fisheries throughout much of southern Britain (although extending in exceptional circumstances northwards to Yorkshire) apparently made available so much additional food in the last 15 years? Well, for one thing we are now seeing the fruits of the massive amount of mineral extraction (i.e. gravel pits!) since the war, needed to build motorways, houses etc., and such waters are particularly fertile. A gravel pit needs a few years to become established, for weedbeds to grow and for the suspended solids to settle, etc. etc. Most of the big tench recently, have been caught in comparatively young pits, but not all. What then, is the explanation for the tremendous fish taken from, amongst others, the Tring reservoirs, and some of the old and long established "park" lakes? Clearly the years between successive winterkills must help but to show weight increases such as we are now seeing, also demands extra food. One such source of food is undoubtedly anglers' baits – more anglers are feeding into our fisheries more bait (food!) than ever before and as in all things in nature there is always an animal which makes best use of the additional food (or better "conditions") and perhaps in this instance the tench is that animal?

It cannot actually matter from which source the food comes, and in some ways anglers' bait, in the context of food, is better than more natural sources in so far as it is *additional* to the fishes' usual diet. The effect of introducing food via angling practises is to increase the potential biomass of the fishery, sometimes by quite remarkable amounts, feeding not only the fish but also the crustacea, nematodes, bacteria etc., thereafter actually increasing the quantity (and possibly the quality) of natural food, available to the tench. It matters not the type of anglers' bait/food introduced because the nitrogen contained therein cannot be destroyed and is used as an energy source by one animal or another.

But, the better the quality of the bait, the greater the impact it has both in terms of ultimate size of the tench and the speed of growth. A good modern HNV bait is very rich in protein, vitamins and minerals which not only provides additional direct food for the tench but also as a secondary food source via invertebrates etc. which eat and benefit from prebaiting activities. In this way the benefit to the tench is twofold.

Earlier, I mentioned an 8oz annual growth increment for tench under accepted "normal" conditions. By regular feeding of high quality bait (food) into an already rich environment I have witnessed that increment increase by up to 100%, and a few examples would not go amiss at this point. A fish taken on June 17th, carrying spawn, at a weight of 6lb 0½oz was recaptured 4 weeks later, *after spawning*, at 6lb 6½oz. A 7lb 3½oz pre-spawning tench was captured 2 summers later, again carrying spawn at 8lb 8oz – this fish after spawning that summer weighed 7lb 7oz. On that same fishery the *average* weight of the tench caught by employing the specialist methods I have outlined in Chapter 9, increased by almost 2lb in 3 years, but weight gain was not the only benefit. These really very big tench improved in condition out of all proportion to the guesstimated age, and size. They were never spawn-bloated, even when carrying 16oz of spawn, and fought quite magnificently. Much of their weight was carried in their shoulders and some have actually been built like carp, with a pronounced "hump" and very thick across the back.

Clearly the reasons behind the very big tench that we are now catching are several and I now put the question "what size is a giant tench?". The shear numbers of tremendous tench taken in the past 6 or 8 years has given rise to a degree of complacency amongst anglers which I find a little irritating. The fact still remains that tench over 6lb are rarely seen, let alone caught, by the vast majority of anglers in Britain. Len Head, writing in 1978 stated that any angler having caught tench over 6lb can hold his head high in any angling company, and without intending to sound vain I still reckon Len has got it right. It is worth remembering that as a percentage of the record weight a 6lb tench is approximately equal to a 25lb carp, and a thirty pound carp is a monster, as is a 2½lb roach, a 3lb plus perch etc. A giant tench is surely any fish weighing over 7lb. There can only be fewer than 20 anglers in Britain today, that is 20 anglers in the history of British coarse fishing, who have caught more than a dozen tench over 7lb, and all the time that situation exists such fish can only be considered as monster tench.

Many of us have believed our waters to hold double figure tench, but the catches of such fish are, even today, so few that probability does not bear out our dreams. To the very best of my knowledge there has never been caught a tench weighing more than 9lb which did not contain spawn and certainly the few over 10lb were all clearly heavy with spawn. The heaviest fish caught in recent years (that is ignoring the dropsical 11lb and 12lb fish from the 1950's and beyond) is a tench of 10lb 10oz by Joe Darville from a pit on the Herts border in 1984. According to regulars on the fishery this particular tench is spawn-bound and in fact they have been watching it increase in weight annually from 8lb to 10lb plus over 3 seasons, presumably as successive years spawn is added to the previous years but not shed or reabsorbed. Other 10 pounders in recent seasons include 2 from Wilstone reservoir in 1982 and one, caught by Eric Edwards from Deans Farm fishery at 10lb 2oz. Additionally of course, we have the Peterborough brick pit fish of 10lb 1oz which was the first double figure tench to actually hold the British record. The fact that ten

13. Fine 6¾lb fish to HNV bait at long range.

14. Big Yorkshire tench taken by B.R. Note tail fin damage in otherwise excellent fish. Damage did *not* occur on this occasion of its capture.

pounds has been beaten only about 5 times, and then by ounces, in the last decade is surely indicative of the fact that we are still close to the top weight achievable in Britain at this present time.

Such was the impact of a 7½lb tench in then early 1970's that Eric Hodson was, in the first edition of this book, given a chapter much to himself to describe its capture. A tremendous fish, of that there is no doubt, and in keeping with the terrific catches of huge tench by Len Head and Ray Webb, amongst very few others, it was caught at a time when only about 30 seven pounds tench had been recorded. I, myself, have now had more than that number and I have details of one fishery which, in one season produced at least 17 authentic 8lb plus tench – and in that same season around 50 seven pounders, of which I landed eleven. A good friend of mine, Ray Bishop, had the dreamlike experience of landing no less than 3 tench over 8lb in one night in 1981 and if that wasn't enough he added two other tench to make a grand total of 5 tench for 35lb! In two successive seasons I have started with a leash of seven pounders (7.2, 7.3 and 7.12 in 1981 and 7.0, 7.3 and 8.5 in 1982) and on several occasions taken 4 and 5 six pounders, even as late as September, which can produce some superb fishing. My first 8 pounder was taken in a catch including fish of 7.13, 6.13, 6.11 and 6.3, but all of this to the ill-informed could seem to make the pioneering catches of Len and Ray seem rather insignificant. But, if anything their catches were infinitely more meritorious coming as they did from an era when only a handful of anglers had ever seen a 6lb tench, and we must never forget that.

CHAPTER 4

# Basic Tackle
*Ray Webb*

IDEALLY the tench angler should be equipped with several rods for the nature of tench swims varies considerably and the type of bite encountered can change from day to day, from season to season. For fishing heavily weeded swims the two-piece 10ft Mark IV Avon type of rod takes some beating though the built cane originally used in the construction of these weapons is beginning to look decidely old fashioned these days. I've largely abandoned it myself on account of the improved durability and harder wearing properties of fibre glass. In spite of their comparatively brittle nature and consequent need for extremely careful nursing, these Avons, with action all the way from tip to butt, do take much of the strain off the line when big fish have to be manhandled through dense beds of lily pads. I've watched Ron Clay literally skulldrag five-pounders out of such spots in a manner that would be piscatorial suicide if attempted with any other type of rod.

To tackle tench in fisheries with a fringe of marginal weed extending some two or three yards out from the bank with clear open water beyond, length is a prime consideration in a suitable rod, length with strength that is, and 14ft or so is needed if the angler is to dictate the terms of the fight and haul the fish out from the weed into the safer snag free area. Fortunately heavy duty 14ft glass rods are marketed by a number of the leading manufacturers these days so the angler can take his pick a vastly improved position from the old days when Spanish Reed and like materials were in use, a rod combining length and power being a rarity indeed at that time. On waters where the tench are encountered in weed and snag-free swims, a 12ft ferruleless hollow glass roach rod is a pleasure to handle, being light and sensitive yet still retaining sufficient power to play out the fish in reasonably quick time. On water like Castle Howard, with tench of medium size up to $3\frac{3}{4}$lb or so, such rods are ideal and even with big fish of 5lb or more I'd be happy to tackle them so armed given

47

similarly clear open water and fifty yards of tried and tested line.

For distance casting, to reach tench at long range, a fixed spool reel is essential and a selection of Mitchell and Abu reels are available to meet all requirements though the price can be somewhat high, in these inflationary days. If anything like hard and regular usage is anticipated it may be worth while paying for the best as most of the cheaper models have a tendency to break at one point or another, the bail arm pick up, the return springs, the handles and the spools being particularly vunerable; while the gears themselves can quickly develop a dangerous tendency to slip or stick due to wear and tear. My own two Mitchell Prince reels, won in big fish competitions with catches of Yorkshire barbel back in 1961 lasted eight or nine years, and with the amount of hard work I gave them to do, it would be hard to think of a better recommendation. Designed as the first, high speed retrieve fixed spool for matchmen I pressed these into service for all types of heavy duty work short of shark fishing, living at such a pace that anything like regular servicing was virtually out of the question.

Yet even with such overloading and abuse it was on one of them that I played out my biggest ever pike, a 29-pounder as recently as July 1970, a powerful acrobatic fish that put up a tremendous battle for a full 15 minutes or more. At this stage, their general condition warranted an honourable retirement but I still use one for snatching small fry and did in fact land a 6lb pike on it early this year, fairly hooked in the mouth on a size 20 hook, single maggot and 1lb breaking strain line. Not all tench are located at long range, however, margin fishing from the bank and boat fishing in many cases sees the fish in close, my long experience of boat fishing leads me to believe that in bright sunny weather the tench come in close for the shade afforded to keep the sun out of their eyes and in much the same way that they move into lily pads for shelter at such times. With the fish in close a centre pin reel is perfectly adequate and many anglers prefer to play fish on this type of reel feeling that they have more direct control over a fish that is taking line. Certainly the danger from badly worn gears is virtually eliminated for the centre pin is made to last indefinitely; an occasional cleaning and a spot of oil on the spindle being all that is required in the way of maintenance. Current prices are astonishingly high, however, for a new centre pin reel, the best value is undoubtedly to be found in a secondhand one as apart from a few scratches here and there the working order is usually first class.

BASIC TACKLE 49

Line strengths must match up to the rod, the size of the tench to be fished for and the presence or otherwise of weed beds and snags. On a water which sustains a large head of tench up to $3\frac{1}{2}$lb or so and plenty of open water line of 3–4lb breaking strain should prove perfectly adequate unless the angler is particularly heavy on the strike, and used in conjunction with a light 12ft ferruleless hollow glass rod, top-class sport can be enjoyed. When tench of 5lb or over are expected however, heavier tackle is called for especially if lily pads are present in the swim. I've seen anglers using $5\frac{1}{2}$lb line snapped up altogether too often in these circumstances and usually employ $6\frac{1}{2}$lb breaking strain myself.

Floats are being manufactured from all sorts of exotic materials these days but the porcupine quill is still as good as any; it casts well, is available in a wide range of sizes and will stand up to years of hard fishing if handled with reasonable care. Where maximum visibility is required however, a peacock quill is to be prefered as it is of roughly the same diameter all along instead of sharply tapered and given a touch of fluorescent paint will stand out vividly in the half light of dawn and dusk. A variety of colours is needed; yellow for dull and rainy weather, orange for bright sunshine and jet black for a thick mist or fog.

For general use an eyed hook of the Model Perfect or Stilletto brand is to be preferred to mass-produced hooks to gut, for if he ties the hook on carefully himself the angler can fish confident that his tackle will not let him down. A range of sizes from 2 to 14 will meet the needs of most situations whether the tench are feeding on lumps of paste the size of golf balls or will look at nothing but a single brandling. In times of finnicky, hesitant feeding it may be necessary to present a single maggot or a tiny bloodworm and for these baits I favour a hook size of 16 or 18 of the spade end pattern. They're a neater looking job than the eyed hooks for such delicate work. It's a good policy to have both bronzed hooks and gilt, the darker variety being used for baits like worm and breadcrust, the lighter for paste and maggots.

A selection of swing and quiver tips, a few Arlesey bombs and lead shot and the tench angler's box is about complete though odd additional items are always cropping up from time to time. Swim feeders and bait droppers to ensure bait and groundbait are on the same spot are worth carrying and a rake or cutter is sometimes essential before one can hope to commence fishing.

## Comment – by Barrie Rickards

In his account above Ray gives a lucid outline of basic tenching tackle: it is, however, a simplistic approach betraying his overall, happy methods of uncluttered angling. Let me paint you a picture of Ray actually fishing. In the first place it must strike the observer that not much tackle is in evidence: a couple of rods resting upon forked sticks as 'idlebacks' (the Sheffield anglers' slang for rod-rests), possibly, but *only* possibly, a basket to sit on, a bag with a few odds and ends in, and a few small tins of bait, plus a loaf of bread. And who can argue with the results?

But there is another approach, perhaps more common today, where it seems the angler has everything but the kitchen sink with him in the swim. And when I mention that Eric Hodgson falls approximately into this category then clearly this approach must also be 'correct'. It is this 'let's take everything' attitude that I wish to explore further for the clues it gives to the idea of having a set of basic tackle with which to go tench hunting. Remember, by the way of preliminary, that most tench angling sessions involve the angler sitting in one swim for several hours so that it really doesn't matter very much how much clobber is carried.

Let's begin with rods. It is so essential to have the two basic types that Ray mentions: a 10ft soft-action type such as the Mark IV carp rod in split cane or fibreglass; and the long, light, hollow glass rod for finer fishing in less snaggy swims. The relative action curves of the two are shown in Fig. 15. Clearly the longer rod is good for getting over the head of the fish and playing him gently away from problems, whereas the 10ft rod is ideal for a battle in tight, snag ridden circumstances.

Personally my light rod is a 14ft Hardy's Fibatube (I also use a 12ft version of the same rod where trees make the long rod difficult to use) and the 10ft rod is a split cane Mark IV Avon, although Bruce and Walker make, or made, a superb glass version at about 10ft that I have used with rare pleasure. It should be added here that the standard Mark IV carp rod is a shade too powerful for tench fishing in most circumstances: but if you find *big* tench in *dense* lilies or bulrush then this rod should probably be used.

I have already mentioned circumstances where it is a help to have more than the two types of rod, and there are situations where it is a help to have *two* Mark IV Avon rods, or two fibretubes. One is where you wish to fish two rods in weeded swims: you'd choose two powerful

BASIC TACKLE

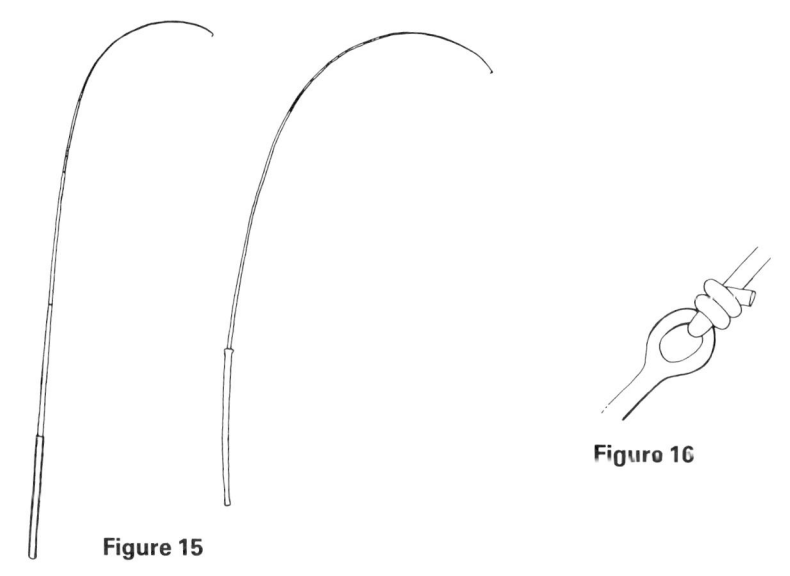

**Figure 15**

**Figure 16**

rods. And in general, if fishing two rods, one is less likely to make a mistake if both outfits are very similar. Thus if I was fishing a swim with a 14ft fibretube, I might just as well be using two. Yet another situation commonly arises when the fish are feeding well. This is just when you get an almighty tangle in the gear, and to save what can be vital minutes it is a terrific help if a second rod is already made up at the bankside. This may seem extravagant to some, although not to an experienced matchman, but when the big tench feed (all too infrequently) you can waste twenty minutes with a bad tangle.

Obviously it is my view that although fishing with two rods it is as well to have other different rods available, and perhaps one already made up in a similar manner to the way you happen to be fishing at the time. All these rods go into a roll-up rod holdall, minus only the reels themselves.

In addition to rods you need reels, and here I agree entirely with Ray's philosophy. So many good ones are available today that it is difficult to go wrong. Almost all the more expensive reels are near-perfect: some have roller pick-ups (e.g. Mitchells and Intrepids) and thus are more favourite with me than other makes. Centre-pins are useful with the 14ft rods when fishing will often be with light float tackle at close range. Nothing could be pleasanter in angling than playing a 3lb tench on 4lb breaking strain line, a centre-pin reel and a light, long rod. We have the pre-swingtip era match anglers to thank for those rods, and probably the big fish angler to thank for the fact that a few good centre-pins are still with us. I have just returned from Poland with an excellent centre-pin costing less than 50p, so perhaps in the future we might see an upsurge of cheap but good foreign centre-pin reels.

My attitude to lines is similar. I'll name my own favourites, Intrepid Superline, Super Maxima, and Platil ordinary, without implying that there are not several other reputedly excellent brands. For all my tench fishing I tie the reel line directly to an eyed hook. For hooks I used Stilletto brand and Goldstrike for their strength of wire, and Richard Walker carp hooks for their small eye, fine wire and good points. I am not satisfied with *any* make of eyed hook, but shy away from from spade ends because I'd prefer to tie them directly to the reel line and cannot do so with facility when actually fishing. The hooks I mention above will not fail you often, but I suspect that like me you will occasionally wish for a smaller eye or a stronger wire!

The hook when tied on should look as in Fig. 16 and should not have a long length of nylon sticking out. Bill Bartles the Sheffield and ex-England matchman tells me that even the tiniest upstanding bristle of nylon is enough to put off tiny roach: if young roach object then big crafty tench will do so all the more. Eric Hodgson's Knot is actually better in this respect than the almost universally used half blood knot.

When it comes to floats we are now superbly catered for in this country. Not only are the traditional bird and porcupine quills still available, both excellent for much of tench angling, but the matchfishing fraternity have provided us with a whole vast range and variety of floats in all shapes and sizes: zoomers, sticks, etc., and they can all have their place in tench angling. Attachment of floats is a matter of simplicity to me: I simply have two or more valve rubbers or tubing of various diameters on the line. The float is attached at both ends, and naturally the float can be changed in a jiffy without breaking down the rest of the tackle. For close range fishing the same system can be used to attach the float at one end only, but for long range fishing, where the angler wants the float attached at one end only, if would be safer to use a clip attachment as shown in Fig. 17. Under these latter circumstances a rubber at one end only risks the float falling off during the cast, and does nothing at all to assist a long

BASIC TACKLE 53

cast. Do not attach a float as shown in Fig. 18: it causes horrible kinks in the line.

Another necessary evil, which can also cause line weakening is split shot. If the line is flattened to a small degree as shown in Fig. 19 then little loss of line strength ocurs, but if soft shot is pressed on to the line so that flattening occurs to the extent of Fig. 20 then the line at that point may tear like a piece of polythene! Avoid really soft shot for it needs a lot of pressure to fix it firm.

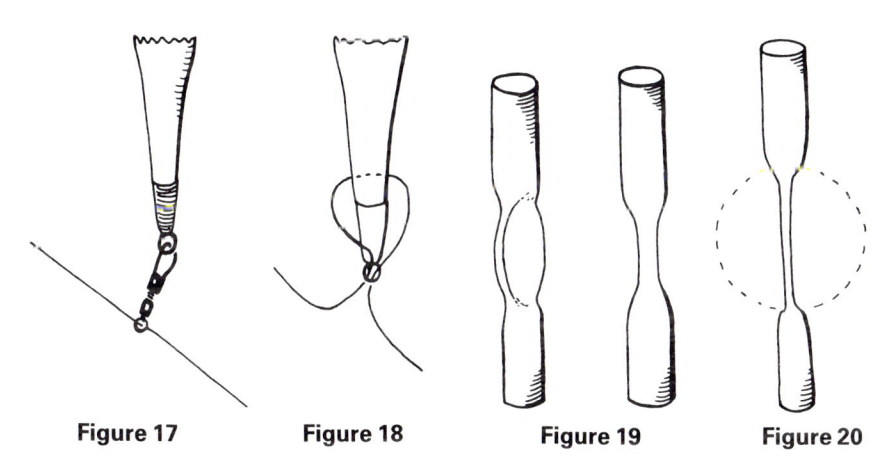

**Figure 17**  **Figure 18**  **Figure 19**  **Figure 20**

In addition to the rods and their attachments outlined above, the tench angler needs a whole suite of peripheral equipment. Never rely on makeshift swim drags, but always use a good one of the types shown in plates 60 and 61. They have to do the job well, either cutting or dragging, and always have them close at hand.

A comfortable seat is of prime importance. Many anglers use a low seat, possibly six inches off the ground, but if enough front cover is available an upright chair lifting you 18in off the ground makes a clean strike much easier; you can really get poised above the rods and lift them cleanly into the air on the strike. Incidently, always try a few practice strikes, and check the position of the rear rod-rest if you are using one, for there is nothing more likely to cause a missed strike than hitting this rod-rest with the butt of the rod as you make the strike. Try to arrange things so that you are seated as in Fig. 21. Note that on the strike the rod comes above, back, and well clear of the rear rod-rest. When fishing from a high seat with no natural front cover such as rush beds, it is a help to construct a hide of the kind

**Figure 21**

**Figure 22**

habitually used by Eric Hodson. This can be as in Fig. 22, and nylon potato sacks, dark green in colour, are probably the best and cheapest things to use. It means you can move about quietly behind the screen without fear of frightening tench feeding very close to the bank.

Personally I use foam rubber on the seat, since I believe in being comfortable. I have a 45in diameter umbrella with a tent which fits over it, made by Roy Thomas and his colleagues at Tamworth. Occasionally I put a bed chair inside and treat the whole thing like a camp, with heater and all home comforts! On finishing a session at, say, 10 o'clock in the morning you can have a snack and then sleep until lunch, and after lunch have a recce around the lake before beginning the evening session. It all makes for comfortable and, therefore, efficient fishing.

You can imagine that we have a fair bundle of tackle in the swim at this stage; rods, landing net, keepnet, screen, rod-rests, seat and brolly, rucksack with floats, hooks, swing tips, quiver tips, swim feeders. And in addition, several polythene bait containers, buckets, and groundbaits. This is the way I like to fish, and others like me, really making a swim my own home for a few hours or a few days. Of course, as we describe elsewhere in this book a lot of work, mental and physical, has gone into the choosing of the swim in the first place. As it happens my recent tenching has been in swims up to which I have been almost able to drive the car. Perhaps just as well. . . .

## BASIC TECHNIQUES
*Ray Webb*

Successful methods for tench are variable though most of them terminate in a bait held hard on the bottom, only very occasionally do we find exceptions to this generally correct rule. In the lakes and ponds in which tench are usually encountered most anglers employ a float of one sort or another and I wouldn't argue against this practice for float fishing for tench is both enjoyable and effective. Sufficient shot to cock the float, bunched together a foot or so away from the hook, with the float set at precisely the right depth for the water is the standard rig (Fig. 23), and when the fish are feeding confidently nothing more elaborate is required.

Notoriously finnicky feeders, there are times when tench will feed anything but confidently, however, nibbling and mouthing the bait only to spit it out several times before a decisive bite is obtained. To meet this exasperating and all too common situation the Taylor brothers employed the lift method with some success, the shot being slid down to a mere 1½in or so away from the hook, a float with maximum buoyancy at the lower end like an inverted goose quill or piece of peacock quill being set at a couple of feet or so in excess of the water's depth, the rod set in a rest and the line reeled tight till the float rests at half cock. Or rather more sensitively as in Fig. 24. An immediate strike is made at the first sign of movement.

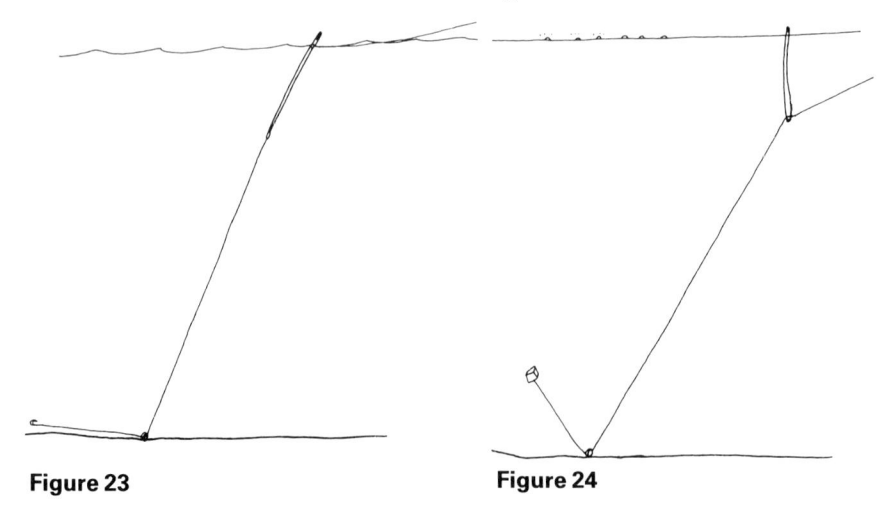

**Figure 23**  **Figure 24**

Though not 100% effective of course, the lift method did bring some improvement, so much so that the Taylor brothers went on to use it even for tench feeding normally. Another answer to finnicky tench that can sometimes produce the desired results is a switch in baits either to a smaller offering of the one in use, or a completely different bait altogether. I well remember back in 1955 my annual fortnight's holiday on the King's Sedgmoor Drain in Somerset, for this was a summer of prolonged drought, conditions that can be guaranteed to produce a nervous, hesitant mood in the tench. And sure enough for the first five days I fished long and hard, dawn to dusk, without obtaining a single bite that could be called in any way decisive. Indeed, had it not been flat calm and scorching hot I wouldn't have been aware of tench activity at all for only the slightest of ripples appeared around the float.

At this stage of the holiday I met up with an angler from London, Mr William Bruty, who was halfway through the second week of his

BASIC TACKLE 57

stay at a nearby hotel, and who assured me he'd taken fish steadily, both tench and bream ever since his arrival. Always keen to learn I abandoned my own fishing that evening and sat observing Mr Bruty in action, to find that he was employing float ledger tackle with a full ounce bomb and a piece of crust for bait. Within minutes, without any preliminary warning his float dipped smartly away out of sight, the answering strike connecting with a lively fish that turned out to be a tench of around the 2½lb mark. An hour later the performance was repeated to finish up with a bream only ounces less in weight on the bank, and just on dusk a third bite saw another fish hooked and lost.

In a mere 3½ hours fishing Mr Bruty's float had registered three really decisive bites, more than I'd experienced in five whole days. Next morning I was casting in at dawn employing exactly the same terminal gear, breadcrust-baited size 10 hook, a 1oz sliding weight and a peacock quill float in place of the standard float, 2BB shot and flake bait that I'd been using all week (Fig. 25). A tench of 2lb 10oz came to the net that morning and for the rest of my stay I averaged two fish a day, a gratifying return in conditions that were all against good fishing. Further experiments with crust for finnicky tench on a variety of waters convinced me beyond all doubt of the superiority of this bait as against flake for producing a more decisive bite, and the full ounce bomb helps of course for whatever the manoeuvres of the tench there's only one way the float can go and that's down.

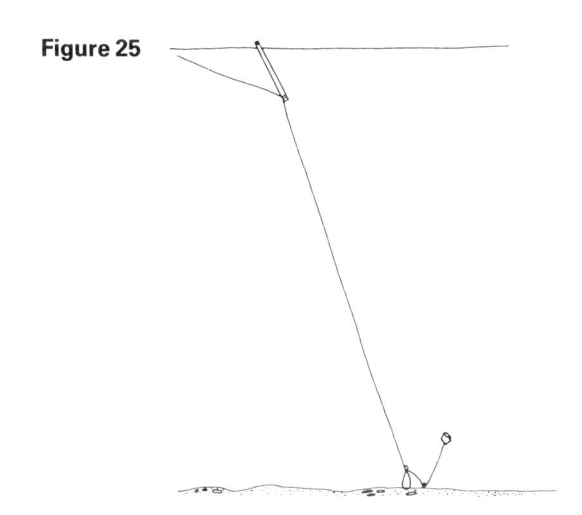

**Figure 25**

In very clear water the best technique of all can sometimes be to freeline the bait employing no float or lead. Especially is this so when fishing from a boat in conditions when a calm unruffled surface allow easy observation. No float tackle, indicator or swing tip can ever be quite so informative as to the correct moment to strike as the sight of the tench actually taking the bait into its mouth. Many times in hot, still weather I've watched tench come right under my boat to take bait and groundbait lying on the bottom eight or nine feet down; and a fascinating sight it is, the easy, leisurely approach of a big tench towards one's baited hook in these conditions being one of the most absorbing spectacles an enthusiast could ever wish for.

If the bait cannot be kept in full view, as when fishing at a distance or in heavily coloured water, freelining can only be really effective when the tench are feeding in a confident and determined fashion. On days when the fish are just mouthing the bait, then spitting it out, the prospects of detecting any indication by watching the line where it enters the water are none too good, especially if there's anything like a wind blowing at the time.

One of the most meritorious examples of angling ingenuity in all my years of pursuing tench occured in 1965 and the bait, a tiny piece of crust, was presented on a small hook and nothing else on the line at all except one small shot, just sufficient to sink the tackle and positioned a mere inch or so from the bait. The weather was hot and still and the tench, after feeding strongly in the early hours of the morning to baits presented on normal float tackle fished hard on the bottom, had steadfastly ignored our efforts for several hours. So much so that most of the boats on the lake headed away to the boathouse, thinking in terms of an afternoon siesta, before resuming operations in the cool of the evening. It must be admitted that after fishing from before dawn, even with a snatched breakfast at about 9 a.m., one begins to get a little tired by mid-day, particularly if the weather is as it was then, namely very hot. It is very tempting, and often sensible, to retire to the base, have an hour or two's sleep, followed by a good wash, a tackle check, and a general potter about until the time comes for an evening meal. Then a final tackle and bait check, and off for the evening session thoroughly refreshed and able to concentrate. Time can also be usefully and refreshingly employed looking at new swims.

Made of sterner stuff, however, Ron Clay and Steve Crawshaw in one boat, and John Weston and I in the other, stuck it out all through the afternoon, and moored a short distance away I became aware that Ron and Steve, peering straight down over the side of the boat, had spotted something on the move. Reeling in their tackle, discarding the float and all but one of the shot they lowered their minute offerings of crust straight down from the end of the rod. No sign of life for half an hour, then suddenly a quick strike, the rod bent double as it usually did when Ron was playing a fish, and in surprisingly quick time a fine tench of just over the 5lb mark was hauled into the boat. Quiet again for a spell then once again a rod took on its action curve as another fine tench was played into the net. And so it went on at intervals all afternoon, though not all the strikes were successful, however, a number of fish being missed.

Finally packing up for tea around half past four, Ron and Steve gave us a detailed account of the afternoon's events. The proceedings started off when, with the aid of polariods, they noticed a shoal of tench margin-patrolling around the small circular bay in which their boat was moored. Working along over a thick weedy bottom some 8ft or so down the fish hove into sight, straight under the boat and kept on travelling out of sight round the bay.

Half an hour later round they came again, a tench sucked in the bait and was successfully struck, so setting the pattern, every time the shoal came round one or possibly two fish would take the crust, but unless the strike was made instantly it was too late, the bait having been ejected as soon as it was taken. With flake or lobworm on the hook, the bait could so easily have been enveloped in weed before the tench appeared on the scene, but the crust remained suspended just clear and proved to be the correct choice for the occasion. On retiring from the water six tench for over 25lb total weight were in the net, a superb catch of fish taken in the middle of an afternoon that was so hot and sunny as to convince a number of good-class tench anglers that they were better off employing their time elsewhere.

Moving baits back along the bottom at intervals – 'twitching' as it is called – is a method recommended by a number of expert tench anglers but it requires a much cleaner, weed- and snag-free bottom than is to be found in most of the swims where I do my tench fishing. A twitched bait covered in pondweed or festooned with lily stalks is unlikely to prove particularly effective; though years ago I did fish several clear, open water swims that produced plenty of tench, if not any really big ones.

Carp men fishing floating crust occasionally take a tench or two and Ted Kershaw did the trick while fly fishing some years ago. Whether actually feeding or not in hot, calm conditions tench do spend quite a fair amount of time near the surface. They are not always grubbing around on the bottom by any means.

In rivers of slow to medium pace, waters which often contain large numbers of tench, the swing tip comes into its own. On these waters it can so often prove far more effective than any of the various float rigs. My own conversion to the swing tip occured in 1970 when I watched Frank Ordoyno take over 20 tench in two days while other anglers nearby, using an assortment of floats, dough bobbins and indicators for bite registration were struggling hard to take one or two. A good-class matchman, as well as big fish hunter, Frank assured me that the tip was more than just a matchman's weapon, it had its uses in specimen hunting too. He very generously presented me with one to give it a try.

Hastily fashioning a second swing tip out of a short length of plastic-covered electrical wire, I soon had both my rods in action again and straight away, after a very decisive bite indication I was into a hard fighting fish that eventually weighed in at 5lb 15oz; as encouraging a start to my swing tipping career as could be hoped for. From that point on I've developed my tackle further and now have a range of swing tips to suit all conditions of weather and water. Having taken four 7lb-plus tench and 13 more over 6lb on the tip since that initial introduction my results are all that is needed to convince even the most doubting sceptic of the efficiency of the method.

For those who prefer it the quiver tip can be extremely deadly too. I've seen some very good catches taken by anglers employing this technique. Harold Pattison of Lucan near Dublin has marketed the Spring Tip which incorporates a fine wire coil spring of extreme sensitivity; the bite registration being positive indeed. For both these tipping techniques, swing and quiver, the rod should be comfortably positioned in rests adjacent to the angler's striking arm, with the rod tip pointing out, down and across the stream. A more positive strike is obtained than if the rod is angled up and across with the exaggerated bow in the line that inevitably follows.

Most swing tip men in the match-fishing world employ the ledger lead at the far extremity of the terminal tackle (Fig. 26) but my results have been obtained with the bait at the final point, the weight being in the form of a link ledger (Figs. 27, 28), a foot or so up from

BASIC TACKLE 61

the hook as a rule but the distance being variable to suit the prevailing conditions. If fishing open water a long 'trail' is worth a try but when one has to cast into small clearings in beds of weeds or lily pads, the lead has to be slid right down to within an inch or two of the hookbait.

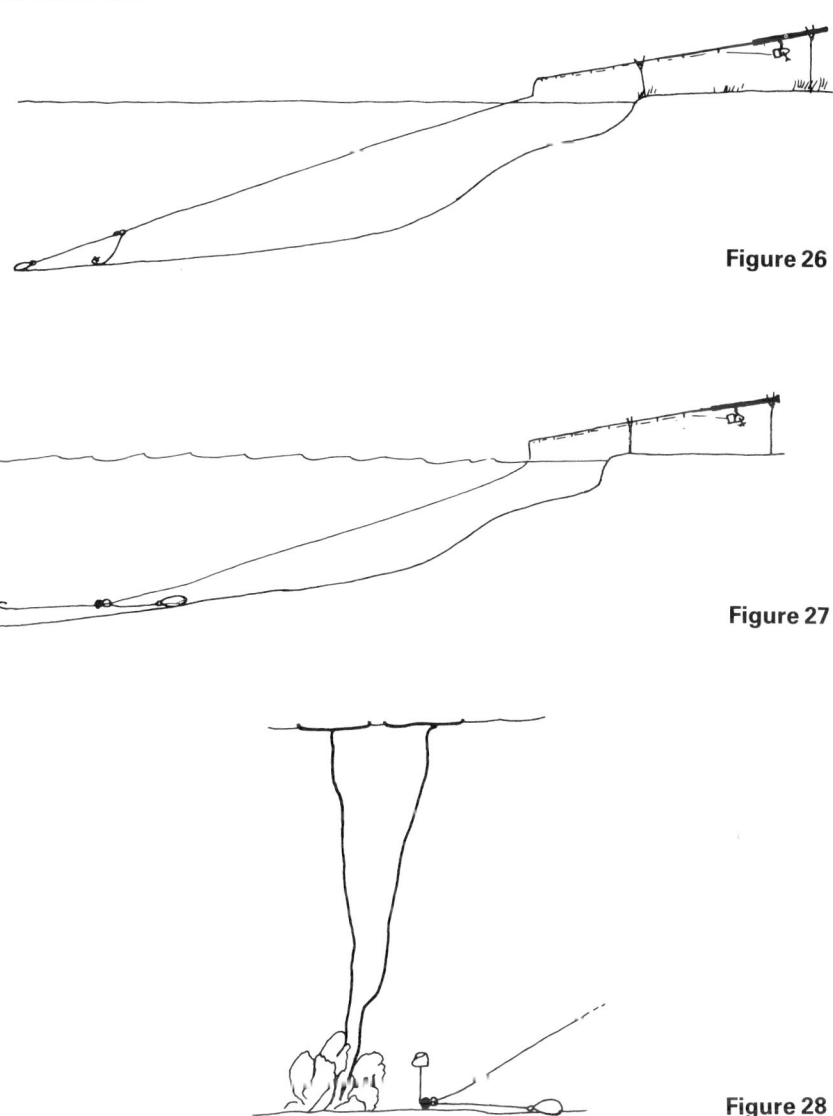

**Figure 26**

**Figure 27**

**Figure 28**

In conditions of prolonged, hot, still weather, baits fished suspended beneath a float in mid-water depths or higher will occasionally take a tench or two, and slow sinking baits presented freeline, no float and no lead, are also worth a try. No big catches are to be expected but an occasional success, taken at a time when the more conventional bottom fished baits are unlikely to prove productive, is all the more welcome in view of the difficulties involved. If the heatwave persists, river tench may eventually move into fast shallow water and in these circumstances long trotting with float tackle can produce results. I've seen this method succeed, in these conditions with maggot or chrysalis for hookbait, when all else failed.

**Comment** – *by Barrie Rickards*

The lift method outlined by Ray, and developed and popularised by the Taylor brothers of Aylesbury, has certainly been one of the innovations of the century as far as tench fishing goes. It has been used for years for other species, such as roach on the River Lea, as pointed out by Richard Walker. I was under the impression that for greatest sensitivity the line should go up almost vertically from the shot to the float (Fig. 29) and that a piece of peacock quill (trimmed with scissors) was chosen so that the shot used (usually a swan shot)

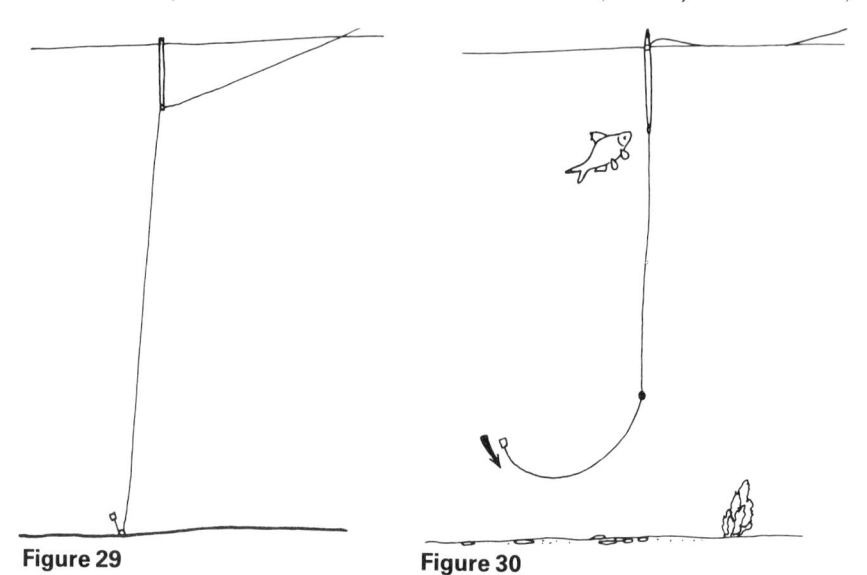

**Figure 29**     **Figure 30**

was *just* enough to slowly sink the float if the tackle was set less than the depth being fished. Certainly it has been my own experience using tiny pieces of crust, a maggot, wheat, and tiny pieces of flake, that this gives the quickest registration of a bite, the peacock quill almost leaping into the air once the shot is picked up.

I remember, some years ago, a great deal of debate as to whether the fish or the float took the weight of the lead, but if the tackle is arranged as I have described there really can be no doubt about it: the float will *not* support the lead under *any* circumstances and the fish itself feels the full weight of the swan shot. The tench must also feel the line dragging gently on its lower lip, which probably wouldn't alarm a fish quite used to digging things out of the bottom. Remember that with stewed wheat the grains may well be *within* the surface layer of mud. It is interesting, incidently, that many tench I have taken on the lift method have been hooked in the lower lip.

The further away from the hook that you place the shot, and the greater you set the float over depth, the nearer the lift rig approaches laying on, the classic tench fishing method. Even with laying on, *sensu stricto*, it is surprising how often you get a flat float bite. Crust can be fished laying on or lift method, and every word Ray says about its use is correct – it really is a killing bait. The bait can be fished various distances above the bottom, simply by letting the crust float up to the distance between shot and hook, or it can be fished slow sinking by carefully choosing the size of crust so that the hook weight is *just* sufficient to sink it. This last trick can be used on ordinary float tackle, with a big shot set to get the crust down through any surface-swimming rudd or roach (Fig. 30): the crust then falling enticingly past the noses of the tench. Tiny baits can be fished this way and I've had a number of five-pounders using the method.

The free-lining system described by Ray certainly has the disadvantage that it is useless when fish are sucking the bait in and out quickly, or are otherwise finnicky, but it does have the terrific advantage that you do not get false bites as so often in straight ledgering or even when laying on. This happens when a fish puts its back under the line (Fig. 31). At one time I had a mania for keeping the line between rod tip and lead very tight indeed: it took me a long time, as always, to appreciate why I got twice as many bites as anybody else and either missed them or brought back a single tiny tench scale on the hook! I've watched Terry Coulson fishing free-line tackle for tench on a lake which has the reputation of finnicky biters, and his success rate is pretty high: it may be that the *almost* free offering, with minimal resistance allays their suspicion and you get a better bite as a result.

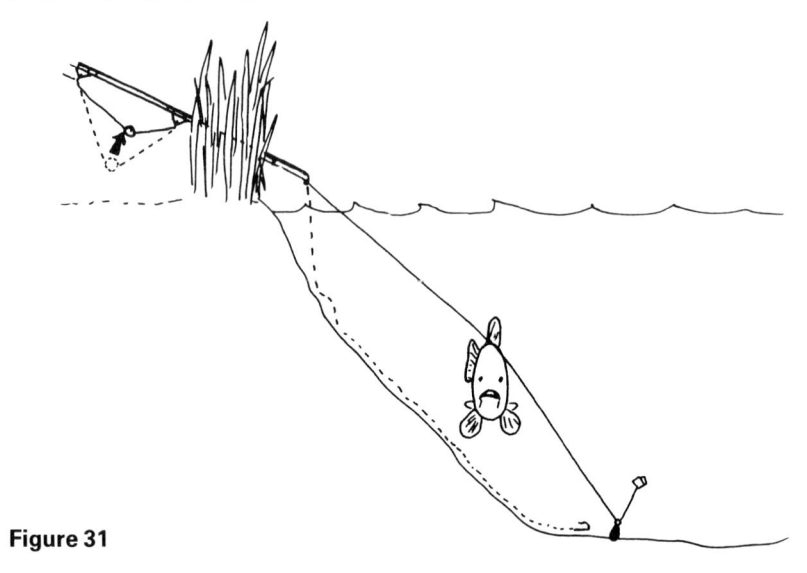

**Figure 31**

There are some purely theoretical disadvantages to the swing tip that it may be as well to mention, although I hasten to add that I've been a convert to its effectiveness ever since I tried it on the Market Weighten Canal many years ago. The obvious disadvantage is that you cannot let the tench run with the bait: there are occasions, using very large lobworms, when it is necessary to let the tench take at least three feet of line before you strike. You cannot do this with a swing tip and, in fact, the strike is made on a total movement of the tip of about 6–12in. Of course, if the distance between shot and hook is 12in also, then the tench may have moved with the bait as little as 1 foot or as much as 3 feet (Figs. 32 and 33). Anglers do use worms on swing tip tackle, but my own feeling is that few anglers use *big* lobworms, whereas many of my own big tench, and those of the Taylor brothers, have actually fallen to really big worms.

Again, valid criticism of the swing tip sensitivity has been made on many occasions by Richard Walker, who points out that touch-ledgering is almost certainly more effective. In fact I've never yet touch-ledgered for tench, but my experiences with roach confirms what he says. Nevertheless you cannot touch-ledger with two rods at

BASIC TACKLE

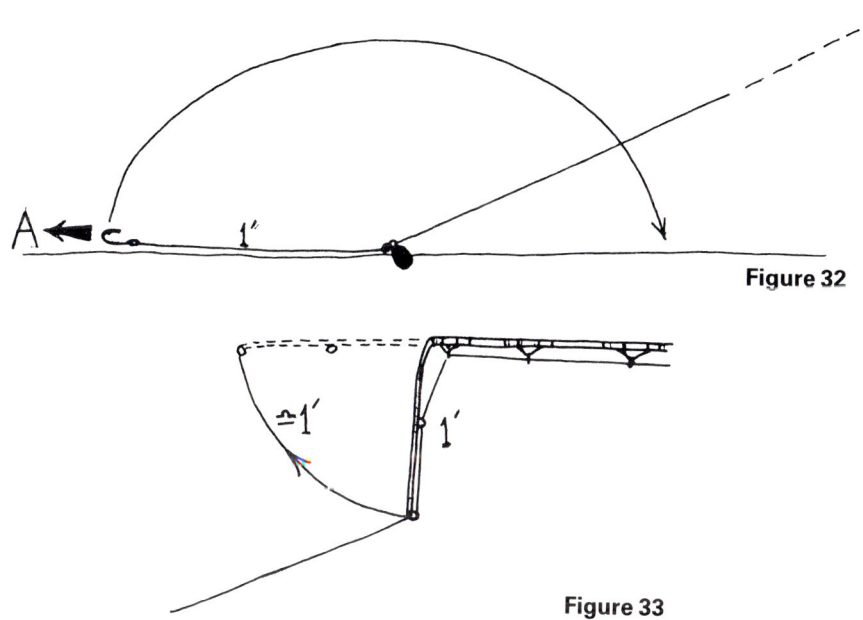

**Figure 32**

**Figure 33**

once, and swing tipping is more confortable over along period. And Ray's results with tench bare witness to its effectiveness.

One other matter worthy of mention in relation to basic techniques is the use of localised groundbait dodges like the swim feeder. The nature of the design of these, and block feeders etc. is too legion for me to go into, and suffice it to give one illustration (Fig. 34). The idea is that the samples of hook bait and groundbait within the feeder eventually fall out in a little pile not far away from the hook bait itself. The fact that the hookbait is very slightly to one side of the attractor probably increases its chance of being snapped up quickly. Swim feeders are extremely effective in tench fishing, whether in still water or rivers, and I first witnessed this on Landbeach Lakes at about the time when the swim feeder first hit the market. I didn't like the way the man in the next swim almost emptied the lake every time he cast (I thought he was cupping hard groundbait round the shot, which is almost as effective as a swimfeeder), but I must admit he was taking two tench to my one, and having had the performance repeated on a few other occasions and in other swims I became converted. Since that date I have watched very big tench feeding on a Yorkshire lake and I think I know *why* the swimfeeder is so effective.

These big fish were feeding, apparently rather casually, in the late morning period *after* a pretty hectic feeding spell at dawn. They wandered aimlessly around and every so often spotted a little patch of remaining groundbait and mopped it up in seconds. But the point is that they had difficulty *seeing* the little piles of groundbait unless they swam within eighteen inches of them. The water was crystal clear, the sun bright, and I think this testifies to the fact that the tench's bright little red eye isn't all that marvellous for seeing with, at least in daylight. Obviously a good size pile of groundbait from a swimfeeder would be more likely to be spotted than a single hookbait offering in an area rather loosely spread with groundbait. So swimfeeders and the like are a must for my tackle box, and if I squash them, a frequent occurrence with me, then I cup a hard ball of groundbait around the shot (and wait for the float to come up if I'm float fishing!).

Another matter basic to tench fishing, and indeed any ledgering, is the nature of the stop shot. Nothing is worse than to have this slip on the strike, for it lets the ledger weight zoom down to the hook and this had the effect of knocking the hook out of the fish's mouth. Actually, when the stop shot slips *on the strike* it probably results in the hook failing to take a hold at all. When the stop shot gives during playing the ledger weight can *easily* knock the hook from its hold: I well remember reading in 'Still Water Angling' how Pete Thomas lost a huge tench when this very thing happened.

All manner of tricks have been resorted to in order to beat this problem, including a string of shots, a portion of matchstick in a valve rubber, and so on, but the most effective is to insert a swivel in the reel line and although this lowers the line strength by a further 10% or so it never fails to stop the lead. Just recently another 'stop shot' has come on the market (Fig. 35). This is made by Custom Tackle and consists of a nylon peg and a nylon sleeve: the sleeve is threaded on to the reel line and the peg pushed home thereby trapping the line. It seems pretty effective, although I haven't fully tried it out as yet, but the peg has to be pushed home so firmly that it slightly flattens the nylon line. This does not reduce the breaking strain of the line, of course (shots have the same effect), but I don't like flats on my line at any time.

The techniques used by Eric Hodgson will clearly be of interest to the reader after his terrific impact in Chapter 2, and he kindly contributes the following:

'I would like to define here the difference between preoccupational

BASIC TACKLE

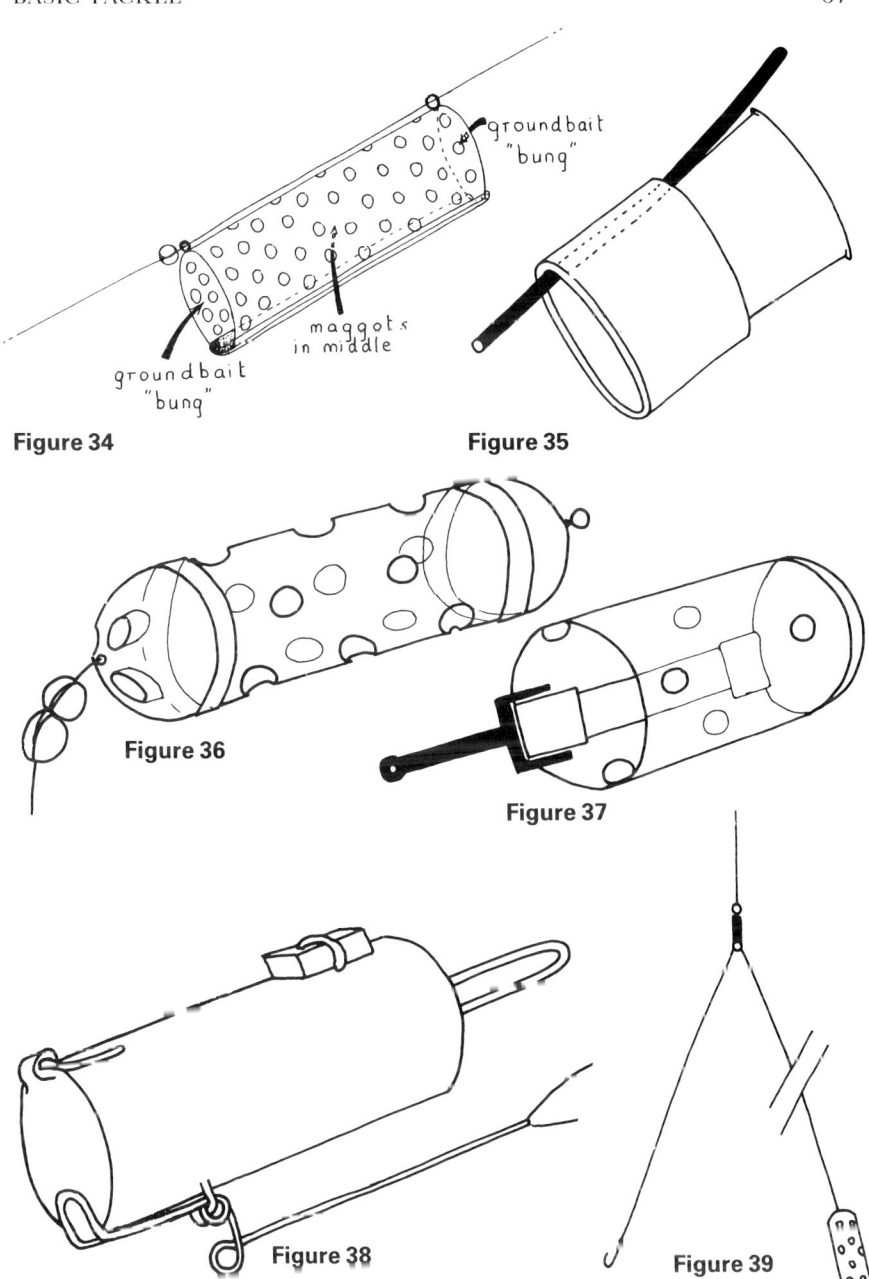

groundbait
"bung"
maggots
in middle
groundbait
"bung"
**Figure 34**

**Figure 35**

**Figure 36**

**Figure 37**

**Figure 38**

**Figure 39**

feeding, which is feeding on natural pond food, and non-preoccupational feeding on baits presented by the angler, e.g. maggots, worms, bread, etc. An examination of the bubble pattern thrown up by tench will give an indication of the type of feeding taking place in the swim at any given time. It is important to recognise these two bubble patterns, since type of bait and bait presentation is of importance if any success is to be achieved. Preoccupational feeding is characterised by large patches of gaseous bubbles coming to the surface, sometimes as big as two or three feet in diameter, and very similar to the effect one would have if detergent was stirred into the water. The bubbles are created by tench foraging in the mud and releasing detritus gases.

'Non-preoccupational feeding is symbolised by small needle-type bubbles breaking the surface. An experienced angler will know that with the latter, clean sail-away bites occur, and hooking the fish is comparatively simple, whereas with the preoccupational-type bite, it is frequently just a pluck at a sensitively rigged float or ledger system.

'Whilst it will be recognised that in general terms preoccupational-type feeding will take place during the high and later summer, non-preccupational feeding will take place in the early weeks of the summer. However, the situation becomes confused when heavy groundbaiting takes place before the start of the season and immediately after, when ground-bait cast in will be found to attract to the area animal life from a large area around. Although this is not a very serious hazard in the early weeks, as it is in the high summer, it can encourage preoccupational feeding to take place early in the season, since the migration of detritus bugs into the swim area, which will be attracted by the groundbait, will encourage tench to seek these bugs and small animals in preference to the hook bait, e.g. maggots cast in as free offerings frequently burrow their way into the mud, drown; and subsequently decay – in the process of nature the small microscopic animals in the mud will devour these as food – tench will frequently suck up maggots purely and simply for the food upon them, and then blow the maggots out. So, the angler is confronted with the dilemma of fishing delicately so as to detect these suck and blow type bites, and whiplash-type reaction is necessary if a hook is to be secured in the mouth of the fish. All too frequently, however, the angler finds that the hook is impailed anywhere in the fish but the mouth.

'There are always exceptions to rules, and on many occasions whilst the tench expert is delicately applying his finely balanced tackle to secure a capture, the young tyro will cast in his large lobworm with his large float, heavy line and big hook in the middle of the afternoon and catch the odd big tench. As mentioned, this is, of course, an exception to the rule, and consistent results will only be obtained with the application of delicate methods.

'The two delicate techniques I use are the balanced lift method or the over-shotted float method. Describing the balance lift method first, I normally use a balsa body float with a 2in antenna, where the balsa body is $\frac{1}{4}$in to 5/16in diameter and measures about 4in long. The idea being with this float that the shots placed on the line at mid-water level should be enough to take the balsa body down below the surface until the point when the body of the float meets with the antenna section. Then, by accurately obtaining the depth where one is fishing, a no. 6 shot is added to take the antenna down until the last $\frac{1}{4}$in of it is showing. Generally speaking, this no. 6 shot is positioned fairly close to the hook and 1in is not too close on occasions, such that when the feeding tench sucks in the bait, an immediate lift occurs from the antenna which should be struck.

'Advice given by angling writers to the effect that one or two swan shots fished on the bottom under a suitably sized porcupine quill in the established lift method, quite frankly is not good enough for bite detection in these conditions mainly, because of the inertia value of the rig. Bearing in mind the fish are merely sucking and blowing out bait particles not solely for the food itself, but for the micro-organisms that have collected on to the bait particles.

'With regard to the over-shotted method, I normally use the short quill float 4in to 5in, which is shotted down with the shots placed mid-water until the tip of the quill breaks the surface. Again taking the depth of the water accurately, I finally place a no. 6 shot on the bottom such that when the fish picks up the bait, which is positioned near the shot (1in is not too near), the extra weight of the shot then is to be carried by the float, and since the float is nearly submerged, one gets a quick registration by the float dipping below the surface. An instant strike will often connect with the fish here when other methods fail.'

CHAPTER 5

# New Tackle & Techniques
*Barrie Rickards*

ALONG with the improved growth and survival of tench into the 1980's has been a considerable change for the better in terms of tackle and techniques. I have referred earlier to the relationships between carp and tench fishing and there can be no doubt whatsoever that tench fishing this decade has benefited from developments in carp fishing. Baits are dealt with in chapter 6 and by Martin Gay in chapter 9, so I shall confine myself to pertinent changes in tackle itself and in the more debateable sphere of techniques.

In 1975 traditional tench fishing outfits were in the process of giving way to techniques essentially deriving from match angling: the use of swing and various other tips, and use of swim feeders was gaining ground. Since then use of swing tips has declined as a specifically tench fishing method although, as with traditional tench fishing and laying-on at close range, it is still a quite valid and effective method. Swim feeders are still widely used, and with good reason for there is now a wide choice of weight, size, and design of feeder, so that the angler can pick his feeder for type and amount of bait needed, for varied release rates, and for close range work or distance casting. For all these improvements feeder fishing remains a clumsy method and one which I personally do not enjoy as much as other techniques. It is, however, one of the most successful of all tench hunting tactics and for this reason above I'll use it as necessary. Figs. 34-38 shows the variety of feeders available, whilst Fig. 39 depicts the basic end rig for their use. I have a strong preference for use of small swivels as stops, rather than the commercial sleeve-and-plug stops or shots, neither of which are 100% slip proof. And a stop which slips on the strike means a missed bite in my experience.

There are many wrinkles which have been developed for feeder fishing, anglers varying the size and position of the lead, the size and position of the holes, and whether to have a blockend feeder, a fully open-ended feeder, or one with one end only blocked. Personally I avoid fully blocked feeders except when I want to cram in as many maggots as possible. I have a feeling that with fine cereal groundbaits, in tench waters that is, most of the bait comes out *on the retrieve*, not as it lies there on the bottom. So I use open ended feeders most of the time. If I use one blocked at one end (Fig. 36) then clearly this is the end nearest the line! In such circumstances I give the feeder a few minutes in one place and then draw it in six inches to let out the attractor. If the hook link length is greater than that of the feeder link, and you have settled the tackle on the bottom skilfully in the first place, such a slight movement backwards will draw the bait very close to the small pile of attractor, whether this latter be fine cereal or portions of hookbait.

Few changes have occurred in getting the heavier loads of groundbait out into the swim except for the manufacture of good spoon-ended throwing sticks which seem occasionally to be available. These will throw large balls not only accurately but a lot further than one can throw by hand! Throwing sticks for maggots or particle baits are much the same, but throwing tubes for boilies *are* used increasingly, as well as catapults. Martin deals with catapults for boilies in Chapter 9, so I'll comment here only on throwing tubes (Fig. 40). These need to be flexible, have a diameter of about one and a half inches (to accommodate varied boilie diameters), and of fibre glass or household plastic drainpipe. The fibre glass – an old blank for example – seems to me to give a little more steely whip and a little more distance and accuracy. I personally prefer catapults, which with today's sophisticated models will give you 80 yards comfortably and with precision. Using, therefore, a combination of throwing sticks and tubes (or catapults) one can bait up more precisely than in the past, and at greater distance, with both heavy groundbait and with hook bait samples.

Tench rods have come a long way in the last decade, but as a direct spin off from other angling, notably carp angling. I still use the full range of rods I mentioned above, namely cane MkIV Avons, fourteen foot Fibatubes, and so on, but I also use with pleasure the very latest rods which in most respects are superior. A few years ago I bought a pair of eleven foot, fast taper Going Brothers blanks especially for fishing boilies at long range for big tench. And this decision exemplifies one of the major changes recently, namely the tendency for most anglers to drift towards eleven foot rods, if glass, and twelve foot rods, if carbon. Partly this is a reflection of the weight of the material. A tip action carbon rod of twelve feet is lighter, nicer to use, and will do all that a glass rod of eleven feet will do. So whereas I used twelve and fourteen foot Fibatube blanks for close range float fishing with fine line, I now find I'm using rods not much shorter on average, for my distance work too – so I might just as well use them for the close work. Many advances in angling tackle and techniques do seem ultimately to lead to a *simplification*, and this has happened in tench fishing today.

As with rods, so with reels. These seem to me to have improved out of all recognition. I shall always use my old favourites, but some of the light weight, dark coloured reels, such as the Sigma Graphite made by Shakespeare, or not dissimilar reels made by Ryobi, are extremely smooth running, robust and aesthetically pleasing in use. These improvements are not a result of changes in carp fishing but of the demands and market of the match fishing scene. As with floats they have made an enormous contribution to us all. It is a delight to play tench on these new reels, whether one uses the slipping clutch, or as I do, rely on the smooth backwind. In fact I am sure in my own mind that they are more suitable for playing middleweight species, such as tench, than other species in the light or heavyweight category.

I do keep referring to the contributions of carp fishing and the demands of carp anglers to the improved tench fishing scene. Nowhere is this more apparent than with reference to peripheral equipment. Whether this is rod rests, optonics, monkey climbers, line clips or things further away from the rods such as brolly covers, bed chairs, seats and tackle boxes, all can be used, naturally, for tench fishing.

For long range ledgering the arrangement of rods and indicators can be exactly as in carp fishing, but you need to know fairly quickly how the tench on your water feed. On some waters you need to let the indicator trundle all the way to the butt ring, and hold for a half a second, before striking: all that time the optonic buzzer may have been sounding. In other instances you get little more than a wobble on the indicator which *may not always* sound the audible alarm. These variations need not only be a result of the manner in which those particular tench are inclined to feed but may in addition reflect the amount of hookbait/groundbait you have put in, the range at which you are fishing, and the amount and type of weed or other obstruction between you and the baited area. Fig. 41 shows a good basic set up for long range ledgering, which may then need to be modified in the light of your own experience.

NEW TACKLE AND TECHNIQUES 73

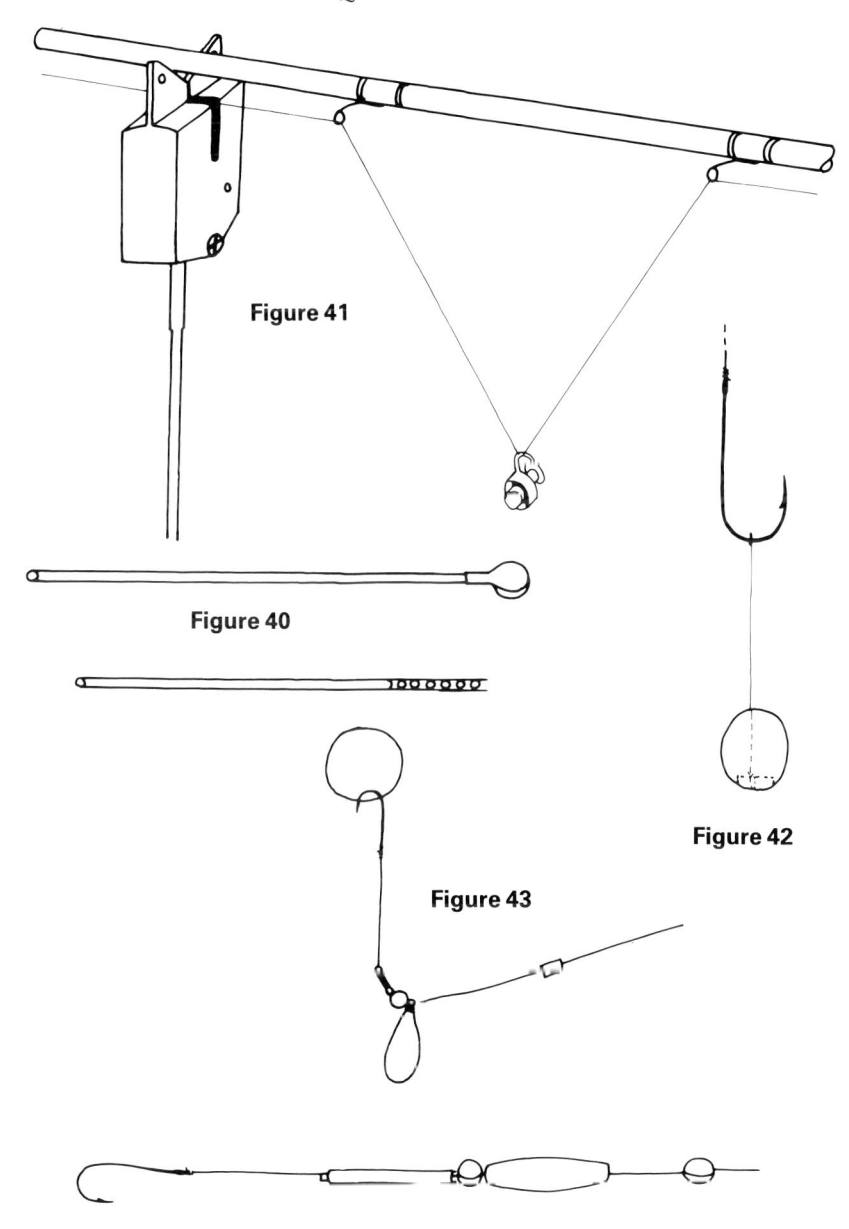

Figure 41

Figure 40

Figure 42

Figure 43

Figure 44 – Shock Rig After Hutchinson (1981)

This leads me to a question that has bothered me for years: that of resistance and the taking fish. Brought up as I was, angling-wise that is, in the 1950's, I fell under the spell of the new specimen hunters and the leading writers of the time such as Richard Walker, Fred Taylor, Frank Guttfield and others. They argued along with many other watercraft principles, that resistance was anathema to the taking fish: eels, pike, tench, carp, all dropped the bait like a hot potato if they felt resistance (which, presumably, they associated with humans and danger). It seems almost an unarguable case even now, to me: if the fish feels no resistance then it will not spook, will it? What bothered me was whether resistance really mattered if the angler had followed good watercraft principles and the fish was quite unaware of his presence. Nevertheless I went along, reluctantly, with the dictates of that era – for such it was. Yet I know a friend who laid night lines for eels, in a water on which I insisted on using free-line, resistance-free, tackle, and he caught far more than I did, and bigger, despite a 4oz lead on the end and 60lb b.s. cotton line with 30lb b.s. monofil droppers. Those eels didn't worry about resistance: they just swallowed the lot. Furthermore, I knew that long liners in Ireland, and sea fishing long liners did exactly the same. And I knew that tench fishers on Carlton Towers used incredibly crude tackle, sometimes involving a fixed 2oz lead, and yet still caught good fish often. I know which approach I *prefer*, but which is best?

It is possible that principles laid down in the 1950s, basically admirable though they are, actually detracted in certain respects from rapid development of one or two techniques in carp fishing which have recently, and similarly, helped transform tenching: I refer to the use of H.P. baits, H.N.V. baits, hair rigs, bolt rigs and shock rigs? The first two have been discussed by Martin above, but the last three are not only important but very interesting.

Consider first of all the basic hair rig (Fig. 42). This was designed (by Lennie Middleton and Kevin Maddocks) because the carp were feeling too much resistance from the stiff line, and because they were gulping the bait down without swimming off and then biting *through* the stiff line with their throat teeth as the angler struck! In fact, exactly the opposite of the frightened fish syndrome. By fitting a "hair" of varying lengths the last thing the fish takes into its mouth is the (necessary) large hook and stiff line, so that the strike is less likely to result in a bite-off or a deep hooked fish. This kind of problem is, incidentally, a result of the times! It didn't happen when we did the first edition because long range ledgering with boilies wasn't practised. Tench can bite-off just as well as carp, and the hair rig works well for tench. I do say this without first-hand experience, having had, so far, no real trouble with bite-offs or deep hooked fish, though I've had several of both during long range fishing. With a bite-off, of course, there is no way of knowing it was a tench!

The bolt rig (Fig. 43) is a refinement, in a way, of the hair rig in that the heavy lead is placed only 1-3 inches away from the hook, the idea being to get the fish to feel the resistance, panic a little, and move off more quickly with the bait. We have a contradiction here. On the one hand I'm claiming that resistance doesn't really bother tench, and here we have a method that claims to *rely* on it (for carp anyway). I think that fish *feel* the resistance but are not frightened by it. In fact their very feeding habits, rooting in mud, silt and weeds, leads them to expect resistance occasionally and they expect to have to pull for their food (you can *see* this in both fish-tank fish and fish in the wild, quite often). So, they feel the resistance and pull like hell. If the resistance is even greater, as in the shock rig with its *fixed* lead (Fig. 44) they pull even harder. If they were frightened they'd spit out the bait in a split second.

You see now how we've come full circle in our thinking. The very latest carping end rigs which work well for tench even though I do not myself now use them, depend to some extent at least on creating a resistance to the take, whereas in days gone by we tried to do exactly the opposite – except for the commercial long-liners who had learnt from experience that resistance often mattered little.

But none of these fish had been spooked: the moment they are then all the above refinements are so much wasted effort. We still try to avoid spooking our tench, by using the modern dark brown or black matt finish lines, for example. Even the hair rig has an element of the non-frightener in it in the sense that as the fish takes the boilie or particle into its mouth the bait *must* feel more natural than one attached to stiff line, that is *if* they expect their boilies and particles to be unattached, which we cannot know on present evidence. What all this comes down to, I think, is that the basic long range ledger rig of Fig. 41 is a good starting point and needs only to be modified as and when it proves defective. It may well be that hair rigs, bolt rigs, and shock rigs, successful though they are with tench, are being used because they are in vogue. I'm sure they are very necessary in carp fishing, but in tench fishing, who knows . . .?

Since 1975 the angler in general has had available a vastly increased range of high quality floats. The kind of home-made attachment of Fig. 17 might by some be deemed unnecessary today because very neat commercial models are available. When close range float fishing for tench is Yorkshire, using antennae floats carrying from 1-5BBs, I change quickly and regularly as the wind shifts. Occasionally I keep only one BB on the line itself and use this as a stop to a tiny swivel. To this swivel I attach a short length of fine line, 1-2 inches, and to this I add or subtract BB shot as necessary. This is a very versatile system because you can fish laid-on, on the drift, or you can fish a slow sinking bait by raising the position of the BB which is on the line. As this is the *only* shot on the line itself there is less risk of damage to the reel line (Figs. 19 & 20). Thus shots and floats can be changed very quickly indeed, and if a switch to ledgering is made the float link can be left on the line though you may wish to effect other changes in respect of the ledger itself.

Hooks have changed relatively little in recent times except that there are available more varieties which purport to be fine-wire, ring-eyed, with good, small barbs. Or barbless. There has been an increasing tendency amongst anglers, and tench anglers are no exception here, to use barbless hooks. In the main anglers are following a fashion, a fetish, rather than thinking it through. I use barbless hooks in tiddler snatching, and pressed barbs in trout fishing, each for a specific reason which needn't concern us here. In other fishing I have, as yet, no use for them and can see no purpose in tench fishing except that it makes hook removal easier. I contend that it also makes hook removal easier for the tench, and I assert that I do *not* cause damage to tench when removing hooks with small barbs or filed down barbs. Whatever one's preferences it is quite easy today to buy what are usually called specialist hooks or specimen hunters hooks from many dealers. Partridge make good ones, as do Peter Drennan Tackle; V.M.C. are good, as are Au Lion D'Or. It's simply a matter of finding the right ones for you. I suspect that very considerable design changes will be effected in hooks during the next decade. The Japanese, for example, use a quite different hook bend to most nations. And I recall a talk by Jim Gibbinson recently where he, in effect, very carefully determines the hook gape and angle, the barb size and shape, and the shank length and "eye" by messing about with manufactured varieties until he gets them just right.

Tench fishing, despite the enormous success in recent years, has not kept pace in its own right with carp fishing, and tackle developments largely derive from the later. This is no bad thing, of course, for the tench fisher today has, as a result, a superb range of tackle and peripheral equipment which he can modify to his own purposes. Some of the latest carp rods are too powerful, at least for close range work, so the tench angler would be well advised to go for test curves in the 1½-1¾lb range, and to stick to lines from 9lb b.s. *downwards*, rather than 6lb b.s. upwards, as circumstances dictate.

CHAPTER 6

# Food of Tench
*Barrie Rickards*

TENCH are classified by biologists as bottom feeders even though they do fairly commonly take food from the surface film, and certainly take water snails from mid-water plants and bankside bullrushes. Most of the time they spend grubbing in the bottom sediment, but not digging deeply like carp and bream with the resultant muddying of the water, but rather taking in mouthfuls of the surface millimetres where their main diet of bloodworms (chironomid larvae) actually live. Like most other species of freshwater fish they do not live on one food alone but will eat shrimps, caddis, snails, and I have even caught one with a whole swan mussel, some three inches long, and complete with shell, in its belly.

Much of the diet of baby tench consists of water fleas (*Daphnia*), *Cyclops*, ostracods (tiny, hopping, weed and mud-loving shelled creatures), and both algae and higher plants; wheras adult tench eat more shrimps (*Asellus* and *Gammarus*), more insects and insect larvae, more molluscs (snails, pea mussels) in addition to the types of creature eaten by baby fish. Occasionally they will eat other fish, including their own offspring (plate 46). The readiness of tench to eat both animal and vegetable matter probably explains why both worms and bread are good baits. Some of the natural food items can never be used or copied by anglers, but bloodworms, shrimps, caddis and snails can certainly, and should be, used more extensively than they are today. A bloodworm does not have to be in the mud, nor a caddis in its case for it to succeed well with tench. Whether any further advantage can be taken of their liking for vegetable matter I do not know, but I remember one angler fishing for a week with sprouts as bait and not getting a run!

## FEEDING AND BEHAVIOUR
*Ray Webb*

Though most tench fishing techniques incorporate a tackle terminating in a bait held hard on the bottom the fish are by no means always to be found at that depth, spending a considerable amount of time in mid-water, or even up on the surface at times. There are waters, in fact, where tench are frequently to be seen rolling at the surface; this habit being of great value to the angler trying to locate the fish before deciding where to commence his pre-baiting campaign. It's not exclusively in shallow areas where rolling occurs, though it is perhaps most commonly encountered here, understandably enough, for I've studied tench surface rolling in 12 foot of water or more. The critical factors seem to be time of day and prevailing weather rather than depth of water.

In common with most other species, in very rough windy conditions or spells of raw cold weather, the tench tend to stay down close to the bottom, but given a spot of settled, calm, warm weather may leave the deeper layers of water to disport themselves, rolling at the surface. Rarely to be seen at midday, most of this surface rolling takes place from dawn through the first couple of hours or so of daylight, and a few early morning fish spotting sessions in suitable conditions before the season opens can pay big dividends once the serious business of angling begins.

Once seen, never forgotten, there is no danger at all of being mistaken for the spectacular surface display of bream, rudd or perch; The tench rolling so smooth and quietly that the surface is barely disturbed at all, just a dark, bronzed, rounded fin showing momentarily, then it's gone; one almost has to be pre-focused on the correct spot to detect the movement at all. Once located, however, the rolling will probably continue in the same area for several weeks at least, weather conditions being suitable, and the spot can be heavily pre-baited confident in the knowledge that for every tench seen on the surface there'll be half a dozen or more down below.

As a supreme example of the results that may ultimately be achieved by a few mornings' observation, one can hardly hope to better Barrie's fantastic bag of 27 tench for 162lb followed up a couple of days or so later with 23 more for 165lb, for tench had been seen rolling in this swim regularly for several weeks, moody and indifferent, before they suddenly came mad on feed with such a vengeance that even I, witness to the frequent day-by-day display, was taken completely aback by the vast number of fish found to be present. In addition to Barrie's catches, other anglers moored alongside were also taking tench one after the other there must have been literally hundreds of them on the bottom as against perhaps a couple of dozen spotted rolling at the surface. Just why do tench roll, are they feeding, coming up for air or what one might wonder? The truth of the matter is I'm sure that neither food nor air provide the motivation, it's purely a form of play or enjoyment just as rabbits play tag, or follow-my-leader, or birds burst forth into song as soon as daylight breaks; all part of the dawn chorus.

Another regular feature of tench behaviour is their habit of sending up masses of bubbles, sometimes in tiny streams, at others in enormous clouds covering several square yards in area. Once again, though other species, bream and carp in particular also indulge in the same habit and the bottom itself discharges gases from time to time there can be no doubt at all when tench are responsible, the needle bubbles, as they are often called, being absolutely distinctive. Though a welcome sign in any tench enthusiast's swim needle bubbles, even in quantity, are no guarantee that the fish will be in feeding mood. The first demonstration I ever had of that was in June 1958 when Dave Mansell and I drove over to fish Castle Howard Lake near Malton in Yorkshire.

Arriving at the waterside late on the Friday night a considerable quantity of groundbait was dumped into a couple of swims that we felt confident were holding a number of tench, and after a short night's sleep we arose at dawn to find both our baited swims a seething mass of bubbles; never to this day have I seen a more furious display. Hastily assembling a couple of rods each, one baited up with worm and the other terminating in a couple of maggots, in next to no time four porcupine floats were sat half-cocked in the middle of all the disturbance, our hopes of a big tench catch riding very high indeed for hadn't I taken fifteen tench in one sitting only a fortnight previously. A slight move of one of Dave's floats resulted in a lightning strike that failed to connect, which was hardly surprising for we didn't normally strike unless a decisive bite was obtained; it was a case of premature action precipitated by the extremely nervous anticipation of the moment.

Before Dave had baited up the hook again I experienced the same type of bite to my maggot baited tackle but firmly resisted the temptation to strike, determined to wait until the float slid completely out of sight. Quite a wait it turned out to be, for though we fished on right through the heat of the day all the way to the point where failing light made it impossible to see our floats any longer, we failed completely to achieve a single decisive bite between the pair of us, though the excessive bubbling ceased just before midday the slight float movements continued all afternoon, though at considerably longer intervals, and we finally packed up beaten after about 18 hours of hard, frustrating effort.

In those early days the lift method was unknown to us, nor had I sufficient experience to have a variety of baits with me in case of such emergencies, so we stuck with our worm and maggot baits on traditional 2BB shot float tackle all day long. Many other later experiences with bubbling tench both at Castle Howard and on a variety of other waters ended up on a far happier note, a catch of 9 fish for 21½lb from Castle Howard on June 30th, 1961 and 4 for 15½lb from Pebley Pond in 1964 being a couple of cases where prolific bubbling took place while the tench were feeding in a firm and decisive fashion. On one occasion, after fishing hard for the five hours from dawn, I'd just about written off all hope of sport for the morning when just after 9 o'clock a single stream of tiny bubbles appeared making steady progress across the 8 or 9 yards of water that separated them from my float, a most heartening situation and sure enough my worm bait was taken almost at once, a 4¾lb tench being hauled protesting all the way to the net.

Unfortunately there were no more bubbles and no further sport for the rest of the day, but that single fish stands out vividly in my mind while many other sizeable catches have faded into oblivion; continually I find myself wondering whether that fish saw or scented the bait and worked its way along for 30ft or more, or whether it was just coincidence that my lob happened to be lying dead in the track that the tench was taking. One of the theories regularly put forward to explain the bubbling phenomena is that the tench are sucking in food, often taking in mouthfuls of mud for the bloodworms and larvae contained, exhaling eventually when the tiny bubbles are formed by the gill rakers, and this seems likely to be the truth of the matter, though whenever I've been able to watch tench feeding on the bottom they have steadfastly refused to push up any bubbles. At Balderton Dip near Newark, however, I did once see a tench come up from 7 ft of water to suck in a mouthful of air from the surface and then slowly move across the pond sinking gradually, and leaving a tell tale stream of bubbles to mark his progress.

Tench are often said to favour swims with a soft, black, muddy bottom and certainly I've caught plenty of fish myself in such places, but many of the best spots I know for really outsize specimens have hard rock or gravely bottoms; at Lanesborough on the Shannon for instance the bed of the river is so hard that one of the major problems confronting the tench enthusiast on this fishery is how to drive in his rod rest, nothing less than a road mender's pneumatic drill being adequate for the job at most points. At another of my early tench waters the bottom was hard sandstone yet the fish thrived on it, growing to 6lb and more in weight, so I never let the lack of gaseous, black tench-ooze worry me. The species is pretty tough and adaptable, well able to prosper in a wide variety of different types of water. One undeniable advantage of soft sludge is for hibernation purposes, however, for no matter how severe the winter weather may prove the tench can easily bury down and keep warm staying there dormant till the warm spring conditions arrive. On fisheries with a firmer, harder type of bottom problems must inevitably arise and fishing one such water for pike in early February a fish that rolled under my companion's rod some 25 yards or so away was eventually spotted trying to bury into a small clump of underwater weed, only his tail being still visible, though that was enough of course for us to identify the species straightaway as obviously a tench instead of the pike we were seeking. A simple matter to scoop the fish out with a landing net and weigh him in at 4lb 11oz, a fine fish for that or any other water, and it swam slowly away, on being released, though still obviously a trifle groggy, suffering from a touch of exposure.

On many waters tench exhibit a distinct tendency towards margin patrolling, and once their regular runs are discovered, provided a cautious stealthy approach is adopted, good catches can be made only a short cast out from the bank. One water I used to fish regularly at one time produced all its best catches to baits fished just over the margin fringe of weed, actual observation of the tench being ruled out on account of the highly coloured nature of the water, but trial and error experiment with one rod fished in close and the other well out almost invariably saw the distant bait finish up as a very poor second, often being ignored completely. Carp anglers have long been aware of the tremendous potential of the marginal weedy areas favoured by their chosen species and tench are in no way different, following along in exactly the same paths so frequently that enormous baits on strong tackle are often taken, not by the outsize carp for which they were intended, but by tench of comparatively modest proportions. One of Dick Walker's big tench, a fish of 5lb 10oz, was taken accidentally in this fashion, accepting a floating crust on 18lb breaking strain line being fished in the middle of the night for carp.

Though primarily a bottom feeder, there are occasions when tench are to be taken on baits presented in mid-water or even right up on the surface itself. Time and again I've watched tench take slowly sinking baits before they reach the bottom and fishing flies at the surface Ted Kershaw successfully hooked and landed tench when all he could have reasonably expected was a good catch of rudd.

Behaviour of this sort is the exception rather than the rule but the competent, experienced tench angler will have sufficient variety in his repertoire of baits, tackle and techniques to seize the opportunity as it occurs, taking a fish or two when the novice would draw a blank. It is, however, the frequent, customary, behaviour and feeding habits that are of paramount importance and the man who has made a thorough study along these lines will usually end up with the right bait, in the right place, at the right time.

## BAITS

*Barrie Rickards*

Between the one extreme dictum which says that baits do not matter, only the approach works, and the other which worships *the* bait, the more secret the better, probably lies the truth that bait is important, but useless if you frightened the tench to death before fishing. Mind you, tench take some frightening. Dragging the swim attracts them very quickly even if the noise of the drag going in initially sends them fleeing. But they soon take off if they see your silhouette against the skyline, and I've seen tench swim off in panic at a handful of maggots hitting the water. The choice of baits is legion, but if I list a few of the better-known ones first, discuss them, and then move on to the more way-out baits you'll begin to get some idea: lobworms; redworms; brandlings; maggots; breadflake; breadpaste; bread crust; stewed wheat.

That list of baits, fished in various ways, will cover most of your tench fishing. If I had to stick to one bait out of that list it would be maggots, but I always carry as much variety as possible. In a single session the tench may go 'off' a bait several times: and when I had that 162lb bag of big tench most of them fell to very large lobworms, but for two periods lasting half an hour each I could only get them to feed on anchored crust.

Lobworms are outstandingly good baits for tench but, in Britain at any rate, suffer from the attentions of eels, pike and perch, although it is true that when the tench really get their heads down perch keep out of the way. Big lobs, and bunches of big lobs I have found to be particularly effective at night, and also towards the end of a morning session as though the tench were grabbing a last big mouthful before moving back to the weed beds. As with all baits, some waters are 'lobworm waters' and it certainly pays to find out how the locals succeed before commencing fishing. A really big lob needs a size 6 or 4 hook, and I prefer to hook them just once, giving plenty of time on the strike for the tench to get it well into its mouth. Slow sinking and mid-water lobs can be highly effective, and if you can get the tench feeding 'on the drop' the bites are of the most positive type. A big lob fished in the middle of the water either below a float, or fished free-line hanging over a water lily pad, can be deadly at times, but most anglers seem to ignore these techniques. All baits fished *in* the weed beds are likely to be more effective during the midday period.

Redworms and brandlings are good at times but I've never been altogether at ease fishing with brandlings and have had few tench on them. Redworms are just like little lobworms and succeed fairly well, but do not have the movement to attract in the way that a big lob does. If I want to use a small bait, as when tench are preoccupied, then I'll use maggots, wheat, puffed wheat or bread, rather than worms. The blue-headed garden worm is a very tough worm, but probably for this reason is not in the same class as a good lobworm. All worms should be relatively short, fat and powerful, rather than long, stringy and limp. For smaller worms, or portions of worms, simply scale down the hook size appropriately.

Maggots are versatile baits, since you can put up a large bait of, say, 20 maggots on a size 6 hook, or fish one maggot on a size 16. Obviously you have a choice of colour, and even type of maggot (squats etc). although the latter may not matter too much. Tench can nip maggots off the hook quite neatly, and I suspect they do this with their thick lips rather than with their throat teeth. You can tell its not roach having a go because the maggots which do come back to you are bruised rather than skins, and roach do not usually nip them off the hook anyway. When tench are doing this I find it is a good idea to scale down the hook size and the number of maggots, and it is rare

45. A good tench taken on sweetcorn.

Tench also eat fish. One [of] the three above ate the little [min]now of a tench at the bottom. [A]lton Towers fish.

Steve Crawshaw and Ray [pr]epare groundbait with blood.

indeed to get the same behaviour when using a single maggot and size 16. I'm very uncertain about maggot colours and usually ring the changes between white, yellow and red. What is important is that the maggots should be big and soft; and old, rubbery maggots are as poor for tench as they are for other fish. Maggots are also used extensively as groundbait, and if it is certain that good numbers of tench are in the swim it is sometimes a good idea to forget about ordinary groundbait and stick to maggots. I doubt if it is possible to put in too many, and the tench usually appear to have no trouble finding the hookbait as well as the free offerings.

One good system is to keep the hookbait gently on the move, either by twitching it at intervals, or by arranging the tackle so that it drags very slowly through the swim. As for hook sizes the thing most people do wrong is to use a hook that is too large. For example a size 16 is probably too large for a single maggot by general angling standards (Bill Bartles, the Sheffield matchman would go down to a size 22 in some cases) but here we are governed to some extent by the need to play the fish amongst snag-ridden swims. But for two maggots you might just as well stay with a size 16, for three go up to size 14: in other words one size smaller throughout than your natural inclinations! It is possible to breed your own maggots, but a good supplier is best except when a huge, soft, white maggot is needed. Then you can use the method outlined some years ago by Fred J. Taylor of allowing bran, soaked in sour milk, to become 'blown' and then leaving it in the sun for a few days. Do check up on the local politics in your neighbourhood before doing this.

Bread baits perhaps need little explanation these days and one thing which has emerged in recent years is that the really giant tench seem to prefer a bread bait to a worm. I remember Terry Coulson coming to this conclusion after statistically analysing the return forms of the Tenchfishers' Club, and it is something which seems to be born out in practice. Everbody has their own way of making breadpaste, but the main thing is that it should be *soft*. After a few minutes in the water a gentle retrieve should see it sliding off the hook. Crust can be fished to any appropriate size of hook and the crust adjusted so that the hook weight just sinks it or the crust just floats: either way it can be deadly and is one of my favourite tench baits. Flake I have more trouble with. Either I squeeze it too gently so that it buoys up in the water, or too hard so that a knob of hard bread forms along the hook shank. I miss more bites than I should on flake and almost lack the art of presenting it properly to fish it. Ideally it should just sink and be soft, but not so soft that the tench can slurp it off the hook without indicating a bite.

Stewed wheat was made famous by the Taylor brothers who used it in conjunction with the lift method (Chpater 4). It is fairly heavy and sinks into the surface of the mud where the tench find it in a very natural way, and begin looking for more. As with hempseed (very little used for tench though it is quite good (Fig. 48)) the wheat can be prepared in hot water in a thermos flask or simple heated in a pan. It is difficult to describe how soft or split it should be, but it should be firm enough to stay on the hook when the latter is hooked into it as shown in Fig. 49. The point should be left clear, in direct contrast to chrysalid (caster) fishing (Fig. 50). I was convinced years ago that with chrysalids the hook point might just as well be fully buried since this causes less restriction when the fish sucks the bait in, but never impedes the strike. If you can get the tench going on sinkers, by heavy feeding, the bites are often really clean and bold and quite unmissable. Tench will also take casters off the surface and a subsurface bait will succeed easily at such times: naturally you get a fair attention from other fish as well. The general rule with caster fishing is to throw plenty into the water as feed.

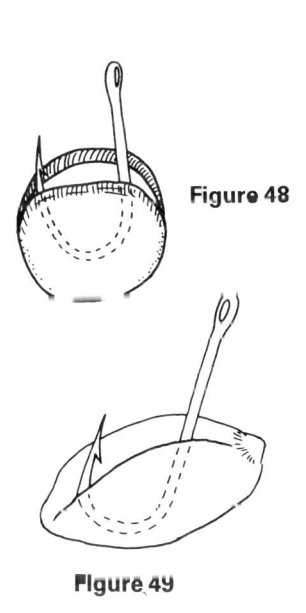

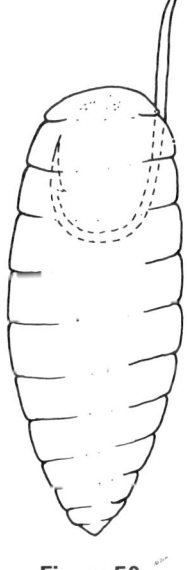

Figure 48

Figure 49

Figure 50

Amongst the more natural baits are many that are certainly under-exploited, such as caddis grubs and shrimps, but the time to try them is not when the tench have almost certainly gone off the feed, but to actually have a full session or two fishing nothing but the trial baits. Of course, everybody's time is short. . . .

Mussels are good baits, even on waters where little or no prebaiting has been done. Various sized lumps should be tried, and a bigger hook than normal fished with plenty of point showing. On waters where the tench rapidly go off big baits after June 16th, mussels can be next to useless and you might just as well stick to maggots etc, but on other waters, and particularly at night, they can result in very bold bites when the usual baits fail. I prefer the softer, squelchier bits of a mussel myself, rather than the tough foot.

Bloodworms are a much-neglected bait, but in this field, as in many others, the matchmen have given us a real lead, and any tench angler not prepared to try them in the future is neglecting a lot of fish. The tackle has to be fine, and the hook small, but we do this anyway when fishing size 16s. Percy Anderson the Cambridge matchman and last year's National winner tells me that the hook to use is a size 18 or 20 for *one* bloodworm, but several can be put on a size 16 or 14. Simply scale down all the tackle and fish them on a *slow* drag at close range.

On some waters I've fished, usually where the tench are stunted, they have a penchant for soft processed cheese. Some of this cheese has just the right consistency for paste, and is a lazy way of 'bread paste' fishing, but a few makes go rather too hard when in the water. Processed cheese is mild-tasting, to my palate anyway, and I have never succeeded when using strong or pongy cheese baits. Cheese is in the nature of a 'change' bait, something to try when the water as a whole seems to be going off the more usual baits, and the same might be said at present of the high protein baits including cat meats, luncheon meat and so on. All these succeed, particularly as large lumps fished at night, and I am sure a pre-baiting programme would pay dividends. Up until the present time I doubt if tench waters have been subjected to the scale of fishing that the (fewer) carp waters have suffered, and 'change' baits have probably never been required. But they may be in the future.

**Comment** – *by Ray Webb*

Crust has long been a favourite tench bait of mine, right back as far as my King's Sedgmoor Drain days, taking many a good fish when flake failed to produce anything in the nature of a strikeable bite. To bait up I insert the hook in from the white crumb side, taking right through and out then back in again from the opposite direction leaving the point just showing.

Though never having tried them in practice there's no doubt in my mind that shrimps would prove an extremely good tench bait at times for they are part of the natural diet of most fish coarse or game. Even pike take them frequently in times of famine, as I found out recently on cleaning and gutting a five pounder for my dinner for all it contained was a large number of shrimps and a few water snails, no wonder it was long, lean and lanky as indeed were all the pike from that particular water where rudd, and other food fish were obviously hard to come by.

## GROUNDBAITS

### Barrie Rickards

The whole question of whether or not to use groundbait is always with us whatever species we happen to be fishing for, but with tench almost all the pundits agree that groundbait is a must. Nevertheless everyone will know the feeling of doubt as you stand there in front of a glassy calm swim on a quiet summer's morning, holding a solid, seemingly cannonball-sized lump of groundbait in your hand. You know that the second it hits the water all the waterhens on the lake will complain: will it scare the tench? So often I have had tench take the bait within seconds of the ground-bait going in that it never worries me nowadays, although from the aesthetic standpoint I dislike disturbing a quiet dawn.

The Taylor brothers thought that you could not have too much groundbait for feeding tench and I am inclined to agree. If you can get in a few buckets before dawn, or even the night before, and then keep feeding regularly during the session, perhaps using a further bucketful, then in general I think you have it about right. Prebaiting is discussed in another section (Chapter 7). The groundbait can be amply laced with the hookbait be it worm, bread, wheat or maggots. Maggots can also be fired out using a throwing stick or catapult so that they fall as a carpet more or less on top of the basic groundbait. Many anglers do not seem to realize that free samples of flake can also be added to the groundbait: when the groundbait opens out on the bottom the lumps of flake (squeezed initially so that they just sink) pop out in a very natural fashion.

But what is the groundbait to be? Wholemeal? Bread? Well, with tench I've never been altogether convinced that it matters much. It has to be something they can eat, not just an attractor. Mashed up stale loaves, dried off with any kind of meal or bran, is probably the best thing. For other kinds of fishing I prefer breadcrumbs to sausage rusk, for example, but for tench fishing sausage rusk makes a good base. I'd be unhappy, however, if I didn't have plenty of bread and bran in it. In Ireland I used sackfuls of crushed oats, a kind of coarse wholemeal, with the flattened oat grains clearly visible. The only disadvantage was that Irish coots can dive more deeply than British coots and I have seen them taking mouthfuls of flattened oat grains from a depth of 12 feet: all the chicks sat in the marginal sedges tweeting merrily away whilst the parents shared out the oat grains, one by one, between them. So in Ireland you need something the coots cannot pick up. In summary I'd use plenty of stale loaves, plenty of meal or bran and a good sprinkling of the expected hookbaits (I use the last word advisedly in the plural).

To prepare the groundbait it needs a good soaking of half an hour or so, since it is surprising how long a rock-like loaf needs to take up water. You can then use the 'treading grapes' technique of walking on the loaves, but better still is to put them in a big polythene bag first since you do not want to loose the smaller particles and the milky liquid. Dry off in the polythene bag until you have the consistency you require: when I'm fishing very close I keep the groundbait fairly sloppy; when it goes in the night before I make it very hard.

The oxblood additive is now famous, and rightly so, even if it does attract eels, pike and perch as well. Ideally you should get the blood fresh from the slaughterhouse or butcher, in liquid form, but you can get it in a gelatinous form which is easier to handle and seems to last a bit longer. It's *all* pretty horrible stuff. Whenever I've had oxblood with me I've felt like the Sheriff who takes a mean baddy to the next county for trial – never, never forget you have it with you. Oxblood *always* waits until your back is turned before it goes off, or leaks. Add the blood at the waterside, try to enjoy the ritual, then *wash out the container* you brought it in. Under no circumstances return the container to the boot of your car before doing this, for, remember, the sun will be up when you pack up fishing.

Groundbait is not only necessary for tench, and probably the quantities you could use are limitless, but it's good fun too. And there is scope for more experiment than has been done in the past. Like many other anglers I hope to find, one day, an additive to beat all additives. Stale loaves can be obtained at a small sum if you make an arrangement with the local baker. Making your own groundbait in this way is much much cheaper than using proprietary brands excellent though some of these are: Pomenteg, for example, would cost me too much if I used it in the quantities I like.

Finally, just a slight word of warning. Although I have watched half a dozen tench clean up a full bucketful of meat-based groundbait in five minutes flat, there may be times when the little-and-often principle works best, as in the autumn and winter, so watch out for changes in feeding habits on your water.

**Comment** – *by Ray Webb*

No doubts at all in my mind either about the need for groundbait when tench fishing. Time and time again I've seen anglers fishing side by side, tackled up and baited up in identical fashion, with one consistently outscoring the other often to the tune of 4 or 5 to 1. With everything else equal the answer was just too obvious; one was groundbaiting heavily and the other not at all, usually complaining about the current high price of bread, bran and the likes. From the point of view of sport obtained however it is false economy to cut down on groundbait, far better for the angler himself to forgo a spot of food rather than let the tench go without theirs.

CHAPTER 7

# Tench Swims
*Ray Webb*

EARLY season on a typical English tench lake with a stream flowing into a shallow, weedy, narrowish neck end, widening out into a broad deep trough right up to the dam wall and with an outflow over a small weir, will see the tench up in the heavily weeded neck end and the depth I try to find at this time of year is around 6′ or so. In late May and early June I've frequently observed tench gathered in such spots for spawning purposes, working their way in and out of weedbeds and lily pads. Sometimes the fish have been grouped together in fours or fives but at others I've come upon 40 or 50 fish gathered together in one big shoal, one such congregation being found one day in clear open water completely devoid of any weed cover at all.

In weedy or open water, however, the controlling common factor has been depth. I've never seen tench spawning in deep water, only from 6ft or shallower. On one occasion in fact I found tench in 12in to 15in of water and have caught them in such depths, good fish of well over the 4lb mark, and a splashy, aerobatic tussle it is in such circumstances; one fish leaping clear out of the water in a manner that would have done credit to a Graffham rainbow. Tench in these weedy shallows can often be heard as well as seen, noisily sucking at the underside of floating lily pads, while searching for snails and insects.

By August, especially so if it is wet and windy, the general movement of fish is away from the shallows and down into the deeper water by the dam wall, where the weed growth is usually slight or absent altogether and the bottom tends to be somewhat firmer than the silty deposit at the upper end of the lake.

In rivers the tench move into the fast, streamy, water to spawn, forsaking their normally placid, sheltered swims for the boil and turbulence of the mill races and weir pools, competing for once with the chub, barbel, trout and other species more commonly associated with the faster reaches. If there are no rapids available the thin

51. Steve Crawshaw caught this idyllic picture of deep tench swims at Garnafailagh on Coosan Lough.

52. Southill Park Lake in Bedfordshire from the dam. Scene of memorable catches to Ray, and Barrie's first four pounder came from here.

fibrous roots of overhanging willow trees are the next likeliest bet to find them but wherever they are located at the start of the season, by the beginning of July they will have retired to their usual quarters in slack, weedy water. One spot above all others is the downstream end of the islands for at this point weed growth usually flourished out of the push of the stream, and the quieter reaches of lock cuttings usually support a thriving bed or two of lily pads that warrant serious investigation. Bulrushes and lily pads are traditionally associated with tench and rightly so, many of the best tench swims I've come across have been thick with this growth but failing these, beds of pondweed or reedmace are good alternatives providing cover from the direct glare of the sun. As midday approaches the tench tend to retire to deeper water or take shelter under weed. I've watched them shielding their eyes under lily pads unlike the pike who will sunbathe in shallow water in brilliant sunshine without suffering any discomfort at all.

Tench in canals are somewhat harder to locate for the uniformity of depth and width of these man-made watercourses makes so much of the water theoretically of equal potential. Features like bridges and lock gates do break up the monotony somewhat and are worth considering as a starting-point, as are the spots where field drains enter the canal. But by and large local knowledge is invaluable to the angler who would do well with canal tench, for certain swims do produce good sport consistently year after year, and the spots that have produced the latest bags of fish will be known. Where the water is clear a spot of survey work in calm sunny conditions can pay dividends, for with the aid of a pair of polaroid glasses tench in the $3\frac{1}{2}$ feet or so of water that one usually finds in canals are not hard to find.

Taking cover behind the bridge of the old Grantham Canal at Hickling Basin one day, I fully expected to see one of the big pike for which this canal was famous in its heyday, for a shoal of small fry had just scattered in all directions, some leaping clear into the air in their panic; but when the marauder finally hove in sight, instead of the anticipated pike it turned out to be a perfectly harmless tench of around the 3lb mark, ambling slowly along in the good natured manner customary to the species. One point that should be borne in mind for canal fishing is that most of the fish and particularly the bigger specimens are usually found beyond the half way mark from the tow path side, the regular disturbance of anglers and sightseers

53. A scene repeated thousands of times on thousands of waters: a typical tench swim in the early morning.

54. Ugly scene, beautiful fish. Lanesborough Power Station outfall where Ray broke the Irish record.

treading the track that was originally made by the horses as they towed the barges along, having pushed the fish across to the quieter, undisturbed water of the far side. Again, on the Grantham Canal, but furthur along towards Belvoir Castle I used regularly to watch shoals of fish, bream and tench patrolling along in a mere 18in of water or so under the far bank, but never once did they come even as close as the midway point, half way across the canal.

My favourite swim in my time in Sheffield, illustrated in Fig. 55 is a splendid example of the classic early season, English pond swim but over on Garnafailagh Lake in Ireland the set up differed dramatically. A small bay off the main body of Lough Ree, Garnafailagh was still bigger than most English ponds, Pebley included, but from a shallow 2ft deep shelf, the bottom dropped abruptly away to 12ft or so. There was no gradual shelving away at all. In the clear fertile limestone water, however, weed growth flourished at greater depths than I ever came across in England; long stemmed lily pads pushing their way up to the surface in 12 or even 15ft of water, though fortunately the stems seemed far more delicate than those of the English lilies, perhaps on account of their length (Fig. 56). A hooked tench could usually be hauled right through a thick bed of them. Some of the lilies seemed to be of a short stemmed variety, never leaving the bottom, and these were nicknamed cabbage patches. Fred Carter, the guest house owner of Garnafailagh figured that the best bet to find a good tench swim was to look for an area where the marginal shelf was thick with bulrush and the cabbages were thick on the bottom some 10 or 12ft down. If there were pads on the top as well to give cover and shade, so much the better, but if the weed on the shelf was the more scanty *Phragmites* insufficient shelter was afforded and the tench just wouldn't stay. Certainly many of the best spots conformed to Fred's requirements and the corner swim at the Athlone end of the lake was an ideal illustration, producing large catches of tench year after year. Many of them were over the 6lb mark.

**Comment** – *by Barrie Rickards*

One of the things I remember Fred Taylor concluding was that apart from picking a swim at the shallow end of the lake in the early part of the season, it was a good idea to choose one reached last by the rays of the early morning sun. My own experiences bear this out, and the tench as a rule feed on longer in the duller swims. Once the

TENCH SWIMS

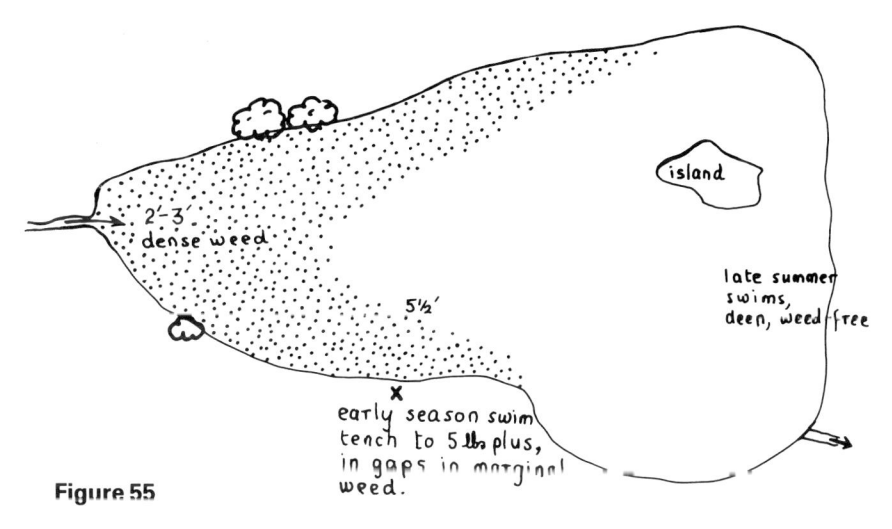

**Figure 55**

*2'-3' dense weed*
*island*
*5½'*
*late summer swims, deep, weed-free*
*x*
*early season swim tench to 5 lb plus, in gaps in marginal weed.*

Pebley Pond, Sheffield showing inflowing and outflowing streams.

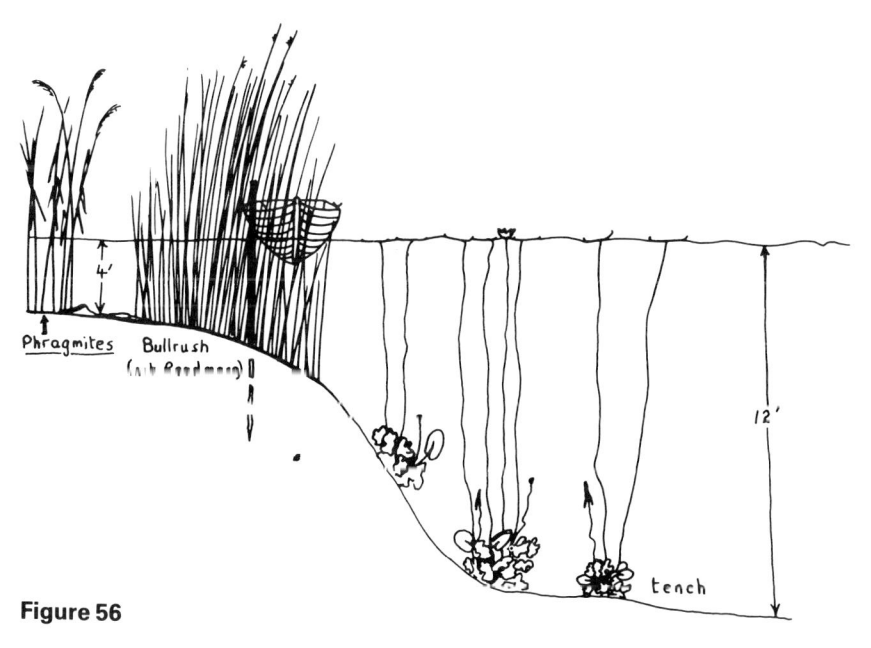

**Figure 56**

*4'*
*Phragmites*  *Bullrush (nib Reedmace)*
*12'*
*tench*

Typical first class Irish Tench swim.

full rays of the sun light up the bottom the tench tend to retreat deep into the weeds or stick their heads under a water lily leaf. However, it shouldn't be forgotten that the tench season in much of the country begins on June 16th and at this time the water has really warmed up to a temperature approaching the spawning temperature (Chapter 17). In other parts of these islands (Yorkshire and Ireland) the season opens earlier and the behaviour of tench can be rather different. For example, last year I watched tench all day long in sunny weather in early June, and it was most noticeable that they *avoided* the shade: on numerous occasions I saw a tench, or groups of tench, swim about one foot into the shadow of a tree, and then immediately turn tail and begin cruising, and feeding, in the bright sunlight. The water temperature was relatively low and the fish *enjoyed* the warmth of the sun. This was in Yorkshire, but the same certainly applies in Ireland where many early season catches are made from swims under a brilliant sun, May and early June often being as nice there as it is over here. It would be interesting to know whether in the autumn the reverse happens – do the tench begin to look for the sun's warmth as the water temperatures slowly drop? I don't yet know the answer to this one.

## SWIM PREPARATION
*Ray Webb*

To get the very best results possible a certain amount of preparatory work must be put in on the selected swim: especially is this so for early season tenching which will be concentrated on the shallower heavily weeded areas. About a month or so before the start of the coming season enough space should be cleared of weed to allow the bait to be presented properly and the hooked fish to be played all the way to the bank. For this sort of work a couple of garden rakes tied back to back are often recommended but progress can be discouragingly slow with this rather undersized weapon. If the weed growth is anything like profuse I've done considerably better by employing a couple of scythe blades which give an overall span of around 8ft or so. If a boat is available one can go a step further and cut a series of lanes all around the fishing area in hopes of leading tench along into the cleared swim.

If extended to cover the whole of the weedy shallows then theoretically all the tench gathering before spawning could be influenced by the prebaiting campaign. Only just sufficient weed

57. Ray and John Weston settled and ready in a ten foot deep tench swim.

58. A superb 7lb 1oz tench caught on HNV paste in September – often a good month.

should be cleared for the purpose and no more and from this point on pre-baiting should be commenced at frequent intervals say 3 or 4 days a week right up to the opening day. If the water holds anything like a big head of tench then overbaiting becomes virtually a physical and financial impossibility. Some of the pre-baiting campaigns are lavish in the extreme, but certainly anything less than 3 or 4 bucketsful per visit is hardly worth considering. Samples of the intended hookbait should be included in the pre-baiting mix, the idea being to get the tench into the habit of gathering in numbers in the expectation of being fed. Additives that have some reputation as tench attractors are oxblood and oil of tar, though the comparative testing of several pre-baiting campaigns running concurrently would be a job of forbidding magnitude.

If the weed is of a quick growing variety further clearance work will have to be done nearer the opening day and this can be carried out without any fear that the disturbance will scatter the collected fish clean out of the area. Indeed there are many highly successful tench anglers who are convinced that the food stirred up out of the bottom by heavy dragging will bring tench into the area without groundbait being used at all, going so far as to insist that the best plan of all is to actually rake vigorously at dawn before the day's fishing begins.

Having the tackle set up ready to cast in immediately the dragging is completed is a good idea, as a quick success or two is more than likely. Certainly tench can overcome their natural caution to satisfy their curiosity, a fact that I once saw demonstrated in a most dramatic fashion while taking a stroll along the tow path of the Chesterfield Stockwith Canal near Retford. It was a calm, bright, sunny day ideal for observation and three quarters of the way across was an object on or near the bottom about 18in long that looked very much like a small pike though then again it might just have been a submerged branch or root of sorts.

Determined to find out for sure I started throwing in small pebbles hoping to galvanise the pike, if such it was, into violent action though without success for there was no response at all. Persisting in my efforts, at the point where about a couple of dozen pebbles had been thrown in 3 tench worked their way out from under the marginal duckweed at my feet, out across the canal to investigate the disturbance, instead of frightening them away the shower of pebbles had brought the tench right across the canal every bit as effectively as if it had been highly priced groundbait.

59. Ray Jackson preparing a plan of a Norfolk tench water from Ray's boat *Tinca*.

60. A cutter designed to clip weed close to the bottom rather than uproot it. Used here on the Old Bedford River.

61. Dragging a new swim to make it fishable. *(Photo Angling Times)*

When the water has been cleared sufficiently a certain amount of bankside work may be necessary too. Branches of overhanging trees need trimming to give comfortable casting but unless really out of control, the marginal reed mace is best left in position; it's well worth putting up with a certain amount of inconvenience for the sake of cover afforded. If the banks are wet and boggy a platform can be constructed to afford the angler a firm base for his operations, a number of logs being all that is necessary to build a useful platform. If there's an old door available to finish off the building work so much the better, for things like ledger weights and disgorgers dropped down in between the logs can be extremely difficult to retrieve.

**Comment** – *by Barrie Rickards*

I think the only reservations I have about extensive swim preparation, particularly the pre-baiting side of things, is that it gets the tench on to small food items right at the very start of the season, so that the opportunity to lay on with lobworm may be rather limited. On the other hand if the intention is to use the lift method and fish wheat, maggot and crust then at least you should have a good shoal of tench frequenting the area. It is certainly advisable to check the weedgrowth in the day or two before fishing because it really seems preferable to *cut* the weeds, rather than raking everything out by the roots, and it always pays to leave clumps of weed in the swim. I usually cut three swathes through the weed towards my fishing position so that I can fish two rods, leave one part of the swim 'fallow', and chop and change the techniques. It also helps, when playing a fish in one part of the swim, if weed growth separates the plunging fish from the other side of the swim where fish may be feeding quite actively.

A similar type of swim preparation is carried out by Eric Hodgson, although he inserts a dark green nylon screen between him and the swim, so that he can move about quickly behind it without any chance of the tench seeing him. Under such circumstances they will come in very close to the bank and can be fished for with light tackle.

In waters holding lots of bream heavy pre-baiting can be quite a waste of time, serving only to attract hordes of bream. (Plate 63 shows Steve Cohen and I preparing a swim on the Old Bedford River in the fens: all we got for our troubles were 35lb of bream per person per night. I've experienced the same elsewhere: I never learn. On a drain like the Old Bedford swim dragging on the day, and moderate

62. Ron Clay using a viewer to inspect the tench swim chosen.

63. Barrie and Steve Cohen pre-baiting an Old Bedford swim, for *bream* as it turned out!

groundbaiting is much more effective. Possibly the best way of all to find the big fish is to wander the banks at dawn, carrying minimal tackle, and watching carefully for the tench rolling. Having found them, move in nearby with cutter and groundbait and then hope that they'll come on the feed by 5.30 or 6 a.m. thereby giving you enough time to take a fish or two before they are off. The only other point relevant to tenching in bream infested waters is that bream, in my own experience, tend to feed earlier than tench (including during the night, of course) often going *off* the feed about 4.30 a.m. So that there is little point in baiting up the night before, unless you want a few bream to begin the day. After they have gone off the feed you can bait up for tench!

One of the enjoyable aspects of swim preparation and pre-baiting is watching how the other fellow goes about it! Nothing is more fun than inspecting the drags used by some anglers. Every single one is different and their manufacture must have contributed considerably to keeping the village blacksmith trade alive prior to the little-girls-on- horses era. But the actual size of a rake can range from one easily chucked out by hand, to one big enough to need a tractor towing it. I do not exaggerate here: on the banks at Twentypence Pits near Cambridge, partly buried in undergrowth that has struggled manfully to overgrow it, is a huge double-sided rake that needed the power of a tractor to move it when really loaded down with weed. I understand also that members of the Tenchfishers had a creature they called The Hedgehog which used to plough a broad and denuded furrow across favourite tench lakes. Anglers 'in drag' are not, in their extremes, to be taken too seriously, but the principle is good enough. Anybody who has witnessed Ray Webb wielding an eight-foot span, double-edge scythe system will know what I mean: a kind of insane Old Father Time.

CHAPTER 8

# Analysis of a New Water
*Barrie Rickards*

PROBABLY most anglers are less conservative than I and trying a new water is something to be taken easily in their strides: to me, moving to a new swim or, even worse, to a new water, is comparable only to moving house. I always fish a swim too long, and flog a water until it is obvious even to me that there is nothing left. But I have worked out an approach to new tench waters that may be helpful to others, and possibly to those who find in a new water nothing but delight and fish it without a care in their heads.

Clearly there are several important matters about which you need information before starting, not least of which is whether or not the water has any tench in it! Naturally this is what drew you to the water in the first place: you heard it was a good tench water. This is the way most anglers find out about a water, by following national press reports for *big* tench, or local newspaper columns for local tench waters going well. It is necessary, however, to find out whether the press reports were accurate, and to do this you visit the water in question, and begin a gentle grilling of the local anglers. Generally speaking I find that if approached politely, local anglers are more than welcoming and are quite happy to let you know what the best bait is, and, often, which are the best swims. In the rather more competitive world of carp and pike fishing I find anglers less forthcoming and, occasionally, this is true of tench fishing. Should you come up against an obvious conspiracy of silence then respect it for what it is, namely anglers worrying about the immediate future of their sport. When, by your subsequent actions, it is clear that you are no threat to their tench pond you'll find that they become quite helpful.

Having located your water, gained permission to fish, and steeped yourself in something of the local history you are then, as it were, on your own. The first job is to get a 1in to 1 mile map which gives the outline of the water very clearly if it is bigger than an acre or so. Or you can take a compass to the pond itself: what you want to know is the position of each bank and swim with respect to North. This is for two main reasons: firstly, you want to know how each particular wind direction will affect the water; and secondly, how the sun's rays will warm up the water. Although the sun's rays will be at a lower angle in the spring and autumn than in the high summer, the change from day to day is so small that you will always know in advance that, if the sun *does* shine, swim A will receive early morning sunlight, and swim B the last rays of sunshine at night. In the accompanying diagram (Fig. 64) the deep water swim at the northern end of the lake will receive sun almost all the time it is shining, except in the shade of the easterly big tree in the early morning and in the shade of the westerly big tree in the evening. This might be a good late season swim offering deep water, *sunlight,* sunlit areas, shade, and some weed.

On the other hand the shallower, weedy end of the lake has a good west bank which will receive the early morning sun and will usually have the wind off your back: the sort of bank you might hope to find a good early season swim if the water were in Ireland or Yorkshire. In Chapter 8 ( point out that before mid-June the tench *love* the sun, and only at the start of the usual season (June 16th) do they begin looking for shady early morning swims. After June 16th the east bank *opposite* the car park might provide better early morning swims, because the hawthorn bushes provide shade over the swims: you would often be fishing *into* the prevailing westerly winds but if these were pushing warm surface water to the east bank then this could be highly advantageous. Should the same westerlies be cooling down the water then the swims along Fred's Arm would be somewhat protected from it, and at the same time would be shaded in the early morning, as well as late in the evening.

You see the nature of my thinking: work out the natural effect of wind direction and strength, and that of the sun's heat, before commencing activities. Remember, your chats with the local anglers will have told you the noted tench swims, so that at this point in our analysis of a new water we have three variables, local knowledge, wind, and sun, to take into account.

Following this part of the appraisal *plumb* the depths. Never, under any circumstances, accept the depths given you by a local informant since these can be inaccurate by several thousand per cent, and vary from the laconic '. . . not enough water to cover a big tench's back . . .' to the fatuous 'bottomless, me boy, bottomless'. Fig. 64 shows a chart

ANALYSIS OF A NEW WATER					107

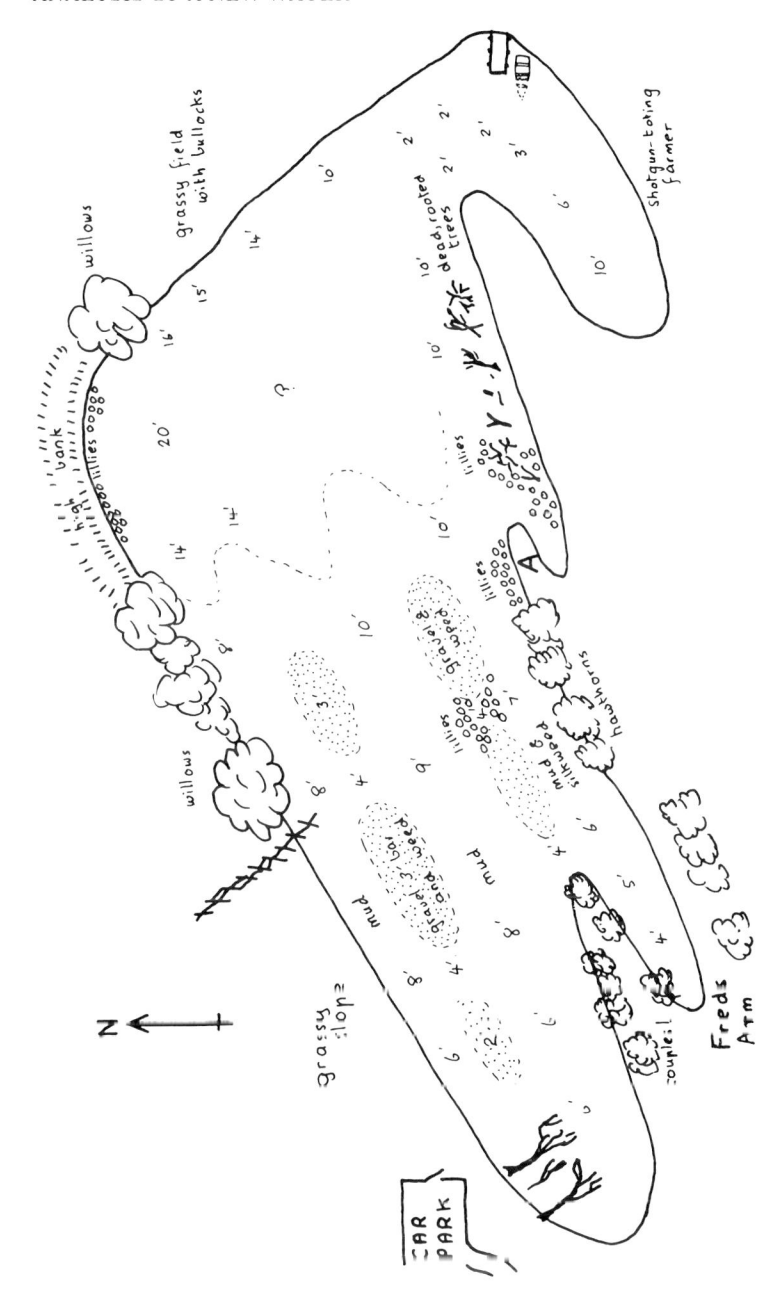

**Figure 64**

produced by plumbing with a rod, float and Arlesey bomb – the dashed area in the centre could not be reached and remained an enigma for big tench were seen rolling there before the season began. Better still is to use a boat and echo-sounder.

Following contouring of the figures you obtain, plot in the positions of the weed beds, and the type of weed present; and then the nature of the bottom sediment, whether it is black, foetid mud, or gravel, or sand. Snags, such as the sunken trees on the south east bank, should be noted too. Personally I go further than this and try to do a pH figure for the water, since I am certain that those waters with a pH of 7.5, 8, 9 or 10 are likely to be better for good tench, as for many other creatures. If you cannot do a pH reading (although I am sure the Water Authority would always do one) then take a really close look at the creatures in the weed: if it houses lots of snails with *big* shells, and big swan mussels, then in all probability the pH is high (i.e. more than 7). Certain weeds, the water soldier and *Chara* for example, also suggest a high lime content.

After all this work, which in fact is not really very time consuming and is always enjoyable and instructive, the next step is to WATCH. Try a few early morning visits, preferably in the Close Season, sit quiet on the bank and watch where the tench roll and when: sometimes you can detect that the fish are generally moving along a beat, although this is much easier with bream than with tench. If the season is already in full swing spend some time watching the locals to see if their claims for particular spots are correct: such things change anyway, both from year to year and week to week.

This completes the analysis, but I'll end the chapter by suggesting an opening campaign: after that you are on your own. If fishing was allowed before June 16th as in Yorkshire and Ireland and a few other places, then I'd pick a shallow-water swim in the region of the car park, or perhaps as far north as the fence. After June 16th a swim along the Hawthorn bank might be better. As the season progressed I would move along the east bank looking for big fish particularly in the region of A where a combination of weed beds, snags, shallows, deeps, sunlit and shaded water, might provide enough variety of choice for bigger tench. During such a campaign I should still watch the results of other anglers, and also make sorties to the west bank to try something quite different: all waters are different in some respects, and no matter how rigorous the analysis it *is* possible to overlook major factors which will affect where the tench feed.

**Comment** – *by Ray Webb*

One of the best ways round the frequently encountered wall of silence and deliberately misleading information is to by-pass the local tench experts altogether and concentrate one's efforts on good class anglers better known for their enthusiasm for other species, bream, roach or carp maybe, for dedicated specialists usually have a fair working knowledge of all round local prospects without any personal incentive to withold information. Other likely sources worth a try are old retired tench men who have finally put away their tackle for the last time, who once again have nothing to lose, though all information obtained must be critically examined for signs of obsolescence.

To look for limestone water the easiest visual check is to inspect the reedmace and bulrushes along the fringes for as the water level drops sway from its winter high a white deposit of limestone powder is left clearly visible, a vigorous shaking being all that is necessary to see it come away in a cloud.

## TYPES OF TENCH WATERS

*Ray Webb*

With just the odd exception my old home county of Yorkshire is about as far north as the serious angler would be advised to travel, the waters of the border counties and Scotland being too cold for tench to really flourish. With this one limitation, however, England has such a widespread distribution of the species that wherever his home the tench enthusiast will have plenty of opportunity to indulge in his favourite sport.

The majority of the Yorkshire tench fisheries are small- to medium-sized ponds and the tench though numerous rarely reach outsize proportions, a fish of 4lb being usually big enough to take the annual prize of the local angling club. Provided one is prepared to settle for good catches of medium-sized fish and tackle up accordingly good sport can be enjoyed: my own best return in this area being a catch of 15 tench for 32lb. Even the unlikely-looking colliery ponds based on a mixture of slag and ash, often hold a good head of tench. One such water near Sheffield, the Tinsley Park Pump Pond, produced a claimant for the English tench record back in the 1950s but on close inspection, though the weight at 9lb was right the species wasn't for the fish turned out to be a carp.

In the north midlands district around Nottingham the lakes of the old stately homes like Welbeck Hall, Hardwick and Belvoir Castle offer better class tench fishing, being larger waters, predominantly shallow with a prolific growth of weed. Permits for a day at Welbeck were hard come by in my time in Sheffield but the tench were present in size and numbers, as was tragically and conclusively proved early in 1963 when barrowloads full of dead fish were taken away, including many specimens of $4\frac{1}{2}$ and 5lb in weight after the coldest winter in recorded history. In Edward Ensom's ('Faddist') inspiring book 'Memorable Coarse Fish' a superb trio of tench is mentioned, fish of $4\frac{1}{2}$, $5\frac{1}{2}$ and $6\frac{1}{4}$lb taken on September 1940 from Clumber Lake by a Mr Sidney Fern; really top-class fishing this but unfortunately the dam was breached shortly after this capture, and the lake remained dry till labour for rebuilding became available again after the war.

South-east to the Fens and my present home town of Downham Market, the tench waters take on a different aspect being for the most part man-made drains, many of which were designed many years ago by the Dutch engineers brought across to help dry out the extremely valuable, but hopelessly waterlogged, growing land. From tiny drains a mere $2\frac{1}{2}$ft deep and 8 yards across to enormous watercourses 12ft deep by 100 yards across the whole area is crossed by countless numbers of such 'cuts' and virtually without exception they offer tench fishing of some sort though the potential varies considerably of course. A far cry from the cosy, heavily-weeded, shallow lakes sheltered from the wind by overhanging trees, so beloved of the tench enthusiasts, these Fenland drains are devoid of cover and windblasted by gales that travel mile after mile without meeting any obstruction. They are, nevertheless, well worth serious investigation for if one learns to get the best of them the results can well justify the effort involved.

One of the best of these Fenland tench drains is the Old Bedford, a water that holds a large head of fish with a fair sprinkling of specimens in the 5 and 6lbs range. 19 miles or so in length, averaging approximately 4ft in depth and of roughly even width, the problem that first confronts the angler is where to start. As an example of one of the smaller, lesser-known drains the Sedge Fen at Southery featured in a big fish competition recently with a specimen of $5\frac{3}{4}$lb and I know of a 6lb 2oz tench taken from the same water; that one ended up swimming in a garden pond. To build up and reinforce the banks of the Fenland drains clay has been dug out at various points and the old workings, known locally as clench or gault pits, frequently develop into good tench fisheries, the one at Manea being an outstanding example having produced fish up to 7lb.

Further east still the Norfolk Broads themselves are tench fisheries of high potential, though offering a fresh challenge in the way of a different type of water which has to be fished almost exclusively from a boat. At the top end of the Thurne, Hickling, the most famous Broad of all, regularly produces numbers of tench around the 4lb mark and occasionally bigger, the shallow, clear water sustaining a heavy growth of weed, providing food and shelter for the fish. As on the Fens persistent high winds can be a very real problem here, whichever way it comes, north, east, south or west there's nothing to stop it and the easterly blow comes straight off the North Sea a mere stone's throw a way. In addition to the stillwater of the Broads themselves the rivers of the area also provide sport for the tench enthusiast with a taste for flowing water; the Thurne from Candle Corner right up to Somerton, being particularly good. Bank fishing is a practical proposition here, unlike on the Broads themselves, but it's advisable to take along a good pair of Wellingtons as the going can get a trifle damp at times.

Further south the Thames at various points contains tench fishing of medium potential, the backwaters around Oxford being far better for this species than is generally realised.

In addition to the main river all along the Thames Valley and that of its tributary the Lea, are gravel workings that have matured into top class fisheries not only for tench but for pike, perch and roach as well. On a brief visit to one such waters on the banks of the Lea recently, a day on which an absolute novice hauled out a fine pike of 17lb, I was informed that through the summer months, the chain of waters alongside had produced a run of big roach to over 2lb and tench of 6lb. An accurate map of the bottom contours is essential to fish these old gravel workings properly, and if a boat and echo sounder are available so much the better. If not the job must be done by rod and plummet. Frequent depth variation is a feature of such waters, often a series of long, parallel, submerged ridges are located (Fig. 65), where the mechanical scoop worked along, and islands either visible above the surface or just submerged beneath are regular

**Figure 65**

occurrences, all of which adds to the interest. I've a very high regard for old gravel pits, both from a sporting potential and an enjoyment point of view.

So many of England's canals, which 30 years ago were fine all-round fisheries yielding good sport with roach, chub, bream, pike, perch, tench and eels, have long since been abandoned as commercial propositions in favour of transport by road and rail. The regular journeyings of the horse drawn barges, which seemed such a curse at the time to an angler who had congregated a shoal of fish and persuaded them to feed, were in fact a blessing in disguise for once they had stopped the canals rapidly silted-up and weeded-up becoming a write off anglingwise almost over night. Fortunately there are one or two exceptions, canals that have managed to retain a reasonable depth of water and good head of fish, the Bridgewater Taunton canal in Somerset being a top class, all round fishery with tench fishing very good in the reaches around Huntworth. The Kennet and Avon canal too can be relied upon to produce tench of prize winning proportions year after year, and long may it continue for I should hate to see these sadly diminished waterways disappear altogether from the angling scene.

Though tench generally manage to forage a good living whatever their enviroment, achieving a worthwhile growth rate, there are occasional exceptions as I found out to my cost way back in 1959 when a vague report of tench mad on the feed in a pond alongside the River Witham at Anton's Gowt sent me heading out at speed on the Boston road one Friday evening, determined to give the water my undivided attention for a full four days or more. Arriving in time to select a swim and put in the groundbait before retiring to the van for the night, I was up at dawn the following morning casting out my light float tackle terminating in a size 12 hook and a sizeable knob of paste as soon as it was light enough to see. Inside the first five minutes my porcupine quill slid decisively away and I hauled out a small tench of around 10oz or so, a quick success but hardly the size I was looking for; nor for that matter was the next one taken 10 minutes later – a perfect replica of the first, they were as alike as peas in a pod. Taking fish steadily at the rate of five to the hour by 9 a.m. I packed up in disgust, having 27 tench in the net with not one over the pound in weight, never in my life before or since, did I see so many small tench at the same time. Obviously this water, a small heavily weeded, soft bottomed pond, was one of those happily rare fisheries where the tench were breeding in numbers far beyond the capacity of the available food supply, for they were definitely not young fish, being small in the body and large in the head, an unfortunate combination resulting in an extremely sick and unprepossessing appearance.

**Comment** – *by Barrie Rickards*

The truth of the matter is that many tench anglers, myself included for a long time, have the idea that a tench water has to be shallow (say up to five feet), weedy, muddy and small: the tench is much more Catholic in his tastes than the angler, however, and will adapt to almost any circumstances including deep pits with no marginal shallows. I am certain a great many tench waters remain to be discovered, for I can think of several immediately which have tench in them, big ones, but which have never yielded tench to a rod and line. Tench show themselves often in shallow waters, but sometimes only during the spawning period on deep waters: in such waters it is possible they spawn less often and grow bigger.

You will probably note, as you read this book, that the methods we advocate are very varied – long range ledgering on the one hand, to incredibly delicate float rigs on the other. This is quite simply because good tench waters *are* so varied in their nature. My *ideal* tench water is at least 4-5 acres in extent, with depths down to over 10 feet for a third of this, with perhaps a quarter to a third of the area shallow, say 3-5 feet, and heavily weeded. If some of the deeper water has heavy weed growth so much the better; and if *moderate* areas of heavy lily growth, mixed in with logs, also exist then the situation could be near perfect for plenty of big tench. Over and above all that, a high pH or lime content is highly desirable, and seems directly linked with rich faunal and floral growth of all kinds.

But as strongly implied by Ray, good tench water is scattered widely over the country, and only someone who travels around fishing for the species can really appreciate just how adaptable the fish is, and how adaptable the techniques have to be.

CHAPTER 9

# Analysis of the finest tench water in history

*Martin Gay*

THE gravel pit described hereafter (Fig. 66) first attracted my attention, as a pike water, in the early 1970's, but quickly it became evident that quite superb big tench fishing was available. In 1974 and '75 numbers of tench to over 5lb were caught with standard tactics, consisting usually of floatfished bread, or maggots, in the margins or close to the several islands and bars present.

Never a prolific water for large bags of tench, the sort of thing that is not uncommonly seen on many "park" and "estate" (shallow and muddy) lakes, it was nevertheless clearly evident that the fish were growing and by 1976 the first of numerous 6lb, and 7lb, tench were taken. Such was the growth rate of the tench that a (rare-ish) 6lb 3oz fish taken whilst carp fishing in August 1976 was the smallest of a 6 fish catch made on opening day 1977. Around eight tench over 7lb were landed in 1977, the best of 20-odd 6lb plus fish. Exactly one year later the largest of 3 fish netted by one angler during opening week weighed a tremendous 8lb 10½oz and heralded the first of three dozen or more eight pounders caught over the following 5 years. Keith Mowberry (9lb 3oz) and Phil Smith (8lb 15oz) took the largest two authentic catches prior to 1984 when a 9lb 7oz fish was taken twice by different anglers about six hours apart!

Even to call the water "the finest tench fishery in history" fails to effectively chronicle the superlative fishing available, which, given the correct approach could yield an average weight of tench taken over the season as high as 6¾lbs. And yet it wasn't because small fish didn't exist. With the maggots-and-swim feeder approach, or particle baits, we have landed tench to as little as 8oz with numerous 2lb to 3lb fish. Using the small/multiple bait approach tench under 5lb outnumbered those over 5lb by around 5 to 1, which gave considerable scope to the specialist big tench angler.

Such a fishery, such fishing, demands a careful description. Covering an area approaching 30 acres in total, the fishery comprises 2 gravel pits connected by a small, 4ft deep, channel. The larger pit (and deeper), more open in aspect covers around 20 acres, the balance being made up by a rather segmented lake to the east of the bigger pit. With depths to between 17 and 21 feet (and which depths have yielded tench not infrequently), although most of the fishery is 4 to 12 feet deep and in effect constitutes one huge tench swim. Several islands, gravel bars and areas of soft weed provide sanctuary to the fish. Out from the west bank of the large lake, and as an extension to a small line of islands is a large "plateau" some 4 to 8 feet in depth and infinitely variable within that range, which provides a tench haunt for most of the 12 months. The only important exception to this is around spawning time (late May to the end of June) when *some* of the tench, along with resident fish from other suitable areas, migrate to the spawning grounds.

There are two particularly good spawning sites – the first at the northern end of the large lake, the second and far more important, at the southern end of the small lake. The previously mentioned spawning migration *can* be almost total, and we have known the larger lake almost devoid of tench (and carp) at the time of opening day, as the fish swim through the gulley and on to the shallows to spawn. Most years this gulley, connecting the two waters, holds some 2-4 feet of water through which any fish can pass. But just occasionally, following a dry winter, the water level is such that little through-passage of fish takes place. This sometimes results in a mass of fish gathering in the mouth of the gulley, and the adjacent bay, knowing that they should be able to pass through but cannot. Anglers who, by careful close season observations, settle into this area on June 16th can make a bumper start!

Here the depth is 8-10 feet, weeded in places and open to the prevailing S.W. wind. The fishing is at its most prolific in this area during the opening weeks of the season when many of the tench frequent the margins, and light-link ledger or float tackle will account for numbers of fish. From mid-late July until the end of September better sport is to be found by fishing at some range, casting 40 to 50 yards out, beyond the mouth of the bay. At this distance you can cover not only patrolling tench, fish keeping well away from the heavily fished margins, but also tench which drop off the shallows at the northern end of the lake.

Careful close season observation tells the angler whether or not tench have passed through the gulley, and a couple of dusk hours spent at the waterside, once or twice each week from late May until

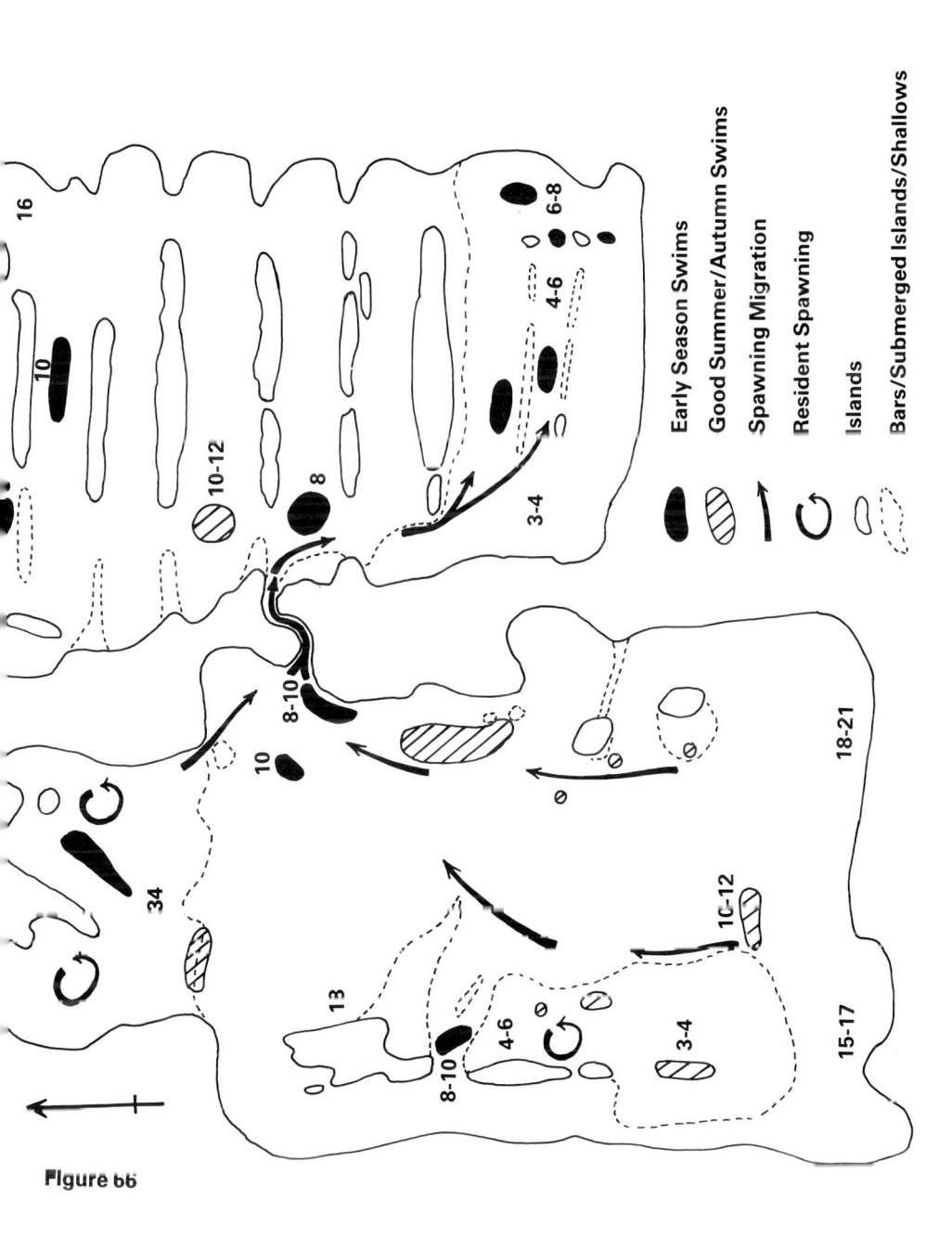

ANALYSIS OF THE FINEST TENCH WATER IN HISTORY 117

Figure 66

opening day can be extremely well rewarded. If the migration has been sucessful then the area to aim for on opening day is anywhere south of the gulley entrance into the smaller lake. In this region the water shallows from 10 feet up to 3 or 4 feet, is heavily weeded (although this is not always apparent) and ideal spawning ground. Spawning is usually witnessed from very late May onwards and quite often some, but never all, of the tench caught on June 16th are empty. Others may not complete this ritual until early July.

The approach to use on and around these and other shallows is to plot the paths of the various gravel bars, which are guaranteed tench patrol routes, and to bait and fish what I can best describe as "catchment" areas. They are formed at a confluence of patrol routes, sometimes by a number of small gravel bars leading in to one bay, sometimes by a break in a long gravel bar. Such a feature causes tench to halt their patrolling, even briefly, and by pre-baiting such a spot they can usually be held down for sufficient time to make a catch.

Some tench spend all the summer and much of the autumn (and occasionally the very end of the season) on the shallows in several areas of both lakes, but their numbers are often severely reduced by a gradual migration to deeper open water and fishing for such fish can be limited to specific times. One of these, and perhaps the most prolific is late morning through to mid afternoon when some tench siesta in the dense weedbeds (mostly *Myriophyllum*). Hectic sport is unlikely but it is often possible to catch the odd fish by casting directly into the weedbed. Tench in weeds seem to be more relaxed during the hottest or brightest part of the day and are more receptive to baits than those in open water. But it *is* to the open water that I look for regular sport (at all other times of the day) from mid July until the onset of winter.

The large expanses of open water, 12 to 15 feet deep, adjacent to weedbeds and bars/islands have produced most consistently over several seasons. In common with many gravel pits heaviest feeding occurs from shortly after dawn until about 11.00am (rather earlier on hot, calm days), and then again in early evening. This period, around "tea time" is often better following a windy afternoon, just as the swell begins to ease. Late evening fishing is almost always slow by comparison with morning fishing (but having said that 3 of my 8 pounders were taken during the evening), but when the occasional bite can produce catches of 6lb plus tench, that slowness is well worth the wait!

Perhaps the most significant change in feeding pattern occurs during September and October at which time night feeding is rather more usual than in early season. Again, open water of between 12ft and 17ft deep has produced most consistently. This night time feeding does not replace a feeding spell at another time, but rather it adds to it – which is a considerable bonus giving some quite excellent catches for an autumn session. One of my best, as I recall, was four tench of 6lb topped by one of 7lb 4½oz plus other action some of which came during the middle of a beautiful late September day. Tench in the autumn fight quite superbly and a haul of 3 or 4 big tench in autumn sunlight has few equals!

I have mentioned elsewhere that, along with the specimen size tench (6lb plus) this pit also contains really quite large numbers of small to medium fish in the 2lb to 4lb bracket. This makes for really nice fishing because you could approach the water with whichever approach you fancy – a so-to-speak casual attitude with light tackle and small baits for tench averaging 3½lb plus the occasional really big fish of maybe even 7lb, or, for the specialist angler, heavier tackle, big specimen orientated baits and a run of magnificent tench unusually under 5lb and more commonly over 6lb. This latter approach was the one I finally settled upon and to give some idea of its effectiveness I'll mention just a couple of catch figures. My first 6 pound tench (6lb 2½oz) was caught on sweetcorn on June 16th 1977. By July 1978 I had taken 10 further tench over 6lb, including three over 7lb, best 7lb 7½oz. In July 1978 I joined forces with Fred Wilton and a few of his mates, Dave Hayes, Chris Paris and Alan King, and by using Fred's HNV bait approach slightly adapted for tench fishing I went on to land, by March 1982 exactly 100 tench over 6lb with 35 seven pounders with 4 over 8lb. The effectiveness of this approach, which I shall shortly describe was, and still is, quite shattering, the quantity of tremendous tench as well as large roach, eels and very big carp, leaving me almost incredulous at times!

I have been particularly fortunate, in my angling to date, to have been party to some superb individual days fishing, but this tench fishing has been part of angling's history – would that everybody had the chance to sample it.

However, enough of the self-indulgence, a word or two about the particle bait approach before going on to more serious things! There are two problems for the specialist tench angler when using small baits (sweetcorn, black eye beans, maggots etc.), the biggest of these being non-selectivity. By which I mean that not only can you not keep away (unwanted) small roach, bream, rudd etc. but it is impossible to be in any way size selective with the tench you catch, and if you want big tench you must single them out and not rely on chance. The second problem concerns tackle strength – small baits really demand small hooks, and if you use small hooks there is little point in employing heavy lines. But I for one don't relish the thought of a 7lb tench on 3lb b.s. line in a snaggy swim. If you approach with care and method, heavy lines, 8lb b.s. say, will not put off big tench but will give you every chance of landing several "fish of a lifetime".

Small, multiple, baits and fine tackle induces twitches and, with twitchers comes an increasing use of fine tackle and sensitive end rigs which rather than solve the problem only aggravate it. One of the common problems concerns bites which, when using ledger tackle, pull the bobbin to within 2 inches of the rod, then stop. In response the angler use a shorter "drop" and so the next bite simply pulls less line and again "stops short" and so on . . . The problem is not one of bite detection but a matter of physical principle. What you have in effect is 2 pulleys (the two adjacent rings between which you suspend the bobbin) about 12 inches apart with the weight (the bobbin) suspended one foot or more below the rod. As the line is pulled (by the fish) so the bobbin rises, but as it rises so its effective weight increases; the fish feels the increasing weight and drops the bait! To beat this simply place 2 rings very much closer together, actually about two inches apart, and suspend it about 6-8 inches (giving 12-16 inches of line to the "take") below the rod. With this set-up many more bites take the bobbin to the rod, but they are often very fast so it's a good idea to use an Optonic bite alarm to give the earliest of warnings.

Obviously another way to combat shy biting tench is to use float tackle, and there is no doubt at all that this is a beautiful way to fish. But, if the tench are at some range or if there is a big wind/swell, or if it is dark you have problems and the way to beat them is not by being bloody-minded and sticking with the float at all costs, but to employ a sensible ledger outfit. In calm conditions and/or at close range use a float by all means, it can often result in a better hooking success rate but it is a method with limitations.

Some twitching tench are shy, feeding fish and can usually be outwitted by changing the bait – simply too many have been caught, but, other twitchers are confident fish which are browsing the baited area casually eating individual baits with little concern. You can

67. A fit 5lb 5½oz male tench.

68. Superb 5lb 5½oz male tench.

aggravate this problem by heavy and tight baiting of a swim which enables fish to pick up loose offerings without needing to move more than an inch or two to the next. Some anglers use bolt rigs to overcome this but I really cannot see the point – you have confident feeding fish in front of you so what is the point in alarming them in order to get a decent bite? I am very doubtful of the long-term value of bolt rigs and hair rigs, not to say the ethics of same, and there are other ways, sometimes requiring a little more thought than slavishly following others, of beating problems. With confidently feeding fish all you usually need to do is bait sparingly so that not only is there less bait laying around but each particle is further away from the next. In this way tench picking up one grain of corn (say) are induced to move some distance, let's say 10 inches, to find the next. If your hook is in the first particle you get a positive pull on your bobbin before it reaches the next item.

To maintain confidence in feeding over several seasons without changing baits you must offer the tench good food, which it can recognise as high in nutritional value. This is precisely the fundamental idea of Fred Wilton's HNV bait approach, and one that I have used to good effect and which I shall now describe.

Invertebrates in their many forms, constitute the staple diet of tench and if you remove the water content from these animals you are left with a meal high in protein content plus minerals and vitamins, the quality of the latter being dependent to some extent on the water quality in which they live. It is perfectly possible to devise a "synthetic" equivalent to this food using selected milk proteins plus other dietary requirements, and to offer this to the fish in bait form. With care in its preparation this will be recognised as good food and which if high enough in nutritional value actually taken in preference to natural food items. The basic components of an HNV bait have little smell (but all smell much the same!) so from our point of view we need to create as near perfect "dietary bait" as possible which can be appreciated by the tench, but we must also introduce a water-soluble "smell" to the bait, unique to that bait, so that the tench can recognise your offerings.

The dry ingredients plus "smell" etc. are mixed with eggs, rolled into balls and skinned by immersing each ball, in batches, in boiling or simmering water for sufficient time to render the outside just tough enough to withstand casting, fish nibbling etc. The longer the immersion the tougher and thicker the skin, although I personally like

69. Bob Church, who wrote the foreword of the first edition, with a huge Sywell fish (male) of 6lb 5oz caught in 1984.

*(Photo Angling Times)*

70. A nice tench netted.

to aim for a consistency not unlike tough putty, which for a bait ball of ¾ inch diameter would require about 40 seconds immersion for summer use, barely 5 seconds for winter use when the water temperature may be as much as 25-30°F cooler.

To get the tench "on" to your baits will require some amount of pre-baiting and whereas it is possible to get takes after only 500 baits have been introduced it is a fact that the more you put in, and the longer the period of pre-baiting the more complete will be the acceptance. A good general guide however would be 150 baits, twice each week for one month prior to fishing. Obviously variations must exist depending on the size of water and the stock of tench – on a big water, say 50 acres, bait only the known tench swims, but on a 5 acre pit, bait the whole water. It is probably almost impossible to over-prebait with a good quality bait especially when balanced against cost and time.

Getting the tench on to your bait is one thing, catching fish of a selected size quite another. But we achieved this, not for some rather silly reasons put forward by people who should know better, but by adapting a carp fishing exercise previously used by Fred. Clearly the mouth of a 3lb tench is smaller than that of a 7 pounder which imposes an upper limit to the size of food items the smaller fish can engulf. We attempted, successfully as it turned out, to feed only those fish over 6lbs by baiting with balls of skinned paste of a sufficiently large size that small tench, being unable to swallow them, were not able to recognise their food value. We settled on a bait size of approximately one inch diameter, which seems huge by tench fishing standards, but even then the occasional smaller than 6lb fish managed to eat them! The catch of 8lb tench taken by my friend Ray Bishop were actually caught on baits 50% larger than this!!

I do all my prebaiting in the evenings, through dusk, for two reasons – firstly I see no good reason to advertise the fact to other anglers; in the close season most waters are devoid of people at dusk, and secondly activity from diving birds (tufted ducks and coots) has just about ceased so there is little opportunity for them to find the bait before morning by which time the tench should have cleared it up!

When actually fishing I "play-it-by-ear" as the saying goes, allowing the tench to dictate the frequency and quantity of baiting. At the start of the session I usually introduce about 2 dozen free baits scattered over an area of about 4 yards square and I then place two hook baits within that area. Baiting accuracy is important but for

71. B.R. with one of his Yorkshire tench of 5½lb.

reasons that I have previously stated I don't groundbait too tightly preferring to force the tench to forage. After the initial baiting up of the swim I don't introduce any more until there is evidence of tench activity, and this can take the form of rolling or bites (although they usually go together). If bites are not forthcoming and no fish are showing there is really no point in putting in more bait – it won't attract fish and, when they do eventually come across your bait you will have simply reduced the odds of a quick take. However, as soon as it is obvious that tench are in the swim I then bait up on a "little-and-often" basis – each time a bite or a fish comes I put out about 12 free baits depending on how many tench I think might be present. Above all else it is imperative that you keep free baits going in and with a large group of tench feeding, 30 or 40 baits each hour quickly will be cleared away. The more bites you are getting, and the more tench being landed, the more free bait should go in. I have never yet reached the point of over-baiting, an almost impossible thing I believe.

I am fishing for large tench in the 6-9lb range, fish which fight particularly well and are often not far from weedbeds or gravel bars. Couple this with the fact that I use large baits which have quite tough "skins" and you can see that strong tackle is required. I have worked my way, by trial-and-error, through a number of rods of not less than 1¾lb test curve (my own are actually 2¼lb!) and 8lb or 9lb b.s. line. This may seem a bit over-gunned but in tricky situations you'll be more than happy and it in no way detracts from enjoying the fight. Despite the large baits I use size 8 Partridge "Specialist" pattern hooks buried in the bait, not side-hooked or "hair-rigged". Much of the reason that I use powerful fast taper rods is because I want to be able to strike quickly straight out of the rests to a fish 40 or 50 yards away, and I prefer the hook to be hidden in the bait. With a good bait which the tench are used to eating there is no call for exposed hook rigs etc.

I can imagine a number of anglers throwing up their hands in horror but I do not not see the need for fancy terminal tackles. The greater majority of my fish have been caught on the standard running link ledger consisting of the lead on a 6 inch link tied to a swivel which runs freely on the reel line. This swivel is stopped by a second swivel about 12 inches from the hook and for most of my fishing on clean bottom swims this is my standard rig. More recently, however, I have been using an even simpler set-up consisting of a lead attached to a swivel via a link (for speedy lead changing if necessary) which, while running freely on the reel line, is stopped by a John Roberts "ledger stop" 4 to 6 inches from the hook. I don't find this arrangement any more sensitive but it is tangle free and efficient. There are two exceptions to these rigs which I use in certain circumstances. If I'm experiencing a number of missed bites I use the fixed link ledger where the lead link is tied directly to the "stop" swivel so that there is no running line to the fish. Generally speaking I have found that this gives a more positive strike even though the lead must be moved simultaneously, but it is not a bolt-rig – the lengths of hook line/lead link remain the same although I do sometimes increase the length of the hook line.

The second end rig variation is for fishing directly into (rooted) weed. In such swims I use a fixed paternoster with the lead on a 36 inch link to the swivel, the hook link 4 to 6 inches, being tied directly to this same swivel which in turn is attached to the reel line. I use the long lead link so that the lead itself hits the weed first, the bait then settling gently *on* the weed some distance behind. By casting directly into the weed there is obviously a risk of dragging the bait into thick weed, which I would prefer not to do! With this in mind I dose the reel line with dilute Fairy Liquid before the cast which breaks up the surface tension and allows the line to sink rapidly – feathering the cast just before the lead hits the water ensures that the line is in a straight line to the bait. All that is then necessary is to carefully take up the slack, put the rod in its rests and attach the indicator.

In all cases strike when the bobbin hits the rod and is held there, don't waste your time striking as the bobbin is rising!

The only remaining item of tackle of particular importance is a good catapult. The "Black Widow" and other sling shot type catapults are very popular with carp anglers using small, very hard baits which can be gripped into the leather "pouch". But I do not use them for two reasons – they are impractical to use with softish baits because the bait is crushed in the "pouch", and secondly I am far from impressed by their accuracy and claimed distances. What you need is an easy actioned catapult with a good sized pouch (perforated for swift travel). Mine is a home made version of the Drennan feeder catapult which has a pouch 2½ inches in diameter attached by swivels to 18 inches of circular (in cross section) latex, which in turn is attached to the U-shaped frame by a swivel and split ring. The use of swivels at the pouch and frame ends of the "elastic" almost eliminates twisting and certainly aids accuracy and distance. I can fire one inch diameter baits, singly or occasionally in pairs 40 to 50 yards with sufficient accuracy to place every bait in 3-4 yard square, which is all that I require.

CHAPTER 10

# Where and When to Fish
*Ray Webb*

ANY list of tench waters stands a very good chance of being obsolete before it appears in print, for angling potential is very delicately balanced and prone to frequent variation, especially on hard fished waters. In addition to this sporting fluctuation, in the keenly competitive, dollar-ruled English angling scene a fishery belonging to a small group of anglers one day may well be leased by a massive Association the next, resulting in a completely different set up as regards day, week or season tickets; even 'no permits available at all' being only too likely. With these circumstances prevailing the following waters are fisheries famous for the good class tench fishing they have provided in the reasonably recent past, the last five years or so say, but the permit situation is left for the angler to ascertain, a simple enough process for a stamped addressed envelope to the secretary of the nearest angling club, whose address is to be found in the Field's annual publication 'Where to Fish' available from the public library, will be all that is necessary to ascertain the current permit situation at the time of enquiry.

One of the latest really hot fisheries to errupt violently onto the tench fishing scene is Alder Fen Broad, a water that first hit the headlines in the angling press in 1970 when a series of really big tench specimens of 6lb and 7lb in weight were taken in a very short spell of highly productive fishing. Previously virtually unknown, suddenly Alder Fen was big news nationally and tench enthusiasts all round the country were thumbing through guide and reference books feverishly seeking information. By July 9th, 1970 two seven-pounders had been recorded, and then Ray Stevenson of Northampton took one of 8lb on a brandling bait on size 12 hook and 7lb breaking strain line. We understand that latterly the fishing has settled down to more 'normal' fishing. Not long after the Alder Fen Broad headlines, private and club lakes in Flintshire came under the spotlight after yielding several fish over 7lb: surely the first time for this county.

Another famous, historic water is the Blenheim Palace fishery at

Woodstock for amongst many other notable catches Frank Murgett's 7lb 12oz tench was taken here in 1952, the biggest officially recorded for the whole of the country at that time. In addition to the top-class tench fishing this water also throws up a regular quota of fine pike, Mr John Cadd taking a 24½-pounder there recently. Also mentioned in the guide books of the area is the fact that Sir Winston Churchill was born here though history fails to record any specimen or even sizeable tench to his credit. Perhaps he was too busy winning the war.

Southill Park Lake is another tench fishery that will forever be associated in the public mind with a nationally famous name, for this was Dick Walker's tench water, the very lake in fact where his regular angling buddy Pete Thomas hooked and lost at the net a monstrous eight-pounder, the split shot splitting at the crucial moment allowing the running weight to slide down the line to knock the hook out of the fish's mouth, clean as a whistle. A most attractive water this, typical of the many lakes around England with pheasant and game abounding in the private grounds and fine old mansion or castle on the hill: the fellows who initiated these set-ups certainly knew a thing or two about stylish living and the long purse necessary to turn their ideas into reality. A vivid example is afforded here of the swing of the predominance of species over a number of years, for around 1935 the water was a tremendous rudd fishery with some good tench while nowadays it's the other way round, a top-class tench water with a few good rudd. My own best tench at Southill was a fine fish of 5lb 4oz.

Still in Bedfordshire some 4 miles or so further south is Henlow Grange an old flooded gravel pit of classical pattern dotted about with islands, pools 15ft or more in depth being separated by ledges a mere 2 or 3ft below the surface. Not an easy water by any means with blank days all too common, the tench nevertheless are big, the angler seeking his first four-pounder could be well advised to persevere here and much bigger specimens still are on the cards; Frank Guttfield's first ever six-pounder being taken from this water in fact way back in 1962.

Over to Hemingford Grey in Huntingdonshire and Jim Eggett's lake, the water that threw up John Salisbury's current English record tench of 9lb 1oz taken in 1963. Actually there are two fisheries here, both shallow waters holding numerous shoals of tench, too numerous perhaps from a big fish point of view, for on a week's holiday there in 1963 Bob Ranby and I took large catches of small- to medium-size tench, 8 or 9 fish each on one day, yet at the end of the stay our best fish weighed in at a mere 2lb 5oz. In spite of the smallish average size the big ones are there too, for prize winning entries of 5lb and 6lb specimens from this fishery have topped the competition lists from time to time. It was here also that the late Bill Keal, well-known angling journalist once took 3 carp over 20lb in one week and on other visits to the water a couple of 29lb pike, one by intent, the other taking a ball of paste ledgered in the hopes of a big carp.

Immediately alongside the river Welland in the Market Deeping area is a sizeable lake, heavily weeded in parts, from which a narrow arm of water extends right up to the foot of the bank of the river itself, known as the Gullet; this small shallow fishery hit the headlines with a bang some years ago. It produced a superb tench of 7lb 6oz, plenty big enough to send a number of keen specimen hunters, myself included heading in that direction and we found that in those days only on the arm itself was fishing allowed, the main body of the water being reserved for duck. My initial companion on the Gullet was Mr John Jeffrey of Peterborough, a man who'd taken a number of very big tench from the water; up to the $5\frac{3}{4}$lb mark and I enjoyed extremely good sport myself with three- and four-pounders. Bread was the bait par excellence for this water, eels and perch proving a nuisance to worm or maggot. Indeed, on one occasion in the middle of an all night session Denis Fullwood's flake bait was taken by a tench powerful enough to make the 7lb 6oz specimen look puny and underdeveloped, only to discover on finally hauling the monster to the surface that it wasn't a tench at all but an eel of $2\frac{1}{2}$lb dragging an assortment of weeds with it. It was on this fishery too that I first saw tench of two distinctly different colourings in the net at the same time, one morning's catch of six fish being comprised of four tinted the normal golden brown shade with the other two a greeny grey.

At Sywell Reservoir near Northampton the tench fishing of recent seasons has been absolutely top class, 4lb and 5lb fish being taken in considerable numbers. A fertile water of naturally high potential. The results obtained have been due to some degree to the good class of angler regularly to be seen fishing the water. Born and bred with the river Nene flowing through the middle of the town, whipping out fish almost before they're able to walk, to win an annual award for the Northampton Specimen Group's Fish of the Year is very nearly necessary to break a national record these days. Many of the best tench taken by Bob Church, weekly columnist of 'Angling Times', have come from Sywell, where one of the most productive techniques is to ledger at long range with a swim feeder, employing maggots for hookbait.

Down in Somerset the King's Sedgmoor Drain where I did so much of my early tench fishing is a water famous throughout the length and breadth of the country for bream as well as tench, so much so that it was chosen as the venue for the All England in 1955 along with the Huntspill and the Gripps River; and Jack Carr's winning weight of 68lb 2oz 4 drams, taken from the King's Sedgmoor Drain set up a new individual record for the event. Though my diaries give an average size for the tench on this water of 2lb 7oz, the species is to be found in numbers for 10 miles or more along the length of the fishery. I've taken them myself from the battlefield length at Weston Zoyland, at Ghedzoy, Middlezoy, Greylake Bridge, near Langport, to the outfall into the River Parrett at Dunball. In addition to consistent sport with medium-sized tench there are big fish to be taken by the angler who studies the water thoroughly, for every year sees a number of four-pounders taken and possibly an occasional specimen topping the 5lb mark. At the extreme top limit the biggest tench I can find recorded from the drain was a superb fish of 6lb 12oz taken by Mr E. Crickmore.

For a water that captures the atmosphere of pure tench fishing, having all the essential qualities that even the most demanding enthusiast could ever ask for, Hawk Lake at Hawkstone Park in Shropshire takes some beating. Long and narrow, heavily weeded, sheltered from the blast of the wind and largely shallow around 4ft in depth, I came away from my visit there in 1962 extremely impressed for even in that most difficult of all tench seasons consistently good sport was enjoyed. With tench over the 4lb mark taken regularly by anglers who know what they're about this is one water that actually is as good as it looks, with crucians over the $1\frac{1}{2}$lb mark also present in considerable numbers.

These then are just a few of the many famous tench waters to be found around and about the country, many more can be located without too much trouble by the angler who is prepared to scout around. In addition to fisheries where the tench fishing potential has been established for many years, new waters are continually being opened up where the species has been only fairly recently introduced, or sometimes only recently discovered, for tench can often be the most unobtrusive of fish living and thriving for many years with their presence completely unsuspected.

On most tench fisheries undoubtedly the most profitable time of the year to fish is at the very beginning of the season from June 16th onwards. Sport can so often start off with really big catches in the first few days, especially is this so after a prolonged pre-baiting programme has been carried out. With just one single exception after thirty years of pursuing tench all round England and over in Ireland, all the catches I've taken, or seen caught, where over half a dozen fish were involved, have been made early on at the start of the season, while the tench were still on the weedy shallows. Once the spawning shoals have split up catches of one or two fish only are the general expectation, possibly three or four if a really favourable condition of weather and water is encountered. Yorkshire anglers commencing their season on June 1st have a bonus fortnight that often yields big dividends, time and again I've taken seven or eight tench at a sitting before the rest of the country had emerged from the close season.

Suddenly, around the middle of July, fishing usually becomes extremely difficult, the fish now deeper in the water being hard to find and if located will generally prove reluctant in the extreme to take a bait. Once this difficult period sets in, it's likely to last a full five or six weeks and one of the theories put forward by way of explanation is that at this time of year the water becomes thick with some type of minute life on which the tench feed to the exclusion of all else and not until the last of them are gone around the end of August will the angler stand much chance of any real sporting prospects. True or false, on just about every tench water I ever fished mid-July to the end of August has been hard going, extremely hard, so much so that I'm inclined to favour a spot of chub or barbel fishing at this point to step up the action somewhat.

Come September and the position begins to improve again, especially so on the waters in Somerset where really consistent catches are on the cards right up to the coming of the first real frosts in November. Considerably warmer, though perhaps wetter too, than the rest of the country during the Autumn months, I was persuaded by the local top man Raymond Perrett to take my holiday down there at this stage of the year, for his records proved conclusively just how good the sport could be. Indeed, his own best ever catch from the King's Sedgmoor Drain, 17 tench for over 50lb total weight if I remember precisely, was taken during one short afternoon of hectic feeding late on in October.

Though it is undoubtedly correct to class tench as primarily a summer feeding species there are nevertheless times and places where the prospects for sport in winter can be quite good. I've seen numerous fish caught through the colder months and taken one or two myself without really trying, being fishing for other species at the time. Winter tenching is a somewhat involved subject, however, so much so that it is discussed at length by Barrie in Chapter 11.

When one switches from considering the best time of the year to the best time of day, using the term in its twice-round-the-clock 24-hour sense, then the position becomes rather more complicated, for there are big variations from water to water, month to month and season to season. In spite of these fluctuations, however, it's generally true to say that on most waters from the beginning of the season to the middle of July the most favourable time to be out on the water would be from around six to eleven in the morning; five hours of concentrated fishing at those times being at least as productive if not more so than the remaining nineteen hours put together.

On fisheries also containing a good head of rudd and bream the usual pattern experienced by the angler out at dawn around 3.30 a.m. say, is for sport to be largely confined to these two species for the first two or three hours but staying with the job in hand, instead of searching around for another swim, somewhere between six and seven the tench will probably start to feed and from that point on they can be fished for with some confidence right through till around eleven o'clock or thereabouts. Occasionally comes a day with weather conditions just right, when the tench continue to feed steadily all the way from dawn till dusk. An opportunity that must be grabbed with both hands when it occurs, for to leave a long sustained session till the morrow, when one is better prepared, is usually fatal; the tench having then reverted to their normal mid-day knocking off time. With just one single exception in thirty years' experience, every time the tench have fed on all through the day there's been a lively breeze blowing; there is little doubt in my mind that the oxygenation of the wind-lashed water is responsible for the continuation of the feeding period right through the afternoon. A fish or two can be expected in the evening session as a general rule at this stage though no water I ever fished provided consistent sport comparable to that obtained before midday.

Knowledge of tench on the King's Sedgmoor Drain enabled me to pick up many a good fish at a time when most anglers had written off all hope of sport. It was only by sheer persistent effort all the way from dawn to dusk that I spotted the pattern in the first place during one of my early visits to the water. Staying at the Silver Fish Hotel in those far off, free-spending days, in common with most of the other guests, I made an early start each morning, but when they retired in the middle of the day to take refreshment and shelter from the heat of the midday sun I stayed with the job in hand fishing on from under the shade of a large umbrella.

It soon became obvious that a large number of small rudd would become suddenly active every afternoon, tearing the bread crust bait to pieces without even offering the angler much chance of connecting on the strike, a most infuriating situation that further convinced the other anglers that they were doing the right thing by giving afternoon angling a miss. For fully two or three hours the rudd would be on to the bait immediately it was cast in. One could literally use up the whole of the crust of a full-sized loaf each afternoon, but by half past three time the rudd activity ceased abruptly as if at a sudden signal, the float then remaining motionless and undisturbed on the glassy surface; not a sign of life to be seen anywhere. After an hour and a half of this absolute inactivity just as one was thinking of heading back to the hotel for tea the float would shoot under suddenly without any advance warning whatsoever and the answering strike connected, not with a tiny rudd, but a solid tench of 3lb or thereabouts. Persistent experiment finally convinced me that a break for tea at this point was indeed the best policy for invariably there was just the single fish and then nothing further till eight o'clock or so as the light began to fade, but by concentrating hard every afternoon about an hour and a half or so after the rudd activity had ceased I was fully prepared for the solitary tench bite when it came, rarely failing to convert it into a fish in the net.

With the coming of Autumn however the position alters somewhat, the big catches of the early morning fishing becoming less and less likely as the weeks go by, with the angler fishing long and hard for just the odd fish here and there, as likely to be picked up in the evening or indeed at mid-afternoon as early on in the day. On the fisheries that provide good tench fishing throughout the winter the afternoon fishing is often the best of all, as was vividly illustrated on March 12th, 1960 when I was doing a spot of pike fishing at Flood's Ferry on the Old River Nene, for on the way back as we crossed over Moreton's Leam near Whittlesey a stop was made to check up on the results obtained by a busload of anglers from my old home town of

Sheffield. Following the invariable custom of those angler's bus parties a cash prize was awarded for the best fish of the day and we arrived just in time to see the winner bringing his catch to the scales and what a surprising net of fish it was; twelve fine tench for 30lb total weight, the biggest just stopping short of the 4lb mark by a mere couple of ounces.

In addition to this remarkable catch a similar bag of tench caught by an angler fishing right alongside the road bridge had just been returned to the water the best of that collection weighing in at 3lb 11oz. All these fish, without exception had been taken in the afternoon session the tench commencing to feed around half past twelve and being taken steadily from that point on all the way through to the whistle for time just before dusk. At Fotheringhay too, fishing a backwater of the Nene in amongst catches of roach, perch and bream, George Roberts, Dennis Fullwood and I took a number of good winter tench on maggot, the fish almost invariably coming to the net an hour or so before dark.

Turning to the question of night fishing for tench the position here is somewhat involved too but as a broad generalisation there's no doubt in my mind that the hours of daylight are superior to the hours of darkness on most waters, most of the time. The same conclusion was reached by Harry Brotherton many years ago as recorded in his book on tench in the 'How to Catch Them' series. Having said that I must go on to explain that there is no shortage of exceptions to the generally correct rule, one of them being the difficult period of mid-July to the end of August, some fisheries producing good returns to the all night angler at this stage while the man who persists in the daylight can so often be struggling.

Then again there are waters that are genuinely better night fished for tench as a regular thing for reasons that are difficult to ascertain, the normal pattern of strong early morning feeding and sporadic nocturnal activity being completely reversed. A gravel pit near London is a supreme example of such a reversal for this water produced a number of 6lb-plus tench some years ago, all the fish being taken in the middle of the night. To further complicate the situation, waters that have regularly been primarily daytime tench waters for a number of years can suddenly cease to provide sport by daylight altogether, the fish switching over to night feeding almost exclusively. The effects of prolonged hard fishing could well be a decisive factor here. On waters of a mere three or four feet in depth, a common enough occurrence in tench fishing if the level fluctuates at all, and a foot or more of water is lost, then once again the fish may turn to night feeding being unwilling to cooperate by day when the level of what is permanently shallow water is reduced even further. Depth of water is a major factor to be taken into consideration when thinking about night fishing, for tench tend to move on to the weedy shallows after dark, having spent the middle hours of the day in fifteen foot or so of water if the weather is at all bright and sunny. Once on the shallows and feeding by night the hesitant, finnicky behaviour so commonly encountered by day is abandoned altogether, large balls of paste or a bunch of lobworms fished on large hooks and strong lines being taken in a positive, decisive fashion reminiscent of bold-biting carp.

Complicated though the position is as regards the right time to be out after tench, the wise angler will weigh up all the many factors involved in the light of his knowledge and experience and come up with the correct answer with sufficient regularity to see him enjoying consistently good-class sport. There are occasions of course, in spells of inactivity when the tench have moved away out of the chosen swim and the problem then is one of location rather than timing, but more often than not the fish are still in residence merely refusing to feed for the time being. Proof of this was afforded me in dramatic fashion one day as I watched a number of tench cruising slowly around in 18in of water completely ignoring my lobworm bait on the bottom for hour after hour all the way through the afternoon. With prospects elsewhere in the area extremely doubtful, for want of anything better to do I decided to stick it out till dark though the thought of witnessing big tench passing by my bait for a further four hours or more was almost too horrible to contemplate.

After putting up with the depressing spectacle till half past six I was almost thinking in terms of abandoning the project altogether when a fine tench that was approaching my bait for the umpteenth time slowly sank down, picked up the lob and started to move away. Scarce able to believe the evidence of my own eyes I had to really discipline myself into striking but the resultant eruption soon convinced me that I wasn't dreaming, for a big tench hooked in such shallow water with dense weed growth all around can keep an angler fully occupied exercising his wits to keep out of trouble. Finally landed and weighed in at 4lb 3oz that fish was followed to the net by two more around the same weight before eight o'clock at which time the feeding spell ended and the tench resumed their patrolling without stopping for food. Out at the same swim the following day the performance was repeated exactly, the tench refusing all baits offered until half past six, then feeding steadily for 90 minutes or so, as truly a dramatic illustration of the importance of the correct time to fish as any angler could ever conceivably hope for.

CHAPTER 11

# Winter Tench
*Barrie Rickards*

IN the discussion of John Ellis's tench paper at the first British Angling Conference the subject of winter tench fishing was well aired and partly inspired, I suspect, by the success at that time of winter carp fishing. In fact fishing in winter for tench has always been on the cards, and is possibly a better prospect than winter carp fishing. However, there are few good carp rivers and the breakthrough here has been with still-water carp. Tench fishing prospects can likewise be divided into the two categories of still and running water, and in the case of the first the prospect with tench may actually be *less* than carp. I remember Fred Taylor succeeding with lake tench some years ago, but he found that the critical factor was water movement: when the lake's controlling sluice gates were opened the tench came on the feed!

It should not be imagined that tench always hibernate in the sense that they bury deep in the mud or allow thick weed to die pretty solidly around them. They often simply go torpid, remain quite upright, and can be quickly active if necessity demands. Indeed, any tench that fully hibernated on some fenland drains and rivers would wake up living with the cods and the crabs if he slept for too long. In many rivers and particularly in winter with their occasional raging floods, a tench can hardly rest up at all, and probably has to feed a little more than his still-water cousins to make up for the energy lost.

The tench in my shallow garden pond never used to bury in the weed or mud no matter how cold the weather became. They were always moderately active in the sense that their gills worked quite strongly and their fins moved continuously. It was quite impossible to catch them in a net for they shot off at a great rate of knots. But they didn't feed much: in summer they could easily be caught on worms and bread, but in winter they barely tackled anything whether a free offering or not. When you think about it a *small* lake full of hibernating tench one winter would be a small lake *without* tench the following summer simply because the pike would have cleaned them

139

up, for it would not take a predator long to learn how to dig out food: hibernating mammals face the same dangers each winter from their enemies.

There is further evidence about winter tench activity as anybody who has been on a winter netting party may know. Tench often turn up in the nets in winter (perhaps slightly more often than in summer, in fact, when they are famous for their net-avoiding tactics) and are seen to be plump, fit and pretty lively. Des Kelsell mentioned this in the discussion of the above-mentioned paper by John Ellis, and I know some lakes in Cambridge which have yielded *very* lively tench to fyke nets.

The very mention of fyke nets reminds me that several years ago Ray and I found a poacher's fyke net of some 60 yards length in that famous little tench lake of Carlton Towers in the West Riding. It was midwinter, the weather cold, yet the net contained quite a few lively tench, pike and eels (another hibernator!). The owner (Countess Beaumont) was very pleased that the poachers had been detected, and from then on the tench could remain torpid in peace, for all they had thrown at them were livebaits, spinners and deadbaits. On the other hand Kennedy and Fitzmaurice (1970) do point out that in some Irish waters the tench bury in the dying weed and also lose some weight.

For still-water tench, therefore, the summer techniques of heavy baiting would clearly be a waste of time, and fine tackle and small baits would be much more likely to succeed. I should think the best way to tempt them (failing sluice gates) would be to try to find the tench first (how?) and then feed them with cloudbait and maggots, hoping to incite them to feed: perhaps a strong-smelling meaty additive to the groundbait might help. It is almost certainly no coincidence that the occasional still-water tench which do turn up in winter are caught on single maggots and small hooks.

River tench are obviously different: they have to be to stay alive. Quite a few rivers have had a reputation for winter tench, going back many years. Thus the Lincolnshire Forty Foot at Swineshead consistently yielded tench to anglers fishing for other species; and in the Fens proper the Sixteen Foot and Ramsey Forty Foot rivers are, today, quite good winter tench waters. It would be unusual *not* to see a tench in the winter match returns on the Sixteen Foot, and I've seen anglers with several tench in the net in the very depths of winter. Of course, the flow on that water is always reasonable, and can be tremendous. The water is also a good depth which could be an influencing factor because the nearby Old Bedford Drain yields very few winter tench despite quite a strong flow. Another famous winter tench water is the River Axe at Bleadon Bridge in Somerset, a water also mentioned, I believe, by Harry Brotherton in the 'How to Catch Them' series. Ray remembers the water well.

The main problem with winter tench is this: how does one go about catching them, and is it really worth it? Well, for Thames expert John Cadd, well known to readers of the angling newspapers during 1974, there was no question about it, because he succeeded with tench in winter on the Thames, but found the going much more difficult in summer! That's the reverse of everybody else's problem which is that the tench are *not* easy to find (they do not roll at the surface for example) and they do not feed avidly. I would say that if you are going to get one tench in three sessions, by employing, say, small bait, fine line tactics, then it really isn't worth it and you'd be better off pike fishing. On the other hand an average of one fish per session would be enough to make me think seriously about persuing the matter further. If, by dint of local knowledge, you could find quite a well-known local swim which consistently yielded tench, then clearly your chances increase. I'm always interested in the unusual approach because it is this which so often produces giant fish in angling. I can imagine, for example, that giant tench, so difficult to coax in summer, might occasionally turn out to be suckers in winter – if only I could find their hidy hole.

John Cadd writing in 'Angling Times' tells us that his best results with the tench of his beloved River Thames invariably come in the colder months of the year, usually from the slacks and backwaters and often at times when the main stream is in flood. In full accordance with all my own experience of similar conditions, fine lines, small hooks, yellow maggots and tiny redworms have proved essential for him to contact the tench with anything like the required frequency, and a lost fish now and again has to be accepted philosophically in the knowledge that stronger tackle would inevitably result in fewer bites. Even with such delicately adjusted gear bites are usually indicated by the very slightest of float movements, which call for an immediate strike, any attempt made at waiting for a decisive slide away being absolutely fatal. Employing such methods and approach Mr Cadd had enjoyed consistent sport with the Thames tench in winter, blanks being a rarity and up to five at a sitting taken when things have gone really well, satisfactory returns indeed from a water that many anglers ignore completely as a tench fishery summer or winter.

Probably there is one further point to be mentioned in connection with winter tench, and that is the artificially heated water of the power station outfalls. For the tench angler these have not yet proved the boon they might have hoped for, all the attention being reserved for carp, but I gather the Electricity Cut at Peterborough did yield a fair number of tench. In lakes a good head of big carp can actually be detrimental to the tench stock, so that with heated outfalls it may be necessary to look at those with little or no carp population. Both the Peterborough and Great Ouse (Barford) outfalls have a good head of carp rather than tench, but perhaps others might be a better prospect, like the famous Irish one at Lanesborough. . . .

**Comment** – *by Ray Webb*

It is unlikely that the Lanesborough hot water cut will ever show really worthwhile results in winter for the tench just are not there, having left the previous July or August time to take up quarters either in the main Shannon itself or out across Lough Ree proper, the river being far and away the likeliest bet to my way of thinking. It is only at spawning time that the tench are prepared to venture into the narrow, shallow, clear water cut putting up with the hazards, disturbances and exposure for the sake of the future of the species. As is to be expected the arrival and departure of the tench in the Cut varies year by year, conditions of weather and water being the two determining factors, but apart from a few stragglers the major shoals of tench usually move in around late April or early May time building up steadily to a numerical peak about the last week or so in May.

CHAPTER 12

# Irish Tench
*Ray Webb*

THOUGH not native fish, tench have certainly been present in Irish waters for well over 200 years being introduced in the 18th century to stock the private ponds of the large manor houses of the period. Largely ignored or forgotten, the species flourished and spread considerably until by 1950, in addition to the originally stocked ponds, tench were present in numbers in the Shannon from Limerick all the way up to Carrick, and in Lough Sheelin, Derravaragh and Iron on the River Inny, and in the Fergus river system around Corofin in County Clare. From 1956 the Inland Fisheries Trust, a government-sponsored organisation originated to preserve and develop the country's angling potential, has introduced tench into suitable waters, rivers, ponds and canals, at all points around Ireland from Bantry down in Cork to Carrickmacross up in County Monaghan, successfully establishing good-class tench fishing on a countrywide basis to meet the demands of a rapidly expanding coarse fishing tourist industry.

Much of the Fisheries Trust's early work was carried out with little in the way of modern equipment, the tench trapped on Sheelin and Derravaragh being transported in sacks and wet grass in the back of a jeep; and one fishery, Killamooney Lake near Cavan, a swampy area of some 2 acres or so in extent, was cleaned out, deepened and stocked by sheer hard slog, developing into a fine water that has since produced many fine catches of tench, the biggest recorded specimen to date going 5lb 10oz. To this day the resounding success of the tench stocking programme stands as a lasting tribute to the wit, initiative and all-out effort of the Trust for achieving so much on extremely limited resources.

All through the 1950s Irish tench fishing continued to attract English visitors in numbers, pleasure anglers looking for good sport with medium-sized fish but the dedicated specimen hunter by and large remained unconvinced that the prospects for fish of over 5lb were better than could be found on their home waters. The clear

143

fertility of the Irish waters, the beauty and charm of the rural scene and the complete absence of frustrating rules and restrictions were hardly sufficient justification to warrant the long journey involved. To add to the big fisherman's problems two of the best fisheries of the time, Balliderry Lake near Moate, Co. Offaly, and Pallas Lake at Tullamore, had to be written off; the former being drained nearly dry and the latter cleared for development as a trout water. My own results of this period confirmed the generally held view on really big tench potential, though I continued to visit Ireland every year. The unlimited individual freedom and lack of restraint was all the inducement required for a man of my temperament.

In 1962, however, the position changed dramatically, the first indication to reach my notice being a photograph in the 'Angling Times' of a guesthouse proprietor near Athlone, Mr Fred Carter and several of his visitors holding very big tench indeed, several of them topping the 6lb mark. My hastily scribbled letter of enquiry expressing admiration for such a superb catch, but wondering if perhaps the weights were estimated, met with a very prompt, detailed and courteous reply informing me that the fish had in fact been accurately weighed and though only taken occasionally after much prolonged hard effort, the tench on his water almost invariably ran big the average size being over $4\frac{1}{2}$lb. It was his first season on the water, however, and the reults so far obtained were as result of the initial, experimental fishing of the pioneers, much remained to be learned to get the very best of it. A bay off the south east corner of Lough Ree, the fishery I was told was known as Garnafailagh Lake, a name that was to have a tremendous impact on the Irish tench fishing scene in the years ahead.

Sufficiently impressed to book in for a week in June 1963, John Neville and I arrived in scorching heatwave conditions, to be greeted by Fred and his wife Clair and then rushed down to the boathouse and shown a catch of 8 tench to $5\frac{3}{4}$lb taken by a couple of anglers from Nuneaton, a breathtaking introduction to the astonishing potential of this remarkable water. Rowing right across the lake to try out a previously unfished swim the Nuneaton men had dropped on the first shoal of Garnafailagh tench ever located. There must have been 40 or 50 of them, at least, packed in together tightly, with at least a similar number of bream in the $5-6\frac{1}{2}$lb range. Right through to their departure on Wednesday the two anglers continued to take 6, 7, or 8 tench a day; big powerful fish of up to 6lb in weight, while

72. A fighting tench is finally beaten and brought to the net.
*(Photo Angling Times)*

Garnafailagh - Specimen tench 1963

| Period | Number of Fish Taken | Average Weight |
|---|---|---|
| July 7-13 | 18 | 5lb 9oz |
| June 30-July 6 | 14 | 5lb 8oz |
| June 16-?? | 12 | 5lb 6oz |
| June 2-8 | 8 | 5lb 5oz |
| June 23-29 | 7 | 5lb 11oz* |
| June 9-15 | 4 | 5lb 7oz |
| May 19-25 | 3 | 5lh 4oz |
| July 16-20 | 1 | 5lb 2oz |
| Total | 67 | 5lb 7oz |

Average Weight of 67 Tench

*Including Record Fish of 7lb 6oz.

74. Photograph of an item of the Garnafailagh House notice board.

73. Ted Kershaw with the old Irish record of 7lb 6oz taken from Coosan Lough at Garnafailagh.

John and I edging as near, or even nearer, than was decently possible, failed to pick up any fish at all, not even small perch, as decisive a demonstration of the importance of the exact spot as I ever came across. We only missed the fish by 3 or 4 yards but miss them we did.

Able to move into the vacated hot swim for the latter half of the week, we found only the remnants of the shoal still in residence for all the big catches had been taken back for weighing and released at the boathouse over a mile away. Still, we did take a good fish or two, if no large numbers of them and a tench of 5lb 6oz was enough to make my holiday, being my personal best for the species up to that time. No sooner had we returned home than a wire from Fred reached us telling of a new Irish Record Tench of 7lb 6oz taken by Ted Kershaw, the second national record of the month from Garnafailagh for a rudd/bream hybrid of 5lb 5oz was taken while John and I were there. Headlines in the angling press convinced the English specimen hunters at this point that here was one Irish water that really did hold outsize tench in numbers and they booked in regularly from then on year after year.

With the better-class anglers on the water 1964 was Garnafailagh's Bonanza year, and more hotspots were discovered; the L-shaped bay swim starting the ball rolling with a tremendous catch by Tom Scates of 21 tench, the fish feeding steadily all through the day as they did a week or two later when I fished the same spot to take 15 tench for 66lb, the best of which, at 6lb 1oz and 6lb 2oz, I hauled out with successive casts. With Ted Kershaw and Steve Crawshaw taking 4 six-pounders each the 1964 season ended with Garnafailagh putting 15 tench over 6lb on the Irish Specimen Fish List and 60 more over 5lb, flooding the market to such an extent that the specimen weight for the species had to be increased from 5 to 6lb.

Year after year, all the way up to 1970 when Fred and Clair sold up to move on to Ballinafid, the tench continued to provide good sport at Garnafailagh, Freddie Lander in particular monopolising a very productive and classically heavily padded corner swim, taking consistently big catches over several seasons. The year 1968 saw the most astonishing return of all, however, when Barrie found a huge shoal in ravenous feeding mood and took 50 tench in two sittings, 27 on the first day and 23 on the second, of which 43 were over the 5lb mark, a truly tremendous haul of fish. Looking back on all the achievements of 9 years of all out effort, Fred must surely chuckle to himself at the property he bought late on in 1961, 'a fine old mansion

75. Tring. All the experts early on the morning of 16th June.

*(Photo Angling Times)*

76. Ray's home-made boat complete with outriggers.

once belonging to Lord Castlemayne himself', so the seller informed him, 'but the lake's a bit of a disappointment, completely devoid of any sign of fishlife whatsover. You'll have to run down to the river at Athlone for a bit of sport'. Buying it regardless, Fred's initial scout round the lake saw a 19lb 14oz pike snap in his spoon bait as soon as he drew away from the boathouse, followed quickly by a five-pounder and another that snapped the tackle, enough to convince Fred he'd made a better buy than the other fellow realised, though just how good a purchase it was to prove even Fred, at that stage, could never have guessed.

Looking back on the Garnafailagh era myself, there are a number of lessons that stand out vividly, from an angling point of view, the most obvious one perhaps being the effect of prolonged hard fishing on a previously virgin water. Prior to my initial visit to Garnafailagh in 1963 most of my tench fishing had been done on the heavily-flogged waters near the big industrial town of the north and midlands-districts of England. These fisheries demanded delicate, finely balanced tackle before anything like a decisive bite could be expected. It came as something of a shock then to see float tackle being pulled away yard after yard in some cases before a strike was made, much after the fashion of a determined run experienced from a taking pike. My own tench were caught ledgering without a float that year, leaving the pick up open and coil after coil of line whipped off at a surprising pace.

Back again in 1964 the tench proved to be still feeding in a bold decisive fashion, but early on in the holiday, several times the bait was dropped just as I was about to engage the pick up to make contact so for the rest of the stay I fished with the pick-up shut and a small loop of line between reel and butt ring with a dough bobbin indicator attached, an arrangement that worked out well, very well indeed. By 1965, however, the dough bobbin was nowhere near sensitive enough and from this point of finely adjusted float tackle became the order of the day at Garnafailagh, only thus could the tench, educated by this time into feeding delicately and circumspectly as on any of the heavily fished English waters, be taken with any regularity at all.

In addition to the changing style of bite, with the passing of the years a changing style of bait came into the 'Garnafailagh picture' the all-conquering worm of the early seasons yielding pride of place to breadflake over the last two or three years. When the 1964 season was analysed, though breadbaits did turn up a tench or two, the prospects were literally ten times better if you had a lively lobworm on offer, but on my rolling up for a final shot in 1970 four fish were being caught on flake to every one taken on worm, years of heavy groundbaiting with bread-based mixtures had reversed the efficiency of the taking baits completely. Another extremely important fact that was conclusively driven home to us was that on a stillwater fishery of Garnafailagh size, say 500 acres or so, the first two or three years of intensive fishing were going to see the best of the prospects, for the biggest specimens at any rate. After that a decline in returns would almost inevitably become apparent. In terms of big tench over the 6lb mark Garnafailagh's first year of 1962 produced six specimens a clear indication of things to come when the fishery was fully exploited. The following year's fishing turned up another six big ones including the new record of 7lb 6oz.

Third time round, the peak year of 1964 saw 15 six-pounders entered on the big fish list and then came the steady decline, eight specimens for 1965; four in 1966 and four again in 1967, two for 1968 and three in 1969. Finally came just one solitary tench of 6lb 5oz for 1970. The significance of these figures just cannot be ignored, for good class anglers were fishing long and hard right up to the very end. Even in the last two or three years, however, consistently good catches of tench up to $4\frac{3}{4}$lb were being made with an occasional five-pounder here and there, but the fish over the 6lb mark had either learned to avoid the anglers' baits or just weren't there any more having moved away to lose themselves in the vast, extensive waters of Lough Ree proper. In other areas we found other examples of the same principle being demonstrated regardless of species, previously unfished waters producing incredibly good returns for the first two or three years then a steady decline; Hornsea Mere in Yorkshire and Horsey Mere on the Norfolk Broads being two classic instances in the pike-fishing scene. Larger waters like Lough Derg or Lower Lough Erne or alternatively rivers of some considerable flow seem perhaps to stand up to a high pressure of angling somewhat better, Lough Ree itself being hammered by the Athlone pike anglers for many years without showing serious signs or ill-effects.

Previously almost exclusively doing my tench fishing from the bank, the boat-fishing-only nature of the Garnafailagh fishery presented new problems and the inadequacy of anchors in water of 12ft or so was quickly brought home to me. But Fred solved this admirably by means of a couple of stiff poles 25ft or so in length driven deep into the muddy bottom, one at each end of the boat. Once firmly tied on the resulting platform was stable enough to allow finely adjusted float tackle to be used even in rough windy weather, the swing and sway experienced when using anchors on 14ft long ropes being eliminated completely. For rowing out to the chosen swims the thole pins fitted on all of Fred's boats proved far superior to the old rowlocks, which worked well enough at a steady pace in calm weather, but whenever real effort had to be put into the rowing to achieve top speed or head up into a strong wind the oars frequently jumped clean into the air, pitching the oarsman violently backwards. So impressed was I that my own boat Tinca was straightway converted from rowlock propulsion to the pin. It surprises me to find that even now the thole pin isn't universally adopted.

With water of high alkalinity and extreme clarity, drab or camouflaged clothing was of prime importance and movement in the boat was reduced to an absolute minimum. Lobworms proved to be a major problem, for the soil around Athlone was hardly rich enough to hold them in any real quantity. We tried to bring enough from England to last out our stay but if they were stored anywhere warm on the ship coming over we were quickly in trouble. Once at Garnafailagh however, safety of our worms was assured, for packed in the moss found on the rocks around the boathouse they rapidly built up into tip-top condition. If the situation became really desperate, brandlings from the town dump in Athlone, or small red worms from under cow pats could be pressed into service, but lobs were far and away the best bet. I used them exclusively whenever available.

Fishing in the Shannon at Clondra in 1966, Edmund Hawksworth broke Ted Kershaw's record with a tench of 7lb 12oz and took a string of specimens, both tench and bream from this area, fishing the parent river and its tributary the Feorish. It was this tremendous breakthrough that set me seriously considering the Shannon river itself for big tench when Garnafailagh House was sold, and with the benefit of a warm water outflow from Electricity Supply Board's power station in the middle of the town, Lanesborough was the obvious place to start. From its initial entry of a 6lb 4oz tench in 1963, Lanesborough had been appearing on the Specimen Fish List with ever increasing frequency and on my arrival in 1970 for a scout round I was fortunate to drop on Frank Ordoyno going strong, having got the tench on the run in no uncertain fashion. Four times in a fortnight he took 10 or 11 fish a day finishing up with the biggest tench of the year for the whole of the country, a beautiful brace of 6lb 13oz and 6lb 14½oz. This was enough to convince me that here was a man whose method I'd be well advised to study.

At this point, as at Garnafailagh in 1963, the serious big fish men arrived at Lanesborough determined to get the very best out of the water, and the results obtained, published every year on the Specimen Fish List, show just how well they have succeeded with Lanesborough (Fig. 77) forging ahead to make it virtually a one-horse race. Indeed in the tench section for 1974 there is no other venue on a list comprised of 30 entries, but the peak year so far was 1972 with Lanesborough producing 40 tench over the 6lb mark, a full half dozen of which went over 7lb a return that will take some

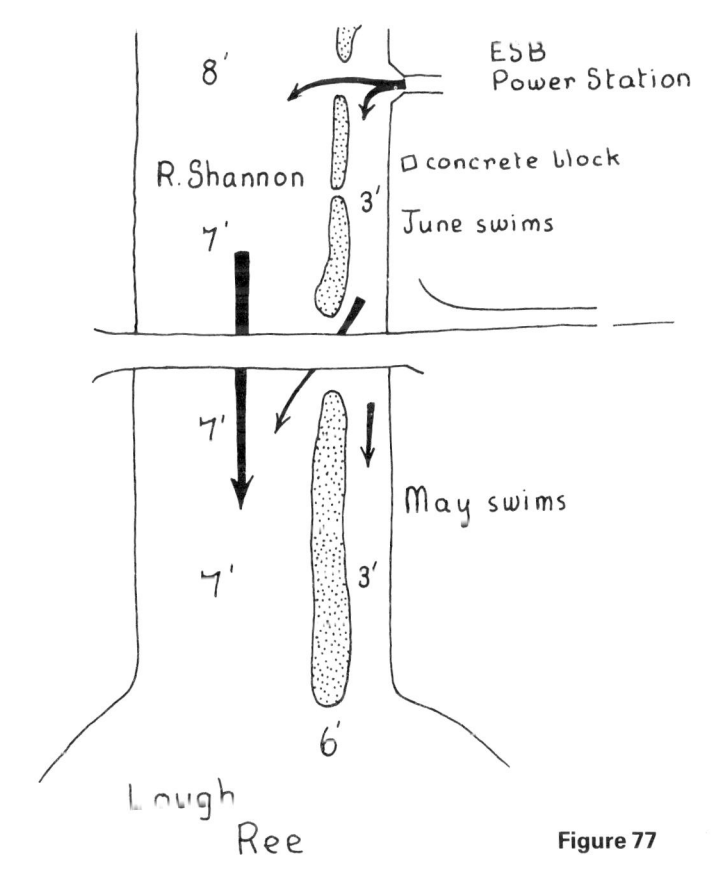

Figure 77

beating by this or any other fishery. My own contribution to this total included two seven-pounders with 10 more over 6lb making 1972 the sort of tench season I'd been studying and working for for over a quarter of a century of dedicated all out effort. Understandably, Lanesborough rates very highly in my estimation and I've hopes that it will continue to dominate the Irish tench scene for many years to come.

In spite of the all conquering pre-eminence of Garnafailagh in the '60s and Lanesborough in the first half of this decade, a considerable number of other venues have put up entries onto the Big Fish List with many more still capable of doing so if fished by the right type of angler for the job. On June 12th, 1959 Clooncorrick Lake at Garrigallen hit the headlines with a new Irish Record tench of 7lb the biggest of a string of specimens from this and the nearby Town Lake. About the same time Reynella Lake, a private water at Bracklyn Mullingar belonging to Mr John Roberts along with the adjoining guest house, consistently fished well and some of the guests also recorded specimens from the Johnstown and Dysart Lakes a few miles away. Below Carrick the River Glogher, running into the Shannon at Drumsna, turned up big tench without a specialized angling approach and Lowfield Lake in the same area also featured in reports.

Out of the news of recent years these Drumsna waters are still top-class fisheries but with Mattie Bourke no longer offering accommodation at Albert Lock, anglers in search of holiday fishing have turned their attentions elsewhere. On the shores of Kilglass the tiny Glooneen Lake alongside Tiernens Guest House put two specimen tench on the List in 1962. A beautiful limestone pond this where tench are as fit and attractive in appearance as they almost invariably are from waters of this calibre. Another lake that sprang into prominence largely as a result of a dramatic, eye-catching feature in the angling press by Frank Gutfield, Lough Patrick at Multyfarnham received a lot of attention from visiting anglers myself included. It turned up enormous catches of medium-sized fish with the odd specimen here and there. From Lough Derry at Carrickmacross in 1970 a beautiful brace of 6lb 4oz and 6lb 12oz clearly indicated the tench potential of this particular water and the following year saw Putiaghan feature prominantly in the List with seven entries, six of which fell to previous record holder Edmund Hawksworth, the best of the bunch going 7lb 4oz.

It was on Putiaghan too, in 1971, only a few days after these

78. The monster of the chapter on Irish tench fishing was responsible for the uprooting of six of these enormous lily roots immediately under Ray's boat in seven feet of water. Ray's companion still looks shaken.

remarkable specimens were taken that I was witness to one of the most astonishing events in the whole history of tench fishing. If I heard the story from someone else I should laugh it off as just about as likely as Jonah and the Whale but being involved in the incident myself I'm unable to discount the evidence of my own eyes, and any possibility of laughter at the time was very definitely out, the experience being anything but amusing. It was early one evening that Ernie Woodhead, his regular angling companion, and myself moored our boat in the middle of a dense bed of lily pads, casting out some 12 yards or so to a small area of cleared water that had regularly been baited up for several weeks. That the tench appreciated the time and effort spent on their behalf was clearly evident by the massive patches of bubbles continually errupting on the surface and we tackled up hopeful of exciting sport ahead.

For a full hour or more we fished hard without reward though the bubbling continued in furious fashion and relaxing concentration momentarily to glance down over the side of the boat where the 7ft of

# Report of the Irish Specimen Fish Committee for the Year 1971

## TENCH

Record 7lb 13¼oz.    Ray Webb.    Specimen weight 6lb.

| Weight lb. oz. | PLACE | DATE | CAPTOR | Method |
|---|---|---|---|---|
| 7 13¼ | R. Shannon, Lanesboro | 25th May | Raymond Webb | Bread flake |
| 7 4 | Putiaghan Lake, Belturbet | 2nd June | Edmund Hawksworth | Maggots |
| 7 3 | R. Shannon, Lanesboro | 19th May | Peter John Mayne | Worm |
| 7 2¾ | R. Shannon, Lanesboro | 25th May | Frank Ordoyno | Bread flake |
| 6 14½ | R. Shannon, Lanesboro | 21st May | Wilfred A. Lister | Bread flake |
| 6 13 | R. Shannon, Lanesboro | 23rd May | James Cheverall, Snr. | 3 Maggots on 16 hook |
| 6 12¾ | R. Shannon, Lanesboro | 20th May | Malcolm Bentley | Worm |
| 6 11 | Putiaghan Lake, Belturbet | 1st June | Edmund Hawksworth | Maggots |
| 6 11 | Coosan Lough, Athlone | 7th June | E. G. Kershaw | Lobworm |
| 6 11 | R. Shannon, Lanesboro | 25th May | Clifford Upton | Bread |
| 6 10¼ | R. Shannon, Lanesboro | 21st May | Peter Andrews | Bread |
| 6 9½ | R. Shannon, Lanesboro | 23rd May | Paul Sullivan | Bread |
| 6 9 | Putiaghan Lake, Belturbet | 1st June | Edmund Hawksworth | Maggots |
| 6 7¾ | R. Shannon, Lanesboro | 23rd May | Paul Sullivan | Bread |
| 6 6½ | R. Shannon, Lanesboro | 26th May | Raymond Webb | Bread flake |
| 6 5½ | R. Shannon, Lanesboro | 21st May | Peter Andrews | Bread |
| 6 4 | R. Shannon, Lanesboro | 25th May | Clifford Upton | Bread |
| 6 3 | Coosan Lough, Athlone | 7th June | J. A. Curtis | Worm |
| 6 2½ | R. Shannon, Lanesboro | 15th May | Stephen Radford | Bread flake |
| 6 2¼ | Lough Ree, Lanesboro | 7th June | Mrs. Elsie Marshall | Worm |
| 6 2 | Putiaghan Lake, Belturbet | 1st June | Edmund Hawsworth | Maggots |
| 6 2 | Putiaghan Lake, Belturbet | 2nd June | S. Phillips | Maggots |
| 6 2 | R. Shannon, Lanesboro | 12th May | Peter Grant | Bunch of 10 maggots |
| 6 1¾ | R. Shannon, Lanesboro | 17th May | Barry Lister | Bread flake |
| 6 1¼ | Putiaghan Lake, Beturbet | 2nd June | Edmund Hawksworth | Maggots |
| 6 1 | Putiaghan Lake, Beturbet | 2nd June | Edmund Hawksworth | Maggots |
| 6 1 | R. Shannon, Lanesboro | 1st May | Malcolm Scott | Maggot |
| 6 0 | Coosan Lough, Athlone | 6th June | E. G. Kershaw | Lobworm |
| 6 0 | R. Shannon, Lanesboro | 28th June | L. Monks | Bread |

# Part of Report of the Irish Specimen Fish Committee for the year 1972

## TENCH

Record 7lb 13¼oz.   Ray Webb.   Specimen weight 6lb.

| Weight lb. oz. | PLACE | DATE | CAPTOR | METHOD |
|---|---|---|---|---|
| 7  7½ | River Shannon, Lanesboro | 22nd June | Charles Murray | Bread flake |
| 7  3¼ | River Shannon, Lanesboro | 13th June | L. C. Vredenbregt | Bread |
| 7  3 | River Shannon, Lanesboro | 5th June | Clifford Upton | Bread |
| 7  1½ | River Shannon, Lanesboro | 12th June | Ray Webb | Maggots |
| 7  1¼ | River Shannon, Lanesboro | 8th June | Frank Ordoyno | Bread |
| 7  0¼ | River Shannon, Lanesboro | 28th June | Ray Webb | Flake |
| 6  15½ | River Shannon, Lanesboro | 23rd June | Ray Webb | Bread crust |
| 6  14 | River Shannon, Lanesboro | 12th June | Ray Webb | Maggots |
| 6  12½ | River Shannon, Lanesboro | 23rd June | Ray Webb | Bread crust |
| 6  9½ | River Shannon, Lanesboro | 6th May | David Cumpstone | Bread crust |
| 6  9 | River Shannon, Lanesboro | 8th June | Jas. Cheverall, Snr | Bread flake |
| 6  8 | River Shannon, Drumsna | 18th May | Rudolf Zimmek | Worm |
| 6  8 | River Shannon, Lanesboro | 12th June | Ray Webb | Maggots |
| 6  7¾ | River Shannon, Lanesboro | 1st June | Frank Ordoyno | Maggots |
| 6  7½ | River Shannon, Lanesboro | 5th June | Clifford Upton | Bead |
| 6  7 | River Shannon, Lanesboro | 20th May | Bernard S. Hanson | Maggot |
| 6  7 | River Shannon, Lanesboro | 13th June | Hugh Gough | Bread flake |
| 6  7 | River Shannon, Lanesboro | 22nd May | Frank Ordoyno | Bread |
| 6  7 | River Shannon, Lanesboro | 6th May | Paul Norris | Bread paste |
| 6  6 | River Shannon, Lanesboro | 13th June | Ray Webb | Bread flake |
| 0  6 | River Shannon, Lanesboro | 24th May | Brian C. Clack | Bread |
| 6  5½ | River Shannon, Lanesboro | 13th June | Ray Webb | Bread flake |
| 6  5 | River Shannon, Lanesboro | 13th June | Ray Webb | Bread flake |
| 6  5 | River Shannon, Lanesboro | 8th June | Frank Ordoyno | Bread |
| 6  4¾ | River Shannon, Lanesboro | 12th June | Ray Webb | Bread flake |
| 6  4¾ | River Shannon, Lanesboro | 12th June | Ray Webb | Bread flake |
| 6  4½ | River Shannon, Lanesboro | 16th May | David Cumpstone | Bread flake |

water was just not quite clear enough to see the bottom, I was amazed to see a violent disturbance taking place directly below, the agitation being so intense that the lily pads were swinging and swaying like palm trees taking the full blast of a roaring hurricane. As the eruption continued to build up, the surface boiled and swirled rocking the 17ft clinker-built boat till we forgot all about fishing for tench, sitting there hanging on to the sides, pale of countenance and wondering whether to up anchor and row smartly away for the shore. For a full three or four minutes the rumpus continued at a peak, during which time I'd visions of an octopus-like tentacle reaching up into the boat to drag one, two or all three of us away down into the deeps. But finally the water calmed down, the boat ceased to rock and all that was left to mark the episode was half a dozen lilies, completely uprooted, floating on the surface.

Still somewhat shaken, though we fished on just the same, we thought it all over carefully and eventually came up with three possible explanations as to what sort of creature working 7ft down could cause a disturbance sufficient to rock a 17ft Shannon longboat for a full four minutes or more.

Ruling out tench altogether, even of record-breaking proportions, we finally concluded that a large pike of 20lb or more, somehow trapped in the lilies and struggling violently to free himself might just possibly be responsible, for the water had produced pike of such calibre and bigger still. Alternatively, if an otter was at work and had seized a big pike the resulting battle might just do it and the third possibility was that a frogman with diving suit, oxygen bottle and all the gear was giving full expression to a rather perverted sense of humour. If our third possibility was the true explanation and some cranky fellow was trying to throw a scare at us I can assure him on behalf of all three of us, he succeeded beyond his wildest dreams.

In addition to the listed waters with officially recorded specimens to their credit there are many other fisheries at various points around Ireland that have provided consistantly good catches of medium-sized tench for a number of years, often fished only by anglers with a carefree, casual approach unlikely to produce anything better. Blackrock Pond and Drumgorman Lake at Drumshambo in County Leitrim are two such waters, and Lough McHugh near Mohill produced 21 tench to one angler in a week's fishing in 1971. At Prosperous on the Grand Canal, medium-sized tench have been taken in numbers since their introduction in 1959, though none have made the Specimen Fish List. Several seasons back, however, a six pounder was eventually taken, but due to inexperience the entry form was incorrectly filled in so the first officially recognised specimen from this venue has still to be taken.

Only discovered a year or so back Lough Carne near Ballyconnel, County Cavan caused something of a stir when featured in the angling press with a large catch of tench, a species that even the Nicholsons of Ardlougher Guest House figured were not to be found locally in sufficient numbers to warrant the serious anglers undivided attention. Not such a surprising find after all, however, for this water was stocked with tench by the Inland Fisheries Trust as far back as 1961.

With such a countrywide distribution and the development work of the Fisheries Trust still going on, the overall picture of Irish tench fishing is an extremely healthy one, still improving year by year. Whether the visiting angler fancies tackling his favourite species in the massive extent of Loughs Ree or Derg, battling it out in the flowing streamy waters of the River Shannon itself or fishing quietly in traditional, old English style from the bank of a small secluded pond or canal there will be little difficulty in suiting his tastes and whatever his final selection the warmth of welcome from the local anglers, though rarely interested in tench fishing themselves, is absolutely assured.

CHAPTER 13

# Weather and Water Conditions
*Ray Webb*

IF I were allowed to choose whatever single weather condition I would like for tench there would be no hesitation in my answer, for of all the various possible permutations of conditions, good, bad or indifferent, one stands out in my mind far-removed from all the rest, for its consistent, never-failing, beneficial effect on the feeding inclinations of the fish. In my 30 years of varied experience on all types of waters, ponds, rivers, lakes and canals, throughout the length and breadth of England and Ireland too, a violent thunderstorm has always been a sure guarantee that the tench will feed strongly in a most decisive fashion, on difficult waters where they have been moody and indifferent for weeks on end.

One of my earliest recollections of tench thus galvanised into violent action was way back in 1953 while fishing the King's Sedgmoor Drain in Somerset. The swim I'd chosen being on the outside of a bend at Weston Zoyland at a point where the Battle of Monmouth had been fought many years previously. All week long I'd been scratching away, working hard without anything inspiring in the way of results, so much so that on the Saturday morning I was in two minds whether to rouse myself at my customary early hour or abandon the fishing in favour of an hour or two's much-needed rest. With my next visit to Somerset, that glorious tench-favoured county, a full 12 months away, however, I did finally decide to be out and about at dawn, being tackled up ready to fish as soon as it was light enough to see the float.

For two hours or so my best efforts went unrewarded, but by 6 o'clock the crash and rumble of an approaching thunderstorm had me regretting I hadn't stayed in bed. There was enough noise and disturbance for it to be the Battle of Monmouth being fought all over again. My dismay was short lived, however, for half an hour later, with the slow moving storm still a long way off my crow quill float slid gently out of sight and I was into a fine tench of 3lb 6oz, following it up shortly after with another just 3oz less, this second fish ensuring my diary would be entered up in letters of red, the first occasion on which I'd taken more than one tench at a sitting. An hour later, with the thunder still rolling, two more quick fish came to the net and at 10 o'clock, just before packing up to dash away for a midday train my fifth tench of the morning sent me on my way completely indifferent to the raging of the storm which was just as well perhaps, for at his point the heavens opened, the rain coming down in an absolute deluge.

A few years later, in 1956 in fact, I left Sheffield one Friday night accompanied by Dennis Fullwood, a regular angling companion of mine at that time, travelling out beyond Newark to an old pit belonging to the Grantham Angling Association; a water that held a good head of extremely fit, healthy looking tench. In two or three seasons of fishing there never once did I see a single fish that showed any blemish or sign of wear and tear; without exception they were like newly minted 2 pence pieces. Perfect in every detail though they were the tench in this water were as bad as I ever encountered anywhere in their habit of mouthing and rejecting a bait. The performance would often continue for several hours, without the angler feeling justified in risking a strike and if action was taken 'on spec' almost invariably there was nothing to show for it.

Our usual procedure on arrival at the water was to fish the last couple of hours till dusk, kip down in the van for a short four hours of sleep and recommence operations at dawn. But on this particular occasion the initial spell of angling was abandoned owing to the sudden bursting of an electric storm immediately overhead; the lightning coming so close that we fled from the van early on to spend the night in a nearby barn, a move of doubtful wisdom according to expert opinion, I was later informed. Still violently active at dawn, the storm was, however, some considerable distance away at this stage, so we headed wearily towards our chosen swim, lack of sleep clearly apparent in our sluggish, leaden-footed approach. Fatigue was quickly forgotten however, when Dennis struck into a fish before my own tackle was fully assembled; a lively tench of $2\frac{1}{2}$lb. Hardly waiting for the bait to settle, on the very first cast my float slid away in real decisive fashion to produce a $2\frac{3}{4}$-pounder and sport continued briskly till we retired to the van somewhat earlier than usual to try and catch up on the sleep we had been denied by the proximity of the thunder and lightning. Even more gratifying than the first rate sport obtained was the firm solid type of bite obtained, the float sinking smartly out of sight with no sign of the dithering, hesitancy that usually proved such a problem on this most attractive of waters.

At a later stage of my angling career Irish tench were found to respond to an electric storm in precisely the same manner as their English brethren; the date in question being Tuesday, June 8th, 1965 when I was over on Garnafailagh Lake staying with Fred Carter. For the first three days of the holiday fishing was slow, unresponsive work, lengthy all-day session being put in on the water with little at the end to show, but on sitting down to Monday night's evening meal I noticed the first distant flash of an approaching storm way over in the south west. Before the dinner was over a number of claps of thunder were proving decidedly too close for comfort for one or two of the guests. But thinking back to my previous experiences of the English tench fisheries, my spirits rose as the storm raged unabated hour after hour, dawn next morning seeing my sprinting down to the boathouse bent on being first out across the lake.

Arriving at the pre-baited swim it quickly became obvious that the tench had been shaken out of their apathetic, indifferent mood and determined to get the very best out of the golden opportunity I fished with feverish concentration to compile a fine catch of nine fish for a total weight of 39lb; the best of the bag going 5lb 2oz. Three acquaintances also out on the lake that day found the sport similarly improved taking 16 tench weighing 78lb, a superb spell of fishing, clearly demonstrating the beneficial effects of the preceding night's storm. At Lanesborough too in 1973, the same principle obviously held true for in a short spell of hectic feeding a party of anglers staying in Eamon Ryan's bungalow took a number of good tench to just fractionally short of the 7lb mark on a day while I was away down Lough Ree fishing for pike. For a full 10 days or more a vast shoal of bream had been proving a nuisance. Whatever bait or technique was tried there seemed to be just no way of avoiding them. A violent thunderstorm burst overhead after I had left the spot, unfortunately I could not get back in time, but tench were then taken steadily through the afternoon and evening, the bream now no problem at all.

Another weather pattern that I keep an eye out for is the first couple of days or so of hot, sunny anticyclonic weather after a period of cold, wet and windy conditions. This also can be a favourable time for the tench enthusiast, extremely favourable indeed. Fishing a water I knew well some 10 or 12 years ago all my knowledge and experience was of no avail for a full five days of all out effort, regular dawn to dusk sessions being put in without reward but the water temperature of 57°F, the result of a full fortnight of dull, cold, windy weather was hardly condusive to good results. Suddenly around mid afternoon on the Thursday the wind died down, a powerful sun broke through the clouds and I stared in astonishment as I watched the thermometer record a rise in the air temperature from 59° to 84°F in a matter of minutes. It rapidly became too hot to fish in anything like comfort. Persevering regardless just before dusk I took a fine brace of tench of 5lb 7oz and 5lb 13oz enough to see me down on the water at dawn the next day in a highly optimistic frame of mind for the weather held warm and sunny and my hopes were fully realised; over half a hundredweight of fish being in the net at the end of the day, a pattern I've seen repeated time and time again, far too often to be coincidence.

Extremely beneficial though the coming of an anticyclone can be the best results have, in my experience, always come in the first couple of days or so, sport tapering off considerably after that. If the heatwave persists for any length of time the water becomes de-oxygenated and stale, the fish refusing all the anglers offerings on a hook or otherwise, which was exactly what happened at Garnafailagh in 1967. A shoal of tench was located by Dave Cumpstone early on in June but with a scorching heatwave settled over the area for the whole of the month sport was so slow as to be virtually non existent. There myself with John Weston for a full week we were able to observe the fish cruising slowly around under our boat day after day, but the inclination to feed had long since gone being literally boiled away. There was nothing to be done but accept the hopeless situation as philosophically as possible.

Continuing for a week or more after we left the anticyclone finally moved away being hustled along by a boisterous wind that eventually reached near gale intensity. As the water temperature dropped and the oxygenating effect of the wind livened up the water, the tench came mad on feed determined to make up for lost time; almost five whole weeks without a good square meal. With no political bias whatsoever the fish celebrated American Independence Day, July 4th with truly fanatical fervour and with the right men in the right place at the right time, Barrie's tremendous total of 162lb set up a new record for the water; one that still stands to this very day.

A warm muggy day with thick, low cloud formations can prove very productive and mornings with a mist rising off the water rarely let me down when I was fishing the Somerset tench waters, an area where these conditions were frequently encountered.

In addition to the weather, water conditions have also to be taken into account having a tremendous influence on the sporting prospects for tench. A vivid illustration of this is afforded in the early '60s when I was spending my holidays on Southill Park Lake in Bedfordshire, a water where the tench were very numerous and of a high average size. My companion at that time, Bob Ranby, and I arrived on the water at the start of the 1961 season to find the water level extremely low and the weed growth absolutely excessive, so much so that we had to drag for several hours before there was any hope of getting down to serious fishing. Once a suitable area of water has been cleared and baited up the weeks sport was off to a flying start when I took a brace of tench 4lb 2oz and 4lb 5oz, following up with a roach only 3oz short of the 2lb mark. Just before the day's fishing came to a close, Bob opened his account with a tench of 3lb 14oz and from this extremely promising beginning, we went from strength to strength, consistently recording good catches day after day. Bob's 5lb 1oz fish ended up as the tench of the week.

With low water and thick weed '61 proved to be a real vintage year at Southill, good enough for local expert Frank Guttfield to be seen on the water from dawn till around 8 a.m. of a midweek morning as a regular thing, taking some fine bags of fish, then dashing away in haste to clock-in for his day's work. Also on the water at the time was John Simpson of Eton, a top-class angler who had fished at Southill regularly for a number of years and with such long and varied experience to call upon he really went to work in the obviously favourable conditions ending up his fortnight's holiday with over 200lb of tench quite a number of which topped the 5lb mark.

After such a highly productive holiday a repeat booking for the following year was an automatic choice but after a bitterly cold, windy spring we rolled up on the opening day 1962 to find the lake up in level and without the slightest vestige of weed growth at all, the bleak barren aspect of the water looking more like a mid winter scene than June 16th. Three or four days' fishing were all that were needed to convince us that the tench were thinking much along the same lines, being conspicuous by their absence, all the sport that we were able to obtain came from perch and small jack pike that took worm and spinner with some frequency. Obviously the word spread quickly that the tench were well and truly off the feed and Frank Guttfield put his time in on a nearby gravel pit, leaving Southill severely alone. John Simpson too found it hard going, his long experience of the water proving of no avail though by the end of his holiday he did have one tench to show for his efforts; a superb specimen of 6lb 4oz, his first-ever six-pounder.

Right through to the end of the season Southill tench fishing proved extremely unrewarding, just as bad in fact as the previous summer had been good and subsequent experience on other waters has confirmed my conviction that persistent, cold, windy condition throughout the vital formative months of spring, resulting in severely reduced weed growth, will almost inevitably produce a poor season for tench, the numbers taken being well below average.

Tench in rivers require the level to be somewhat higher than normal and carrying a spot of extra colour if they are to provide anything exceptional in the way of sport. Low, clear, water make the fish moody and difficult to tempt. On the Shannon in 1971 my Irish record breaker plus another tremendous tench of 7lb 2¾oz taken on the same day by Frank Ordoyno had us thinking in terms of fantastic returns ahead. Obviously there were really big fish around but the level dropped rapidly away over the following two days and a truly exceptional prospect was ruined overnight, the fishing proving so unproductive that after a further week's all out effort we abandoned the river altogether turning our attentions towards the still-water fisheries.

Back again at Lanesborough the following year just the opposite obtained as regards water conditions, the Shannon being up in flood after an incredibly wet and windy spring with the exception of a mere 3 or 4 days warm dry spell the rain poured down non stop from early on in March all the way to June 8th bringing fishing virtually to a standstill all round the country even in ponds and canals. Day after day, week after week the cold, pushing, highly coloured water kept the tench off feed and the usual holding swims became too fast to support fish life at all, but eventually the Ordoyno party discovered two back eddies slightly slower in pace and the tench that were normally distributed over 250 yards of river were now congregated into a mere couple of swims. Fishing on through wind and rain, even in a force-nine gale, Frank and his companions battled through to take a number of specimen tench, fish of 6lb and 7lb in weight, but living rough in a tiny five-hundredweight van at the time I had to be content and view the proceedings from the sidelines, having no hot baths or drying rooms awaiting me in the five-star-rated Lough Ree Arms at the end of the day. Regular observation and interrogation established, however, that the tench were reluctant to take breadbaits, usually the best bet for the water and in the cold dirty water it was only by scaling down line strengths and hook sizes, offering a couple of maggots on a size 14 that there was any real hope at all, which was hardly to be wondered at for maggots often prove superior to bread when the temperature is below normal as I'd found out myself on a number of English tench waters.

Almost to the day that the Ordoyno party left for home the rain stopped and I emerged, somewhat cramped from my restricted living quarters, to move into the best of the two slightly slacker water back eddies and fishing two rods, one with fine tackle and maggots, the other on 6lb line and breadflake. I took three tench a day for four consecutive days up to a top weight of $5\frac{1}{2}$lbs; all the fish without exception falling to the maggot, the breadflake being left severely alone. Throughout this spell of fishing the weather, though dry at last, had remained cold and windy but at dawn on the fifth day I was out on the bank to find it flat calm with every indication of a hot sunny day ahead. My prayers had been answered and the long awaited anticyclone had arrived.

In addition to the weather being right the water was now beginning to fine down after a three-month-long flood, still somewhat up above normal level, with a touch of extra colour and pace, but getting warmer slower and clearer every day; every factor in the equation was right, weather conditions, water conditions, the fish all packed tight into one little corner. There wasn't the slightest doubt in my mind that this was the opportunity of a lifetime and I determined to fish as I'd never fished before. Had there been anyone in my chosen swim I'd have hacked him to pieces with me gaff, confident in the knowledge that no jury in the country would convict me. But the odd few tench men left in the area were all still in bed, obviously unaware of the significance of the sudden change in weather.

Settling down to fish the two contrasting tackles, groundbait was introduced in the swim in liberal quantities and bream, rudd and hybrids fed steadily all the way from dawn till half past nine by which time the heat was beginning to melt the tar out of the boats moored along the river. It really was a fiercesome hot day without a breath of wind. Still the breadbait lay untouched; all the fish being taken on maggot and the same bait produced a bite dead on the stroke of 10 o'clock that obviously wasn't a bream, the slow ponderous power of the fight proclaiming tench just as surely as if I'd seen the fish itself. On such light tackle the situation was critical and the only angler I could turn to for assistance with the net was 100 yards away and he stone deaf at that. Determined to wade into the river myself if need be the battle seemed interminable, but eventually the tiring fish was in the net – a most heartening specimen of 7lb 1½oz. An hour later a second tench of 6lb 8oz and from that point on the bream seemed to leave the swim completely, it was tench all the way. The last five or six tench came on breadflake, the effectiveness of this bait obviously increasing as the temperature continued to rise.

By the end of the day I'd around 120lb of fish in the net, a catch that included, in addition to the two specimens already mentioned, three more big tench of 6lb 4¾oz, 6lb 4¾oz and 6lb 14oz. The following day in similar conditions, once again fishing hard from dawn till dusk I'd another hectic day's sport finishing up with three more specimen tench of 6lb 5oz, 6lb 5½oz and 6lb 6oz; eight over the 6lb mark in the two-day all-out attack being more than reward enough for the non-stop effort involved. It was perhaps as well that the anticyclone drifted away and sport slowed down on the third day, it enabled me to take time off for a good square meal, badly needed by this time, for I'd survived on Complan, the meal in a cup, for a full 48 hours, determined not to miss a minute's fishing of what I knew was a golden opportunity unlikely ever to be repeated.

To sum up briefly, my ideal day would be a hot, still June morning the first of such following a fortnight's cold wet, windy weather, terminated by a violent thunderstorm the preceding evening as the temperature started to rise. If fishing a still water, a lower level and thicker weed growth than normal following a warm, early spring with the year's growth, grass, leaves, flowers and such like ahead of schedule. If in a river, a water level some four days or so after the peak of a prolonged spell of intensive flooding; the pace and colour fining down nicely but still somewhat above normal. Given these conditions and perhaps a fine drizzle from thick low cloud and a slight breeze to just ripple the surface about midday as the fish tended to become a trifle cagey, I'd buckle down to fishing with my heart really in it, confident that conditions were to my, or rather the tench's liking if this happened. Is it too much to ask one might query? Apart from just the odd occasion, once in a blue moon, there's no doubt about the answer at all, obviously it darn well is.

CHAPTER 14

# Playing Tench
*Barrie Rickards*

I CAN say one thing without fear of contradiction, that tench are just about the most consistently good fighters an angler could hope to come across. Thinking back I cannot actually recall a tench that fought badly, although once they get their heads solidly enmeshed in soft weed they can be led to the net with great ease provided, of course, you can dislodge the weed and get it on the move. I used to fish a swim at Carlton Towers which had a heavy growth of water lilies amongst logs to the left, and a mass of soft weed to the right. If a tench got into the lilies it was 10-1 against it coming out again, so I used to hold very hard if they went in this direction and as often as not they turned tail and dived into the soft weed. After this it was just a question of pulling steadily until the weed around the fish came free of the main mass. Generally speaking it is not advisable to allow a fish to weed itself, as a tench really can bury itself deeply: there is no more frustrating sight in angling than the taught line leading into a mass of weed 10 yards away, and a hooked tench sending up clouds of bubbles and mud some 20 yards further on.

When a tench makes an unstoppable bolt for the weed beds it is advisable to keep as much pressure on as possible, keep the rod held as high as possible, and try to keep the tench moving by 'bashing' it with the rod top. By this last point I mean that if it shows any sign of slowing give as much of a jerk as you dare to try to knock it off balance a little. I suggest holding the rod high so that the taught line is as little in the water as possible and tends to cut through the weeds. Laying the rod low, and applying sidestrain in the classic manner can be fatal if a tench bolts along a hole under the weed beds. All that happens is that sidestrain pulls the line and fish deeper into the weeds, and eventually the weight of weed will be too much for the line.

Should a tench get everything jammed up solid, a not uncommon occurrence despite everything you do to prevent it, then do not stand there jerking the rod over your head in a series of mini-strikes, but

79. *Above*—Steve Crawshaw captured this classic shot of Ted Kershaw, ex-holder of the Irish Tench record, playing a big tench on Coosan Lough. The water liiles are growing in at least 9' of water.

80. It's a sobering thought that this tench, only a few seasons ago, would have held the British record! And it isn't even Martin Gay's biggest.

firstly try slackening off to see if the fish swims on of its own accord. This works sometimes but not often. If it fails then take the line in your hands and give a few niggling little tugs to try to irritate the fish into moving a little. Failing that give a slow, steady and gradually increasing pull with the line wrapped around your sleeve, not directly from the reel, in the hope that the line will cut the weed or the weed itself shift. Once the tench comes free do not assume that it has weed around its head, but take up the rod quickly and treat it as though you had just struck.

The worst case I ever had was getting a 5lb-plus tench out of bulrush beds. These rushes were rooted in 5ft of water and extended above the surface by a further 5ft or so: each stem was about 4in to 5in apart at the water surface. The tench were *in* the bulrushes, not in the open swim, probably because an otter had the habit of working that bank each morning. Anyway, they fed in the bulrushes and periodically you could see the tall rush stems wobble as the tench grubbed at them for food (snails?). To fish for these fish I used a 13ft rod (so that I could get *over* the fish), a self-cocking float set at four feet, and slow sinking big lobworm. I threw the whole lot about a foot or two into the rush beds, the float cocked quickly and the lob sank slowly down, usually with the line around one or two stems. The takes were good, but to get the fish out I had to really hammer them into the open water. I found that 6lb line wasn't strong enough, and eventually got them out using 11lb line. The best went 5lb 8oz.

Usually the use of thick line puts off tench, particularly after the first few days of the season, and I suppose my tendency these days is to use 5 and 6lb breaking strain if I can get away with it, but more commonly I use 4 and 5lb b.s. This is quite a difference, when fishing weeded swims, and whereas you can be very confident using 6lb breaking strain you have to be extremely careful when using 4lb line. The initial lunge of a big female tench is quite dramatic and you can feel the tackle strained to its utmost: often you have to let them run deep into the weed beds simply because you have no choice in the matter. It's quite a helpless feeling, and yet if you up the strength of the gear you get far fewer bites.

Males and females fight differently, and generally the males fight much better. Not only do they make the same runs and plunges but they really jag the tackle at every and all opportunities. They seem to change direction several times each second! A lot of the fish-that-got-away stories connected with tench fishing are a result of

81. Not one of the calm tenching dawns this scene, but Ray Webb attempting to keep a big fish out of the bulrush beds. Ron Clay watches sleepily.

82. A difficult but productive swim in the lilies.

hard-fighting males, and not the giant female that the angler hoped for. Look at it like this: you are fishing weedy swims and catching really good females of 5lb-plus and perhaps the odd male round about 2½lb; then you hit a really big male of 4lb, and it smashes you to smithereens. You wouldn't be human if you didn't put the colossal run down to a 10lb (female) tench. This actually happened to me once, but the tench when caught later was a relatively small male and it still had the hook in its lips. It has been suggested that the big scoop-like fins of the male (probably shaped for spreading milt during spawning) are the deciding factor: not only does the female have to move a fatter body but its pelvic fins are actually smaller. Nevertheless the initial rush of a big female is probably a little bit, just a wee bit, better than that of the male. In his otherwise tremendous book, 'My Fishing Days and Fishing Ways', J. W. Martin ('Trent Otter') made the mistake of thinking that the larger tench were males, an error one still comes across when listening to anglers talking.

It is obvious from the foregoing that playing is fraught with difficulties. I've already given a few tips, but another general point is to use as long a rod as is reasonable in the circumstances. It makes quite a difference to be able to get the rod tip over the fish's head, and I remember once astounding some colleagues whilst playing a river tench of 4lb by not giving any line at all during the fight. They had been having to yield up to 15 yards in one rush. I'd hooked the fish at close range and had the upper hand (literally) from the word go. It was simply a matter of waiting for the tench to dash around in ever-decreasing circles until I popped it up to the surface and into a waiting net.

Netting tench is relatively easy compared to pike and carp fishing where a really big net is needed. Personally I still use as big a net as I can carry without trouble, which often means in practice that I use my pike net. Once the tench is over the middle of the net you can slacken off, and gently lift the net at the same time, at which point the tench usually dives deeply into the mesh. There's little doubt that the tench sees the net as a way of escape, so rather than have the net bright yellow, the colour is dark green or brown. It's aesthetically more pleasing anyway: bright or garish colours in the countryside is the domain of mountaineers and boating people, not of anglers, who should blend with the surroundings.

The final stage is unhooking the fish. The only important point here is to try to get into the habit of using artery forceps. Even when the fish

83. A historic shot this: Ray playing a big tench in the swim from which he broke the Irish record. The mighty Shannon is just beyond the bulrush beds.

84. The net is brushed to one side as a very large tench makes a final bolt for freedom. Steve Crawshaw stood up in the boat as he was about to net this fish.

is lip-hooked it can be difficult to get the hook out with your fingers since they do not have the ability to centralize the pull properly, and the tench has tough lips. The fish can be held down with firm pressure on the net as it lays over the fish's flanks. I think micromesh netting is to be avoided in landing nets for, although it is soft, it seems to remove more body slime than the traditional knotted type. The fish should be returned quickly or placed in a good keepnet (preferably knotless, but, again, not micromesh which gets easily slime-coated). The photography if desired can be done at the end of the session. This usually means that the fish is fully recovered by the time you are ready for photographs, and at the time it is to be returned to the water. Wet the grass thoroughly, or use a soft, plastic sheet, before photography. It is a good idea to set the whole scene, including camera on tripod, before putting the fish on stage. They'll be pretty jumpy and after putting them where you want them cover them up with the keepnet until they quieten down.

Tench are probably better out of water than any other fish, but never keep them out for more than three or four minutes. It is quite unneccessary anyway if you get organised first.

**Comment** – *by Ray Webb*

The final and ultimate answer to a heavily weeded tench is of course a boat, for once directly over the fish one can prod about with long-handled gaffs, oars and the like usually managing to get things moving one way or another. If one is actually fishing from a boat it is just a question of up anchoring and moving across, but the fully prepared bank angler will have a boat moored alongside so that he can jump aboard, rod in hand, once a hooked fish has run into serious trouble, a technique that was used successfully by Richard Walker many years ago when one of his 30lb-plus carp went to weed at Redmire. Handlining has proved remarkably effective for me, however, whenever there has been no boat available, only a couple of days ago in fact it resulted in a fine specimen of 5lb 14oz being successfully brought to the net, the tench having bolted away at speed on being struck to bury itself deep into a bed of soft clogging weed. Caught napping without waders I finished up soaked to the knees but remained firmly convinced that the end justified the means.

CHAPTER 15

# A Tench Trip
*Ray Webb*

To illustrate the way in which the points discussed and information given in preceding chapters can be built up into a full day's tench fishing I can do no better than to extract an entry from my diary for June 1963. This was a year when I was putting in a lot of time and effort at Carlton Towers near Selby in Yorkshire, a fishery near enough to Sheffield for regular midweek trips, dawn to midday sessions being fitted in three days a week or so before heading back home for a short siesta and in to work at 6 p.m. Employed as a night telephonist at the G.P.O. in those days, these midweek angling trips, with the lake all to myself, were one of the perks of the job, one of the many that is, for the working schedule was tailor-made to the requirements of a dedicated angler; which was the reason for my being there of course.

For the particular trip in question, however, I was off work for the whole of the day and the preceding evening saw me heading the old van out of Sheffield on the main Doncaster road, then on to Carlton, arriving at the lakeside with half an hour of daylight left. Just enough for a good scout round and to put in a spot of groundbait. With the prevailing south-west wind forecast to continue for several days a swim was selected in the north-eastern section of the bank to take advantage of the oxygenating effects of the waves, a factor that could be of paramount inportance on such a shallow, silted up, stagnant type of water. With no deep water anywhere on the lake the spot I'd chosen was a mere 2ft 9in deep, heavily lily padded on the surface and thick with Canadian Pondweed on the bottom, an area offering shade, security and shelter to fish that would elsewhere be vulnerable and exposed, and for a full month or more I'd been regularly thinning the weedgrowth down with a drag and putting in quantities of groundbait, both in my chosen swim and several others at various points around the lake. With a water temperature of 61°F and thick banks of low cloud to cut down heat losses through the night, prospects looked extremely favourable, and a couple of large buckets full of bread and bran groundbait in each of two swims, one for myself and the other for an old angling pal Dave Mansell scheduled to roll up early next morning, completed the preparations for the day. No need to pitch a tent, my Morris Minor van was never without a bed made up in those days and setting the alarm for 3.15 a.m. I retired to snatch a few hours well-earned rest.

Up just as dawn was breaking, the lake at that time was absolutely calm, not a ripple to be seen and with the overnight cloud having moved away, the day promised to be bright and sunny. Faced with such a dense growth of weed and lily I elected to fish with a couple of 10ft Avon type rods. Tench at Carlton, though present in large numbers, didn't grow big and a four-pounder would usually have been enough to finish up as the fish of the year. The idea of shattering the peace and calm by hurling my drag out to the still glassy surface of the lake was just too much to contemplate, though I must confess a sneaking admiration for the angler capable of doing so. I elected to adopt the opposite approach altogether choosing to fish for the first half hour at least without putting in any groundbait at all, leaving the water completely undisturbed. In view of later experiences it was a mistake *not* to rake and groundbait.

Established by previous experience as a good worm water I tied on a size 8 bronzed Stilletto-eyed hook for fishing the lob on one rod, and a gilt size 12 for flake on the other, swinging both tackles gently out about 10 or 12 yards from the bank. Setting the rods in rests and reeling in to take up slack line I squatted down on a cushion at ground level to make myself as inconspicuous as possible and settled in to concentrate on the brilliant orange peacock quill tips, sitting up half cocked a mere 5ft or so apart. For a full hour I fished hard to no avail, not a bite to show, at which point I felt safe in introducing a spot of groundbait as my completely silent approach had failed to pay off; and, as the appetising mix went in, the sound of a high powered sports car announced Dave's arrival, somewhat behind schedule as a result of a hectic session at his local Palais De Danse the previous evening. Explaining the preparations I had made on his behalf, and showing exactly where to cast, as I turned to retrace my steps a tench rolled out across the lake, a frequent habit of the species on still, warm mornings.

Back at my own swim I'd no sooner settled down once again than my lobworm bait was taken on the run, the float sliding smartly out of sight without any previous warning whatsoever. A quick strike met with solid resistance and firm handling was necessary to avoid being badly weeded, but keeping up a relentless pressure all went well and the first tench of the day was successfully hauled in to the net, a fish of 2lb 14oz. With Dave in and fishing by the time the tench was unhooked and in the net, we fished on without any further action, apart from the occasional rolling fish breaking the surface with easily recognisable dorsal or tail fin, till around about half past six when both our worm baited tackles produced fish at the same time, 2lb 1oz for me and 2lb 9oz to Dave.

With handfuls of groundbait going in every 10 minutes or so clusters of tiny needle bubbles signified the presence of tench rooting around in our swims and for the next couple of hours we were kept busy, the bites coming at frequent intervals till by 8 o'clock 11 tench had been brought to the net, six to my worm baited rod and five to Dave, his also falling to the lob. As so often happens early on in the season the lob was being taken in bold and decisive fashion, only one bite to each of us failing to produce contact on the strike though I did hit into a further fish that shook the hook free after a brief couple of seconds play. A slack, biteless period at this point enabled me to fire up the Primus stove, an old museum piece bought for 17s 6d some 30 years or so ago, and a bowl of hot porridge proved to be just what the doctor ordered, for by this time the early-morning sun had disappeared completely behind a heavy bank of cloud, a rather coolish wind springing up and bringing with it a spot of light drizzle. All through the breakfast interval we kept an eye on the floats, but the bites had ceased fairly abruptly with the coming of the wind and by 9 o'clock with no further action, even the bubbling and rolling having ceased as it so often does when the early morning calm gives way to the rising ripple of the waves. It began to look very much as though sport was over for the day.

Following my invariable policy of the time of fishing on till mid-day, regardless of how doubtful the prospects appeared to be, 10 minutes' vigorous raking was put in on each of our swims before we resumed our angling in earnest but at the end of a further hour of all out effort there was nothing more to show, not a single bite between the pair of us. With the headwind quite strong by this time some difficulty was being experienced in casting accurately into the cleared areas in among the dense beds of lily pads, and at this point I opted for a switch in tackle replacing one of the BB shot with an Arlesey Bomb of ½oz in weight and advising Dave to do the same. Keeping the groundbait going in frequently, our fishing proved completely without reward till suddenly at 11-30 Dave's second float shot away to the pull of a tench that was finally weighed in at 3lb 1oz, the best fish of the day so far. The bait that did the trick was a couple of maggots, a success that saw me switch my own second terminal tackle from the size 12 eyed hook baited with breadflake to a size 16 spade end and a couple of maggots.

Inside the first 10 minutes the move paid off as I achieved my first bite for three whole hours of effort; my maggot bait being taken by a lively $2\frac{1}{4}$-pounder, enough to convince us that a liberal quantity of maggots should be mixed into the groundbait from this point on, though our supply was somewhat limited for a project of this kind. Though never as hectic as in the early morning pre-breakfast period, the bites came steadily at intervals all through the midday and afternoon fishing, our interest being maintained as it never would have been past the midday mark had the tench gone completely off feed. Late on around 6 p.m. Dave's lobworm bait, fished on what had now become his second-string tackle, was taken decisively and somewhat off his guard the tench was tangled up fast in the middle of the lily pads almost before he knew what was happening. Applying maximum pressure with the rod Dave moved along the bank in both directions to vary the angle of pull but without success, no line being retrieved at, nor were we able to ascertain whether the fish was still on at this stage there was just no sign of life at all. Putting down the rod altogether and taking up the line in his fingers, having first put on a pair of stout leather gloves, Dave steadily built up pressure till the line was obviously just short of breaking point at which a certain amount of give in the weed, coupled with a spot of pulling from the other end, resulted in a gradual retrieving of line and eventually a tench of 1lb 14oz and a full half-hundred weight of weed was hauled up the bank. Two or three more fish like that and we should have opened up another swim!

Feeling at this stage that we'd had enough for one day, tackle was quickly taken down and stacked away, the cameras being brought out to record the catch before the light failed altogether; it had been none too good even at mid-day what with the rain and cloud. Counted up the catch comprised 25 tench, 14 to Dave and 11 to myself, the total weight going $51\frac{1}{2}$lb and Dave's 3lb 1oz fish the best of the day. The camera work completed, the fish were returned to the water, a little wiser but none the worse for the day's adventure.

Thinking over the events of the day I'd have been well advised perhaps to fish maggot on both rods for the afternoon session for past experience had proved to my satisfaction at least that with the coolish wind chilling the water down the maggot was to be expected to come into its own. I'd seen it happen on a number of occasions on a variety of waters. Breadflake fished on my second rod all morning was aimed at selecting a bigger stamp of fish, as it so often does, but to see it at its best the water temperature needs to be holding steady or rising slowly, not falling slightly as it was in this case. Even in ideal conditions it was inevitably something of a long shot at Carlton for big tench over the 4lb mark were few and far between. In two or three seasons of regular fishing there, the best I saw caught fell 5oz short. All in all, however, an enjoyable and instructive day's fishing, an occasional session with medium-sized tench well on feed can be well worth while, a pleasant change from the fierce hard slog of all-out specimen hunting.

CHAPTER 16

# The Tenchfishers
*David Mawer*

WHEN the authors of this book on tench fishing asked me to write about the Tenchfishers, I immediately had visions of scribbling until my pen disintegrated or hell froze. However, the reality and the dream are irreconcilable and although I consider the group to be the best angling organisation of its kind in the country I must not yield to base instincts: therefore, instead of the 10,000 words of text I had planned, there follows a summary of the group's activities past and present.

Following the tremendous success of the original pre-1952 Carp Catchers Club, a group of well-known anglers, John Ellis, Maurice Ingham, John Roberts, Norman Woodward, Frank Murgett and Fred J. Taylor, decided to direct their collective efforts towards the formation of a tench angling group. They recognised that whilst big tench were more common than was generally supposed, very few were caught. The original Carp Catchers also encountered problems of a similar nature. Consequently the Tenchfishers was formed in January 1954, as a club for anglers specialising in tench fiishing with the aim of providing a means of pooling the knowledge and experience of its members, each contributing in turn to matters under consideration. Whilst this worked well enough, the growth of the club was severely inhibited since the larger the membership, the slower the Rotary Letter circulated, and the infusion of new energies in the form of substantial numbers of new members was impossible. Inevitably, the club became inactive in the course of time.

During the early and mid-sixties 'Specimen Groups' were being formed at an increasing rate, and comparatively large numbers of anglers were concerning themselves with the capture of big fish. In this atmosphere, Dr Terence Coulson, already prominent with the National Anguilla Club, entered into discussions with John Ellis with a view to reforming the Tenchfishers along its original lines, but incorporating an additional, long-term, science-based, reporting project, in which members submitted details of their angling sessions for statistical analysis. In 1967 the Tenchfishers was reconstituted and by 1970 some 40 members throughout Britain were engaged upon this work. The type and nature of the projects undertaken during this period, were promoted by AIMS clause of the Tenchfishers constitution, and here I quote:

*Group Aims*
To promote the study of tench and tench fishing, to this end:
1. To provide an organisation which will enable specialist tench anglers to associate together, and to pool their knowledge and experience.
2. To take whatever steps seem appropriate to enhance the status of tench fishing in particular and angling in general, and to join with other bodies engaged with these aims.
3. To define and describe the areas in which knowledge of tench is incomplete, and to devise and conduct projects to remedy these deficiencies.
4. To conduct collectively experiments to test angling theories.

Stimulated by these objectives the group took its first great stride forwards as its members subscribed to a variety of projects including:
1. The writing of a very detailed report (on a pre-printed questionnaire form) on every Tench session, productive or unproductive, undertaken by each individual member. (Information on weight, length, girth and sex of any fish captured – also weather and water temperature details.)
2. Historical big Tench captures study. (Retrieval of suitable information from relevant angling publications.)
3. A study of the tench population in the low pond at Wold Dale.
4. Periodicals report scheme, analysing the weekly tench captures as reported to the weekly angling newspapers.
5. The submission of tench carcasses for scientific analysis by the zoological departments of two universities.
6. And the initiation of a new series of Rotary Letters: the articles which appeared in the first Rotary Letter were subsequently reprinted in an influential monthly angling magazine.

During this period the group members not only received their Rotary Letters, but they were also the recipients of a regular flow of informative Bulletins. The information from these projects was reported in the Bulletin and also disseminated at group meetings, thus giving the group members some very interesting and useful data on which to base their subsequent tench fishing efforts. Unfortunately, the sheer volume of work that these projects imposed on the committee members, and the general down turn in interest shown for the 'scientific method approach' to angling, led to a general re-appraisal of the group's projects between 1971 and 1972.

Building on the invaluable experience already gained, the group adopted a more practical and general approach to tench fishing. The Rotary Letter was discontinued and a combined Bulletin/Rotary Letter was born. This revised Bulletin was and still is, issued at quarterly intervals. It contains the collective results of the whole group; articles of topical and internal tench fishing interest and also the usual group notices. All members in the course of time submit articles to the Bulletin and these contributions appear in alphabetical membership order. The content of these articles varies from humorous narratives to serious appraisals of tench fisheries and the techniques needed to capture tench from such fisheries.

At about this time we grafted a new project (still in existence) called the Geographical Location of Big Tench to the existing Periodicals Reporting scheme and this combined project has and still is, proving to be of tremendous benefit to the members. Perhaps the most dramatic changes in this period came when we re-styled our session reports scheme and simplified the report form. Results extracted from the session report form are entered in log books 1 and 2. Log book 1 records all male tench over 4lb and female tench over 5lb, whilst log book 2 records all female fish under 5lb and male fish under 4lb. These projects were orientated towards locating good tench fisheries and the use of the accumulated group bait data, to determine the most productive baits in terms of quality fish.

Some typical results are shown below:

|  | 1972 | 1973 |
|---|---|---|
| Tench over 6.0 | 9 | 9 |
| Between 5.0–6.0 | 65 | 76 |
| Between 4.0–5.0 | 125 | 199 |
| Tench under 4.0 | 525 | 578 |
| Total tench taken | 722 | 862 |

In 1974 we recorded our most spectacular tench capture when a group member Mr L. A. Head (secretary) reported our two biggest English tench: these two fish weighed 7.3 and 7.10 respectively. This session report scheme is still in operation at the time of writing.

In 1973 we recorded one of our most notable achievements, when a 'high circulation' weekly angling newspaper published a series of articles which were essentially about the Tenchfishers' projects and the groups approach to the capture of quality tench. These articles were very original in content and constituted a radical departure in angling writing. The articles were headed:
— Acquiring the know-how about tench
— When the leger pay off best
— Pin-pointing the big fish waters
— Seven basic float rigs for tench
— Sorting out the real giants
— First find your swim
— Developments in tench tackle
— Urgent need for tench conservation
— Maggots lead top three tench baits

After the success of these articles, it was decided to initiate a Tenchfishers' award scheme, whereby a certificate is issued by the group to the captor of a specimen tench; providing his capture is reported in the angling press and that it is proven to be genuine. We awarded five certificates in 1974. Two new schemes have been added to our present formidable list of projects and these are: the reading of tench scales to determine age and growth rates and a comprehensive tench fishing guide. The scale reading study is proving to be the most difficult task we have engaged upon since our re-formation.

Currently there are two activities which the Tenchfishers particularly encourage; one is the art of angling; the other is the science of tench. The dedicated tench angler is the man who as a result of extensive experience which includes thoughtful experimentation with different kinds of baits, methods of bait presentation, bait location and much practical observation, distills a recipe for success which he passes on for comment and criticism by his fellow group members. This is the art and science of angling.

The successful tench angler who can also, by intelligent observation, comment in depth on the behaviour of his quarry, is not only a good angler but is well on the way to becoming a useful fish scientist as well.

This is a message the group tries to get across and it is a philosophy which is reflected in some of the projects which they undertake. While it is appreciated that the fundamental biology of the tench is a study best left to professional icthyologists (with their associated laboratory facilities) it is nevertheless true that this group has a vital interest in understanding the ecology of its preferred species. Thus the Tenchfishers have for many years been carefully recording the parameters of every tench caught at a large number of fisheries with a view to identifying why certain fisheries produce specimen fish whilst others are very unproductive.

Recent studies have attempted to take this observational role one stage further, by examining relationships between the age and weight of fish from a few selected high-quality fisheries, with a view to identifying these waters which may be capable of producing fish in the record-breaking class (thus enabling effort to be concentrated on these waters). This investigatory work is slow and painstaking and is hampered by a fundamental lack of knowledge of the biology of the tench. Because, or in spite of the fact that I am the chairman of the Tenchfishers, I am very proud of our achievements both past and present. I leave you therefore with my closing statement. The group, with its new policies and projects intact is now entering its eighth year; because it has shown – through its subscriptions to the N.A.C./A.C.A. causes and also the frequent tench lectures given to angling societies – a sense of responsibility, it deserves to continue to its eighty eighth year enjoying the same success: especially when that success has been achieved with an average membership of 35 anglers.

CHAPTER 17

# Biology of the Tench
*Barrie Rickards*

THE tench was described scientifically by Linnaeus, the famous Swedish naturalist, in 1758, although it was well known as one of the main food dishes of monks long before that date. Linnaeus used the scientific name *Cyprinus tinca* clearly indicating its close relationship to the carp by placing it in the same genus *(Cyprinus carpio* is the common carp). Subsequently, however, the tench was considered sufficiently different from other carp to be given its own generic name, the same, in fact, as Linnaeus' species name *tinca;* and the tench became *Tinca tinca,* probably one of the few scientific fish names known and revered by all the freshwater fisherman in these islands. Like many other fishermen Ray Webb named his fishing boat *Tinca*. Actually the full scientific title of the tench is *Tinca tinca* (Linnaeus, 1758), the author's name in brackets indicating a change in the generic, or surname, of the tench.

The word *tench* not only bears close resemblance to *tinca,* but also to the French word *tanche,* and the Spanish *tenca,* and perhaps indicates to a degree the widespread distribution of this tough and adaptable species which is found through much of Europe (growing very big in Italy's Lake Como, for example), parts of Russia and even further afield in Tasmania. Most writers consider the Irish tench to be introduced by man (see, for example, Went, 1966) as are the Tasmanian fish of course. But the tench of the rest of Europe are part of a post-glacial (post-Ice Age) indigenous population. Tench are warmer water fish than many others (such as the grayling and chub) which colonised Britain after the ice sheets retreated northwards, and even today they are absent or rare in the most north terrains including most of Scotland, Norway, Finland; and they do not occur in rivers draining into the Arctic Ocean.

During the retreat of the ice Britain was connected to Europe by a land bridge and river system (ancestral to the present River Rhine) across the English Channel, but Ireland became separated from Britain whilst the climate was still very cold and before the tench could spread northwards. Hence the tench was introduced to Ireland

183

in historical times, rather than spreading naturally in pre-historical times. As a warmth-loving species the tench also occurs further south in Europe than other species, where it may attain greater sizes (up to 15lb) than in the more northerly climes. In Britain, for example, the upper weight limit is around 10lb, more or less, and the current rod-caught British Record stands at 9lb 1oz.

It is of interest that *Tinca* has a longer geological record than the carp, *Cyprinus*: *Tinca* occurs from the Oligocene to the present day, a period of some 30 million years, whilst *Cyprinus* occurs in rocks only as old as the Miocene, that is up to 20 million years ago. In these ancient times many parts of Europe and Britain were in a near-tropical climate, which tends to confirm that *Tinca* is a warmth lover.

The adult tench is probably the most distinctive and easily recognised of all British freshwater species and a full description would be out of place here but, briefly, it can be said to be a most solid, plump, carp-like fish but lacks the hump-backed appearance of many carp whilst the body is laterally somewhat flatter but still oval in cross-section; the back is olive-green, occasionally almost black, shading down the flanks to a yellowish-green, occasionally more gold than yellow, and with an underside that is usually yellowish-orange, but may at the one extreme be almost white and at the other vermilion; the fins are all rather thick and 'fleshy', the dorsal short, high and rounded (as is the anal), the tail broad and with only a slight V and the scoop-shaped pelvic fins with thickened anterior margins; the small eyes are a most distinctive orange-red; the mouth is relatively small, with thick lips, and two small barbules, one descending from each corner like a neat moustachios. The male tench is easily distinguished from the female in that the former have much larger, more spoon-shaped pelvic fins, with a thicker leading edge and thicker fin roots within the body wall. On the whole the female looks a plumper, smoother, more streamlined and neater creature than the male.

When one studies the actual measurements such as scale counts, usually used to define and distinguish fish species, one comes across discrepancies and apparent lack of precision from one authority to another. The tench has numerous tiny scales set in a tough skin, and protected by a mucus layer which is occasionally thick and slimy, though never so much as in the bream. Holčik *et al.* (1968) give 87-115 scales along the lateral line, whereas Jones and Tombleson (1964) give 95-110 and the 'Angling Times' Know your Fish guide gives 95-120.

85. A fine brace of big male tench taken by Martin Gay in Essex. Note the fin rays.

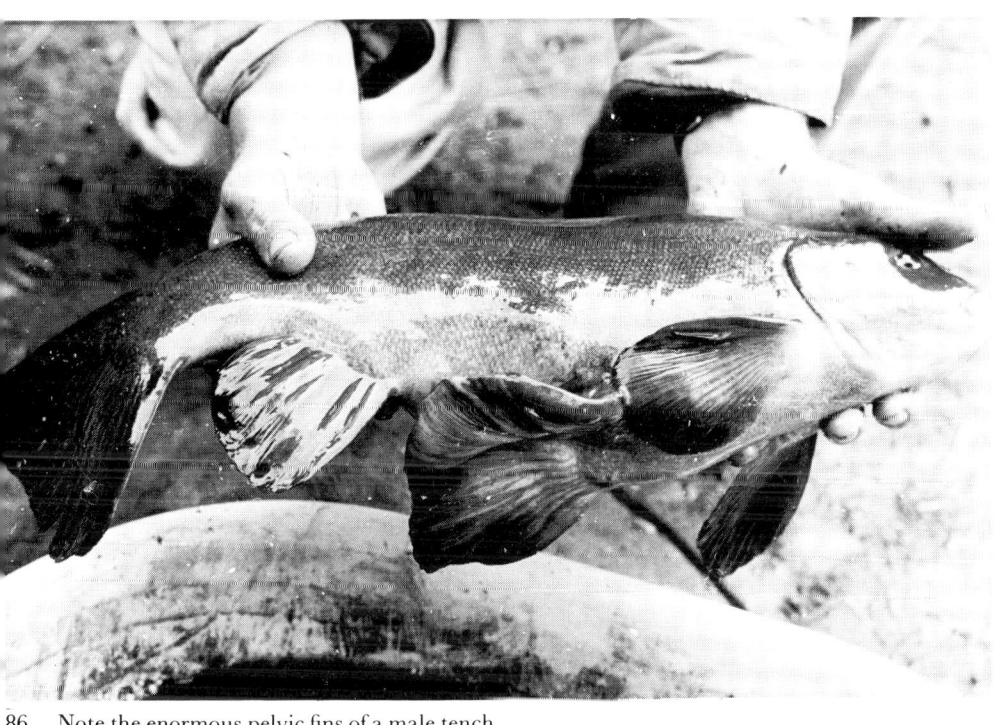

86. Note the enormous pelvic fins of a male tench.

Weatherley (1961) gives 93-108 for some British tench and 91-105 for Tasmanian tench. As with all other coarse fish species there is clearly a need for modern biometric analysis: there may, for example, be considerable geographical variation in such measurements. The other measurements, fin ray counts and so on, also show 'discrepancies', but unfortunately none of these matters need worry the angler very much for, as pointed out above, the tench is most distinctive in its shape and colouring.

It should be added that in addition to the above colouration of tench, there is an increasingly common Golden Tench, which is the very beautiful bright yellowish fish seen in almost all pet-shop fish tanks. Some pits around Cambridge have a few, a few have always occured naturally, and Church (1974) has noted the occurrence of substantial populations of these fish in some waters. I should think most anglers, myself included, would regard such a beautiful fish as an asset to any water: as long as we do not get blotchy yellow-cum-greenish fish! Golden Tench can be produced by selective breeding from the occasional naturally occurring near-albino tench with yellow colouration. I have seen very yellow-bellied tench when fishing the Clowne pond in Sheffield, but these were not Golden Tench in the strict sense: the locals called them the Banana Tench. Vermilion-bellied tench are not uncommon and I remember Dug Taylor showing me a picture of one such fish from a water near York. They should not be confused with those tench showing redness of the belly around the pelvic, anal fin, and anus; a condition often seen as spawning time approaches, or with fish that have been badly crowded in angler's keepnets.

In most waters in which they occur, whether with a good growth rate or not tench usually appear to be plump, healthy fish, and whilst special conditions of space, water depth and pH are probably required to grow big tench, the very adaptability of these tough fish ensures that they get a fairly good living even in rather adverse circumstances.

*SPAWNING.* As far as the angler is concerned tench are ornery creatures, almost always spawning during the open season some time from the end of June to early August. It is very common to find the fish on June 16th fat, full of fight and feeding quite well, and yet after one to three weeks of fishing the tench go 'off' and begin spawning. There is obviously some relationship to the weather: the end of May and early June often sees warm sunny weather which causes the tench to become

87. Unusually low levels on this northern water show the willow roots upon which tench sometimes lay their eggs.

active and to feed well prior to spawning; the middle of June, round about the opening of the season often has variable gusty winds, variable pressure systems, and may be quite cold at times; at the end of June the temperature rises (if nothing else) and at this time or shortly after the main body of the lake, and particularly the shallows, reaches the optimum spawning temperature.

Those are my general feelings having fished around Britain for tench, but to be more specific Kennedy and Fitzmaurice (1968) found that in some tested Irish waters spawning took place some time in the period mid-June to late July being delayed until August if temperatures or water levels were wrong. In Russia tench seem to spawn a little earlier in mid-May to late June (Berg, 1964), which is perhaps surprising for a continental environment. Elsewhere, as in France the spawning period is much the same as in Britain and Ireland. The actual spawning water temperature seems to be round about 20°C (68°F) but some authorities give as low as 18°C and others the range from 20–24°C. The temperature for actual ripening of the eggs may be slightly higher though there is little direct evidence on this score. The earliest spawning month I have been able to find recorded is that given by Holčik *et al.* (1968) of April, but since they took into account southern European tench this is perhaps not too surprising.

All anglers are familiar with the spectacle of spawning tench with considerable shoals of fish chasing through the weed and reed beds of the shallows, periodically erupting at the water surface, rolling and torpedoing. A depth of about 2–5 feet is usually chosen, but in some waters, of course, it could be less or much greater. One thing is certain, and that is that during the actual act of spawning, and probably for a day or two before and after, the tench do not feed much and really go 'off' as far as the angler is concerned: a happily built in protection mechanism. It is rare indeed to catch a tench actually leaking spawn (contrast pike) though male tench shedding milt are taken not uncommonly. After spawning the tench lose weight but become very fit within a couple of weeks or so. A fish of 5¾lb will have up to 12oz of spawn, and after spawning will weigh not much over 5lb.

Female tench do not appear to rely on the pressure of vegetation upon their flanks to shed spawn (contrast roach, rudd, etc.) but shed it over a wide area as the chase by two or three attendant males reaches a crescendo. A group of males may service several females in this way, and Kennedy and Fitzmaurice (1968) point out the similarity of such behaviour in that of pike spawning.

Tench mature much earlier than other carp species and may be sexually mature and ready for spawning after two years. Since the tench spawns later than most other carp species and in a manner different from most carp species it is perhaps unlikely that tench will often produce viable hybrids, although in Russia the tench is thought to hybridize with Crucian Carp. I have never heard of tench hybrids being recorded in these islands.

*FECUNDITY.* European estimates vary considerably from 150,000 eggs per 500g of female tench, to 300,000; or in terms of the eggs deposited by individual fish from 280,000–287,000. In any event, a considerable number of eggs: survival, as with most creatures with such fecundity figures, is probably less than 1%.

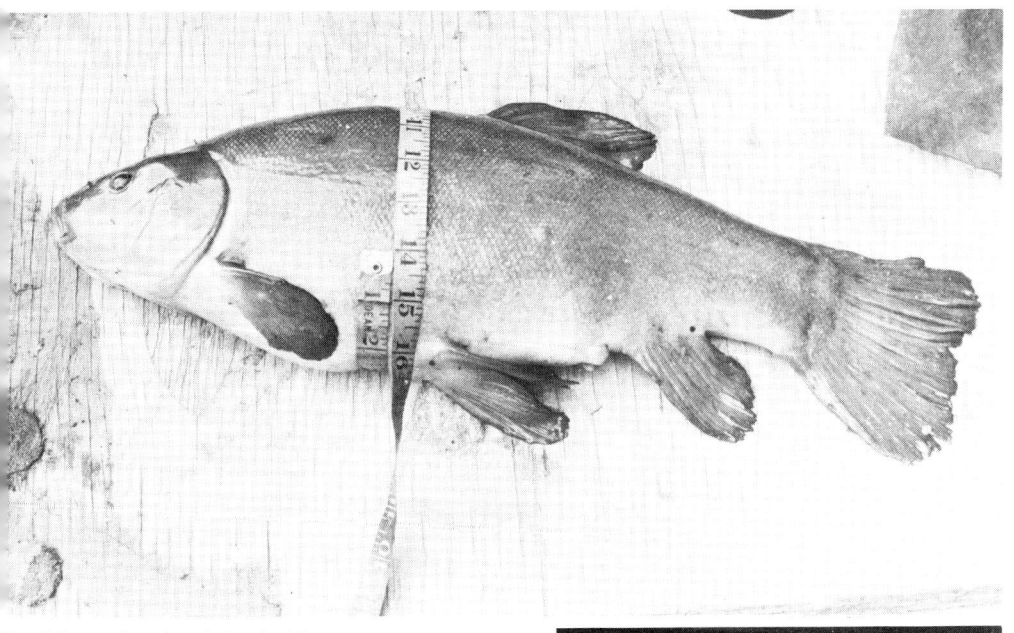

9. Measuring the girth of a big Yorkshire tench as part of a detailed scientific study carried out by Dr Jerry Coulson.

88. Growth rings clearly visible on this scale from a tench of 5lbs 14oz. An age of 10+ years is suggested.

9. Hope for the future! Small tench going into a northern water.

*DEVELOPMENT.* Tench eggs are usually smaller than rudd eggs, for example, and larger tench eggs in Britain and Ireland have a diameter of 1·30–1·40mm. This is rather larger than eggs of Continental tench (1·0–1·2mm). Tench eggs are transparent with a pale yellow yolk, and probably take rather less than a week to hatch. Tench larvae are initially up to 5mm in length with a yolk-sac (Fig. 91) which may last up to ten days: loss of the yolk-sac is conveniently taken as the end of the larval phase. The larval tench has adhesive glands on the head by which it suspends vertically from vegetation; the dark stripe provides camouflage in grassy weed. The larval circulatory network may be particularly adapted to life in a stagnant environment.

From about 10 days to five weeks or so the tench are in the post-larval, pre-fry stage, that is they do not have well-developed fins until the end of this period approaches. During this period, and after, the tench is much less active, more secretive than other members of the carp family. It seeks the shelter of weeds and stones, and is clearly not designed for competition with rudd and bream in the open water. Thus from the earliest periods of their lives tench set a behaviour pattern which will persist until they are several years old: how very rarely are tiny tench caught on rod and line by anglers, but how often they turn up during dredging operations in thick weed beds.

Growth of tench, and in particular its significance for the angler, is discussed in the chapter on Modern Research, but suffice it to say here that after three years of life females begin to outstrip the males and become eventually bigger, fatter fish, and male tench over 4lb weight are uncommon except in the very best waters. Since males tend to outnumber females by almost 2:1, the size of males caught can perhaps more quickly give a guide to the potential record-breaking prospects of a water. Not that a giant fish is one's only reason for going tenching, of course.

BIOLOGY OF THE TENCH 191

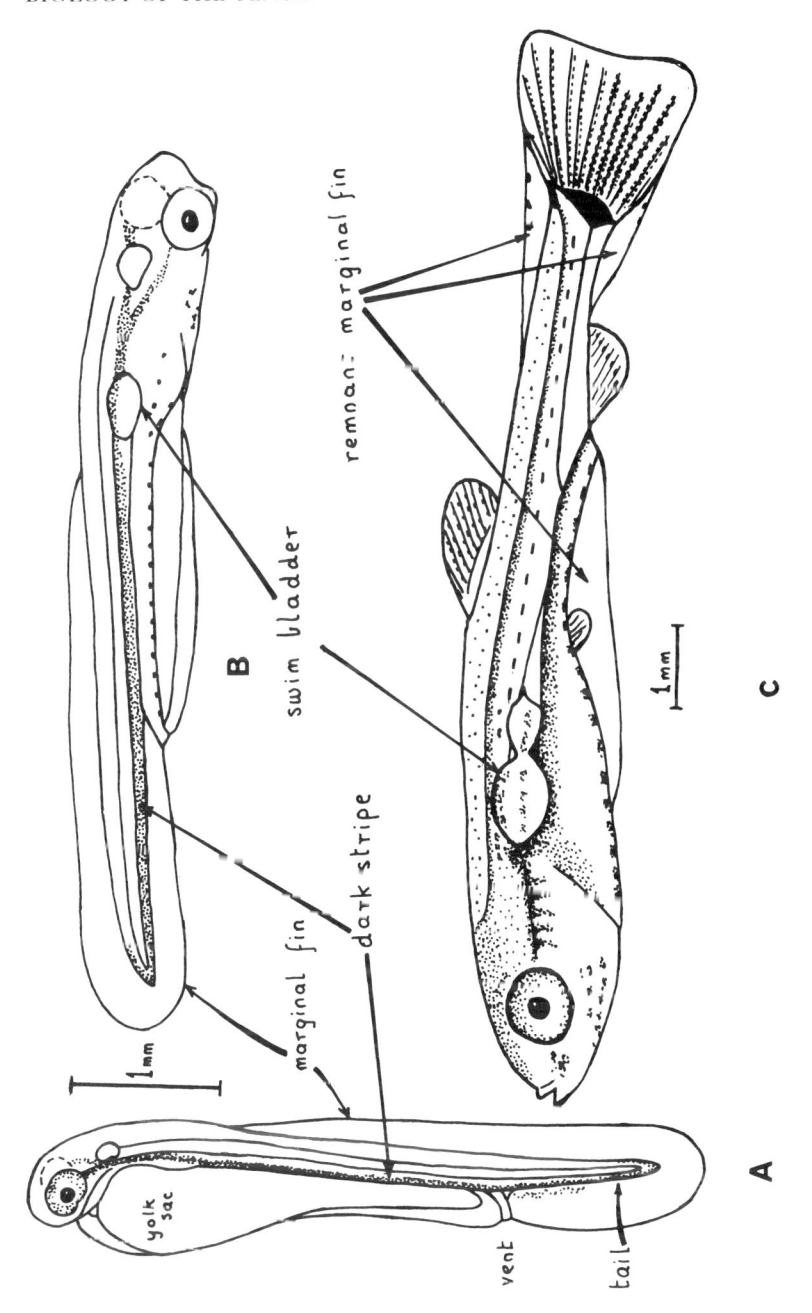

Figure 91

CHAPTER 18

# Modern Research
*Barrie Rickards & Terry Coulson*

SCIENTIFIC research into coarse fish was sadly neglected for many years, particularly in Britain, and many anglers couldn't care less anyway. But quite a few results have been beneficial to angling, not least of which is the breeding and rearing of fish, so the adverse view point of many anglers about 'scientific angling' is rather short sighted. I think they're frightened of science, if the truth be known; which is rather silly since condensed and simplified versions of scientific reports can always be made available. At the first British Angling Conference (run by the N.A.S.G.) John Ellis called for more research into tench and mentioned that in Ireland work was already going ahead under the auspices of the Inland Fisheries Trust. On this work, at places like Coosan Lough, anglers were able to participate by helping Dr Kennedy and Fred Carter, and were fortunate to have the research programme explained to them. This work was eventually published by Kennedy and Fitzmaurice (1970) in a most readable form. The only other important works relating to tench are by Vostradovsky (1965) on Russian tench, and Weatherly (1959) on Tasmanian tench.

However, the anglers have been doing quite a lot with direct implications for the tench angler. Foremost in this work has been Dr Terry Coulson, firstly in his association with the Tenchfishers' Club, and latterly in association with Eric Hodgson (of Chapter 2 fame). His work with the Tenchfishers comprised two parts: firstly the design of a reporting scheme which recorded weight, length, girth, date, bait, air and water temperature and several other factors; and secondly a rigorous mathematical analysis of the data obtained. Many anglers thought the whole thing went too far: it was too complicated, they said, and it wasn't really fishing anyway. Others objected to the use of computors to analyse the data. This last point was amply countered by John Ellis in the discussion of the above paper: quite simply, if you have collected a lot of information, why not study it in the easiest possible way.

But some interesting conclusions were reached, for example that tench of about 3lb tended to prefer 'meaty' baits (that is, worms, maggots, etc.) whereas tench above about 4lb tended to prefer 'mealy' baits (that is, bread-based baits such as flake, paste, etc.). The experience of Ray and myself bear this out. Many big tench *have* been caught on cereal baits of one sort or another. More detailed conclusions concerning *rates of catch* were as follows:

(1) In terms of catching *any* tench, regardless of size, large and small, maggots turned out clearly to be the best bait overall.
(2) Flake and paste were superior to lobworms for all except a narrow weight-range around the 3lb mark. This was particularly apparent below about 2lb – that is, lobs tend to discriminate against the smaller tench.
(3) There was little to choose between flake and paste for the smaller tench, but flake was superior to paste for the larger tench.
(4) As expected, the tench were found to become fairly steadily more difficult to catch as the season progressed from June to October.
(5) There was limited evidence that maggots performed best at the beginning and again towards the end of the season, whilst giving their poorest performance in July. Conversely, lobworms tended to give their best results in the middle part of the season. Contrary to common belief, bread-based baits appeared to give their best results early in the season, in June.
(6) The tench were caught most freely during the dawn and early morning period, less so later in the morning and a little less freely still in the evening. They were generally caught least freely during the night and afternoon.
(7) There was little to choose between the various baits considered in the afternoon and evening periods, but lobworms tended to be inferior to the rest at other times. Unexpectedly, there seemed to be no advantage for small baits in the afternoon. Equally surprising, bread-based baits performed well for the larger tench at night, when some movement in the bait might have been thought advantageous.

These conclusions, as examples, were reached from an analysis of over 900 tench taken in 1967 and 1968, and could be regarded as the equivalent of the experience of *one average angler fishing for 80 years!*

The conclusions were presented in tentative form and it was felt that much more data stretching over a greater number of years and an even wider variety of waters and conditions, were needed to conclude the work on a statistically valid basis. Nevertheless, whatever one's reservations about the conclusions, it is worth asking oneself what other angling information is based on detailed records of anything approaching 900 tench? The mathematics, and even the generous work of people like Terry Coulson, needn't concern the average angler. But the conclusions should.

At a later date the Tenchfishers opted for a simplified reporting scheme with more limited aims, and Terry, a Leicestershire man, continued his research with Eric Hodgson, the Sheffield expert. This work is progressing and may be published eventually but in the meantime Terry has kindly given us a plain language preview, but an accurate one, of his findings:

'It must be obvious to every angler that he can and does benefit from many different kinds of scientific endeavour. Obviously, useful information can be obtained from the zoologist, the natural historian, the fishery management scientist, and so on. Equally obvious benefits come from the chemist who develops and manufactures nylon monofilament and the synthetic resins used in the production of glass-fibre rods, and from the engineer who designs and makes rods, reels and other tackle items.

'It's not so obvious, perhaps, that the statistics has any particular relevance to angling. Yet there is a statistical basis which is as important in angling as in games such as dice, cards, crown-and-anchor and the like.

'Reflect, for a moment, on some of the things we tench anglers all do. We recall the amount of time we have spent fishing and the quantity and quality of the tench we have caught in the different months of the season, over the years, and we draw conclusions about how the tench prospects tend to vary during the season. We do the same sort of thing with the different times of day. We all make deductions from our experience about the relative merits of different baits and about how those merits differ from one water to another, from one time of year to another, and so on. If we try out a new water, we eventually mark it down as good, bad or indifferent on the basis of a necessarily limited number of tench that we and our friends catch from it. And so on.

'In all such things, consciously or not, we are playing the part of the statistician. It's statistics by the seat of the pants, perhaps; but it's statistics, nevertheless. On occasion, we may spot an individual fish and cast a bait under its nose; but that sort of thing is the exception for most anglers, not the rule. Usually, we are thinking in terms of probabilities, basing our tactics on ideas about what the "average tench", so to speak, is likely to be doing – and this is equally true even if our chosen tactics are to avoid the "average tench".

'Most of the anglers I know are perfectly happy to admit that they know little or nothing about the statistics and care even less. Well, there's nothing wrong in that. You don't have to be a polymer chemist to make good use of a glass-fibre rod! I'm not trying to persuade anyone to carry a statistics textbook in his tackle box; I only want to establish that there is a very real statistical basis to angling, that when an angler makes generalised deductions from his experience (that is, from the observations he has made) he is actually doing a bit of rough-and-ready, intuitive statistical analysis.

'This common-sense, intuitive approach is quite effective, of course. But if the same sort of thing were to be done on a systematic, scientific basis, there's no doubt it would be many times more effective. It simply means making angling observations in a systematic and preferably numerical form; recording instead of remembering them; and analysing them so as to extract their true inner meaning by proper statistical methods instead of intuitively. No aspect of angling has been more woefully neglected, nowhere is there such an opportunity to carry out investigations of immediate practical benefit to the angler. No one has more than scratched the surface yet.

"The great scientist, Kelvin, remarked many years ago that we don't really know much about anything until we can measure it and express our knowledge in numbers. For my money, that's as true of angling knowledge as of any other kind.

'Suppose, for example, that you are interested in some aspect of tench fishing – choice of bait, let us say. If you were to take a dozen angling books from your bookcase or from your local library, I would take considerable odds that you would find each author expressing a slightly different opinion on the matter from each of the others. I mean no discourtesy to the authors; I'm sure they are genuinely trying to convey a distillation of their experience to the reader. But unless you and I are of a very different turn of mind, you will be left wondering where the underlying truth lies and how the contradiction may be reconciled. Over what variety of waters does the author's experience range, over what times of the season and of the day? How extensively did he test the different baits in forming his opinion, were conditions and circumstances comparable, and what numbers and sizes of fish did he actually catch?

'Of course, it is not the custom to give this sort of information in angling books. Anglers simply don't collect it in the first place. But if this sort of information were given, any statistician could reconcile the differences of opinion: he would simply point out that there was nowhere near enough data to justify the conclusions presented. The principle of what the angler is trying to do is all right; but frankly, few if any anglers – even if they fished for a single species for the whole of their angling lives – could hope to accumulate enough data (that is, catch enough fish in sufficient variety of circumstances and conditions) to yield statistically significant conclusions on such complex questions as, say, choice of bait.

'That's not to say we can't make pretty shrewd common-sense judgements on the basis of what little we do know. And, thank goodness, we manage to cane a few fish out, in spite of the limitations in our knowledge. But it wouldn't have satisfied Kelvin, and there's no reason why it should satisfy us.

'The work in which I was involved with The Tenchfishers in 1967/8, referred to in the introduction to this chapter, concerned details of the capture of over 900 tench, caught by a variety of anglers from diverse waters, using the tackle, bait and tactics of their choice, at all hours of the day and night throughout the season. From this mass of information – as much as an individual tench angler might accumulate, if he recorded it, in the whole of his angling life – it was possible to reach the interesting and potentially useful conclusions already summarised. It was a novel situation – not because the conclusions were particularly unexpected, but because they were objective and quantitative. However, several more years' collection of similar data would have been necessary to establish firm conclusions on a statistically significant basis.

'Eric Hodgson and I have been carrying out a more modest exercise of this sort for the last few years. With only two anglers involved, the rate at which the data accumulates is necessarily limited, and the scope of the work is also constrained by the fact that it relates to a single water and by our decision to keep to a strict short-list of observations so as to ensure that the tasks of recording at the waterside and of analysing the data are not too burdensome. It is early days with no firm conclusions yet, but I would like to tell you a little about it, if only by way of illustration.

'Even recording only the sex, weight, length and girth of the fish and the bait, date and time of capture, provides a wealth of analytical possibilities. One of the simplest is the numerical ratio of the two sexes in the catch. It is well known that female tench grow larger than the males, so it could be of angling interest to know whether females are relatively more likely to be caught at certain times, or on particular baits. Or, again, some authorities say that the males may somewhat outnumber the females with advantage in breeding, so it could be of interest from a fishery viewpoint to find out whether the ratio of the sexes in the angler's catch gives any guidance to the longer-term breeding potential.

'Now, the overall ratio of males: females in our data so far is 77:97, the females outnumbering the males. However, after a few moments calculation, any statistician would be able to say that those two numbers do not differ significantly from equality – or, in other words, they provide no good reason for supposing that our chances of catching males and females were anything other than equal. If pressed, he will add that he is pretty confident (99% confident, to be precise) that, when we finally terminate the exercise sometime in the future, the ratio of males to females will prove to lie somewhere in the range from 0.5:1 and 1.2:1, always assuming that no progressive trend is occuring. If you say that the statistics have only shown that we have not proved anything yet – then so be it! What folly it would be to turn one's back on the statistician and merely deceive oneself about the meaning of the data.

'We also know that there have been no significant differences in the proportion of males to females from one month to another, or between evening and morning catches, though the raw data might suggest otherwise at face value. It may be that, in due course, significant differences of one sort or another will turn up – wherein lies the interest of the exercise. It will also be of value to investigate how the ratio in our angling catch compares with those found by other sampling methods – but that's another story.

'Turning to another time-of-day aspect, it is of angling interest to enquire how the prospects, in a more general sense, differ between the morning and evening periods, as revealed by comparison of our records of actual results at these times. In making this comparison, one must bear in mind that it may differ from one season to another, from one part of the season to another, from one pitch in the fishery to another, from one bait to another, and so on. When a sufficiently large number of captures have been recorded, the data may be broken down and analysed so as to show whether or not there is any underlying difference between morning and evening results and whether or not that difference varies during the season, from one bait to another, etc. It is vital, of course, that the analysis should be done by the proper statistical methods which show whether an apparent difference is significant or not, because a rule-of-thumb approach can lead to misleading conclusions.

'In our case, we are still far from the stage where a complete breakdown of data is possible, but we can go part of the way. To eliminate any differences which may occur from one bait to another, let us confine attention to results on maggots only, and state, for males and females separately, the number caught, their average size, and the spread of size around that average, for mornings and evenings. This information is straightforwardly set out in the following simple table. Two things about the table need a word of explanation. Firstly, we have represented size in terms of length instead of the more usual weight. The reason for this is that the weights of the fish fluctuate during the season due to the effects of spawning and we do not yet have enough data to permit any breakdown which would take this into account. The lengths, however, are not affected by spawning, and the length data can be treated as a whole; and we can always convert the lengths into their corresponding weights for any part of the season, if we wish, from our condition statistics (see below). Secondly, there is the intimidating statistical term "standard deviation". We will not bother with the precise definition; suffice it to say that it is merely a measure of the spread or scatter of the lengths above and below their averages (three SDs on either side of the average encompasses almost all – about 99.74% – of the data).

|  |  | *Morning* | *Evening* |
|---|---|---|---|
|  | Number of Tench | 21 | 7 |
| MALES | Average length, inches | 16.95 | 17.48 |
|  | Standard deviation | 1.21 | 0.80 |

|  | Number of Tench | 25 | 16 |
|---|---|---|---|
| FEMALES | Average length, inches | 17.93 | 17.88 |
|  | Standard deviation | 1.34 | 1.57 |

'Plainly, the males averaged a bit larger in the evenings and the females averaged a bit larger in the mornings. Conversely, the males were spread over a wider size range in the mornings and the females were spread over a wider range in the evenings. But the important question is whether, having regard to the weight of evidence, these differences are real or whether they might have arisen by chance. The appropriate statistical analysis tells us that neither the males nor the females differed significantly either in their average size or their spread around the average, as between morning and evening. So at this stage of the investigation, it is a case of "not proven" as they say in the Scottish courts, and it remains to be seen, as more data are collected, how the picture changes, whether other baits produce similar comparisons, and so on. I need hardly add that no intuitive or common-sense appraisal of these results could lead to the realisation that no significant difference has been demonstrated and that the investigation must go on.

'Finally, it's worth remarking that a comparison of average size and spread for morning and evening, whatever it may eventually turn out to be, is by no means the end of the story. Angling prospects depend not only on the average size and spread but also on the rate at which you can expect to catch them. For example, one might find that there are twice as many five pounders in the evening catch than in the morning catch; but if you cane them out twice as frequently in the mornings, expectations would be equal. To investigate this aspect, one needs to take into account some rough measure of "angling effort" to permit some sort of rate-of-catch estimate to be made. I use the infamous rod-hour for this purpose. So far as I can see, there's no even remotely reasonable alternative. Oddly enough, this concept of the rod-hour, which I devised for my own private convenience in trying to make sense out of angling data, has led to some astonishing bitter and ill-informed polemics! I hasten to add that I didn't take part in the polemics, simply because the question of whether the rod-hour provides a useful statistic is not to be settled like some political issue by debate, be it never so impassioned. It is a factual question which can only be settled by an objective statistical study, and the fact is that the statistical evidence demonstrates convincingly that the rod-hour serves its purpose admirably.

'In some zoological studies, the horse-power of trawlers has been used with success as a measure of fishing effort, so it's scarcely surprising that the angler's rod-hour turns out to be a usable measuring-stick.

'Investigations involving this rate-of-catch element have provided some fascinating insights into the behaviour of tench as revealed by the angler's results and, if they are continued, I'm confident they will eventually yield information of interest to the angler in very real and practical ways.

'Another exercise the data provide for is a running study of the "condition" of the tench. When an angler speaks of "condition", he usually has in mind things like the appearance of the fish, the regularity of scaling, colour, evidence of injury or disease, the fight the fish gave, etc. However, in scientific work, "condition" is defined quantitatively in relation solely to the weight and length of the fish. A little – a very little – is known about the condition statistics of tench in a few waters around the country and in Eire, and we have been able to show that the tench in our water compare favourably in condition with those elsewhere, and that there has been no significant change in their condition during the time we have had them under study. One water I was concerned with about 10 years ago suffered a disastrous influx of pesticides, and statistics on its tench clearly showed the catastrophic effect on this pollution on their condition. So, by keeping a watchful eye on the condition of our tench, we are able to assure ourselves that our water is not polluted in this way, and we have an effective "early warning system" which will alert us should anything amiss occur in the future.

'To give an idea of how striking such changes in condition can be, an average July female tench of $17\frac{1}{2}$in length (nose to fork) in our water weighs 3lb $4\frac{1}{4}$oz, whereas such a tench from the polluted water weighed only 2lb $7\frac{1}{2}$oz. Obviously, figures like these can turn suspicion into certainty and lead to prompt action, to find the source of pollution and put a stop to it.

'Incidentally, it is scarcely feasible to do a worthwhile investigation of condition by the old "condition coefficient" type of method, such as underlies useless monstrosities like Mona's Pike Scale and similar tables. The proper statistical method goes by the intimidating name of Regression Analysis which is the process of calculating the "best fit

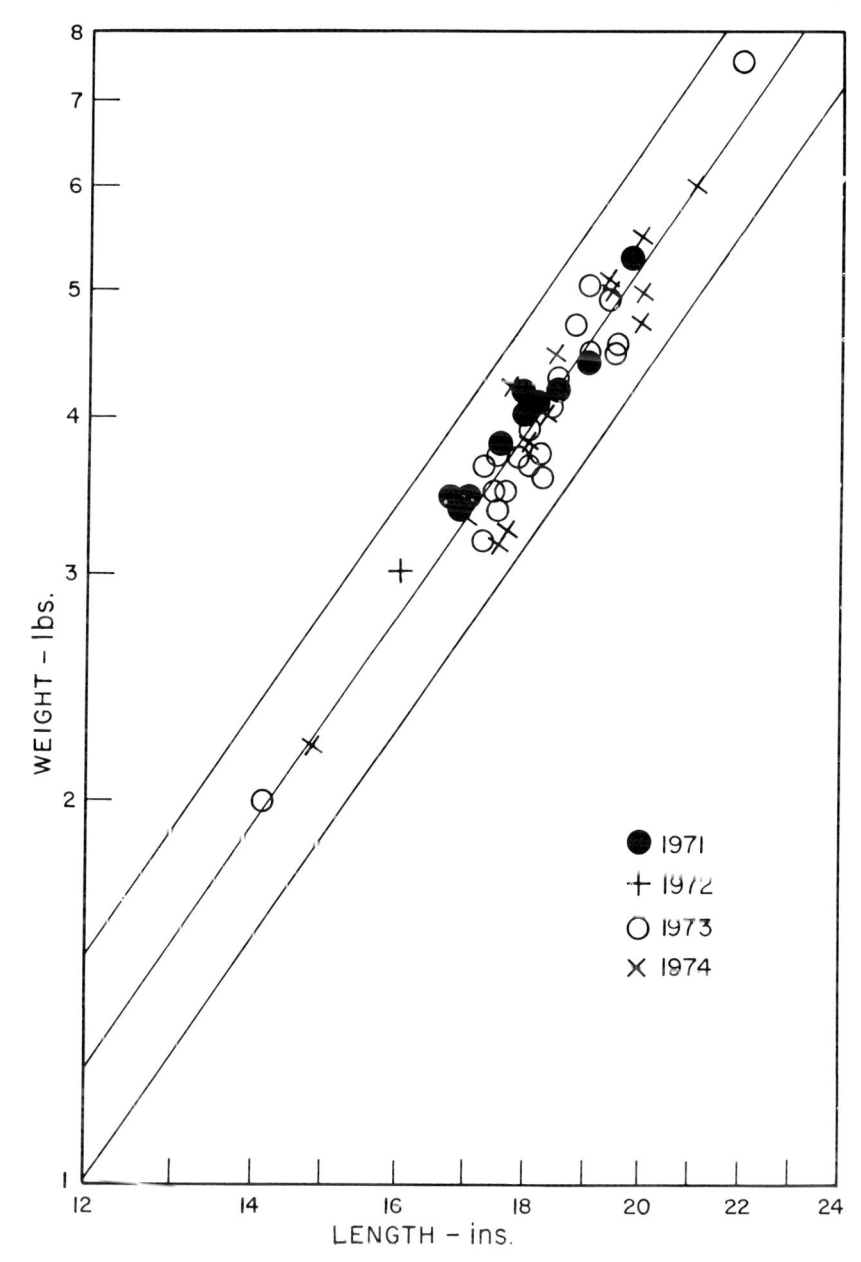

Condition regression – June female tench

line" – that is, the unique line which, running through the scattered cloud of weight/length measurements minimises the sum total of the differences (strictly, the *squares* of the differences) from the observed weight/lengths. The regression line is therefore rather like an average, with the observations scattered around it, and the method of calculation provides the means not only of describing the data succinctly, but also of testing the significance of differences from other such regressions and degrees of scatter.

'For interest, the graph illustrates the regression line for our June female tench, bracketed by limit lines which are characteristics of the scatter and are related to the standard deviation mentioned above in connection with ordinary averages. In case the impression has been gained that statistics always gives a "not significant" verdict, let me add that our data do show a significant difference in condition between males and females, and also between June and July females, both as expected.

'I hope the illustrations above will at least serve to show that statistics is a very practical matter, concerned not merely with describing numerical information compactly but also judging the strength or weakness of evidence, assessing the true significance of comparisons and guiding us away from misleading ourselves about the meaning of the data we collect. It certainly shows dramatically that it can be necessary to catch and record numerical facts about quite large numbers of fish to obtain convincing (i.e. statistically significant) evidence, even on such apparently simple questions as the ratio of males to females. More complex questions can require the capture not of a few hundreds but of many thousands of fish for there to be any prospect of a meaningful analysis.

'Nevertheless, it is by no means impossible for groups of anglers with access to the services of someone versed in the necessary elementary statistical skills, to make worth-while headway. The cumulative effect would be a contribution to angling knowledge of an unprecedented kind and of incalculable value.'

CHAPTER 19

# Tench Fishing – The Future
Barrie Rickards

THERE surely cannot be an angler in Britain who does not wish the tench and tench fishing a happy future. The sport has become as important a facet of angling as roach, or pike or trout fishing, and only north of Yorkshire does good tenching become a little thin on the ground. This last problem, whilst reflecting a *natural* northern limit on the species, could certainly be improved upon by a little judicious stocking: remember that even small and stunted tench (as small as half a pound) put up a terrific fight compared to most species, and are rarely in competion with other species in terms of food supply since roach, trout and pike do not spend their time grubbing out bloodworms from foetid black mud. One immediate step forward, therefore, would be to stock more waters with tench, particularly the more northerly waters.

Other aspects of the future for tench are, to my mind, more connected with the dangers which exist. Take, for example, the requirements of big tench or a healthy stock of good-sized tench: *mud, variation* in depth, *weed,* and at least some part of the lake with an unpenetrable mass of weeds, logs, etc. Now contrast this with the requirements of big clubs and commercial enterprises who cater largely for match anglers: easy bank access to the whole water, with no parts of the river or lake unreachable or unfishable; no snags; no weed. The two simply do not go together, and the general tendency today, in the commercial world we live in, is for more water of match-fishing type. Tench have, of course, been a good fish for matchmen at times past, but not for the big-time matchmen, more the local club match. There is some hope here, however, for even on a big match bream-cum-roach river, the tench would interfere little with match anglers' requirements except in taking too long to land perhaps. But by and large I expect tench to survive in small lakes and ponds run by small clubs, in the larger lakes and gravel pits, and perhaps also in the reservoirs with a head of coarse fish.

In many waters which *do* have inaccessible areas or snag-ridden parts, tench may go unnoticed for many years, unless the angler happens to be around at spawning time. I remember one small East Yorkshire lake near Newport where in all the years I fished it not a single tench was taken as far as I know. The water was renowned for its small 'skimmer' bream and hybrids which went up to about 1¼lb. One close season at the end of May I happened to be walking around the lake (a common occupation of mine) when I saw a huge tench, certainly in excess of 6lb, spawning in the *Potomogeton* beds. Those tench were never caught, and I left the area shortly afterwards. I'm sure I could catch them now! But it emphasizes a point for the future tench angler: a little diligence might uncover 'new' waters, small and large; and with some encouragement the Water Authorities might be persuaded to start to stock more widely with tench in order to safeguard the future of tench stocks and tench angling.

The trouble with big reservoirs is that tench fishing might be extremely difficult. For a start there are often severe restrictions on angling methods and access, as at Abberton, and yet that water has reputedly yielded tench to the traps in excess of the present record. Public access areas are not usually going to be those places beloved of tench partly because of human disturbance, and partly because the snags and weedbeds are likely to be elsewhere. So if tench men are to get anything at all out of the vast waters very good liason will be needed with those in charge. And I wonder how likely that is. It *is* possible to fish huge waters, as we have explained in this book but full access by boat is vital.

There is another slant on all this, namely that waters often go in cycles: Alder Fen Broad used to be good years ago, and it came good again in 1970 yielding tench up to around 8lb in weight. Yet others remain consistently good, such as Southill Lake in Bedfordshire which has been producing good tench from before the days when Peter Thomas, Richard Walker and, later, Frank Guttfield fished there. It pays, therefore, to watch carefully tench waters with old reputations: tench waters go in roughly ten-year cycles and things could come around again in time for you. . . .

**Comment** – *by Ray Webb*

In terms of prospects for new tench waters to be opened up in the years ahead Ireland is richly endowed indeed, one of the most exciting of all such fisheries being the hot water outflow area of the

Shannon by the Shannonbridge power station. For several years now a small number of enthusiastic anglers have been taking large numbers of bream together with the odd tench or two from this area, 100lb between two anglers at one sitting being a very distinct possibility. With the output of hot water scheduled to be increased considerably in the very near future the tench potential from that point on will soar dramatically the species being drawn into the area from long-established holding spots downstream. Once the effects of the increased flow are fully operative the results at Shannonbridge could well equal those obtained of recent seasons at the fabulously productive hot-water stream fishery at Lanesborough.

Another water that could hit the headlines in the very near future is Greggan Lough on the eastern side of Lough Ree, situated some six miles or so south-west of Ballymahon. Already established as a fishery all this water needs is the anglers, for it's literally unfished even in these days when top-class tench fishing is so eagerly sought after. For many years the longliners after eels were taking 6lb tench regularly by accident and returning them as of no commercial value and with this technique illegal for the past six years or more the fishery has been left severely alone, undisturbed by anglers, boatmen or even swimmers. Present as a witness at a sample netting of the water recently I weighed and photographed specimens up to 6lb 6oz, a really impressive haul and with clear, pure limestone water, a shallow shelf covered with *Phragmites* terminating in bullrushes and lily pads as the depth drops rapidly away to 12 foot or more plus stream connection with the main body of Lough Ree itself this fishery could well turn out to be a second Garnafailagh, given a man of Fred Carter's initiative and organising ability in the immediate vicinity that is.

Down in County Clare too, are a number of fisheries holding sizeable populations of tench some of which are well into the specimen weight class, the most promising of the many good prospects in the area being the series of interconnected waters known as the Gullaun Chain of Lakes. Way back in 1969 one of these waters, the White Stones Lake, sprang into prominence by putting several bream on the Specimen Fish List, the biggest of which went 9lb 10oz, a return that was impressive enough to have all serious big fish men jotting the fishery down on the list of waters to be visited in the immediate future. What wasn't so commonly known however was the fact that two tench over 6lb were also included in amongst those bream but due to inexperience, the local officials, Paddy White and Tim Quealy of Tulla, didn't record them officially assuming that the specimen weight for tench would be 7lb 8oz as for bream. Having had a close look at the waters myself, taking six fine tench over the 5lb mark without too much trouble, I'm firmly convinced that the tench potential of this area is absolutely tremendous every bit as good as Garnafailagh was in its heyday way back in 1964, if not even better.

It follows from our remarks in earlier chapters that tench fishing is on an all-time high, with good quality fish being caught almost nationwide and huge fish from several waters. Without doubt there are waters with big tench whose presence is, as yet, unsuspected. But we are long overdue a bad winter! This seems to me to be the cloud on the horizon. A freeze-up in excess of five or six weeks could cause severe winterkill, and the main sufferers would surely be the very large fish. It is possible that some of the relatively modern, deep, gravel pits will survive winterkill better than those waters that traditionally hold tench, namely shallow muddy lakes: if this happens then fish in the 12-14lb bracket could be with us by 1988/89, or earlier if the winters continue as mild as in the early 1980s. It is strange that interest in tench is not *exactly* related to the quality of fish being caught. In the 1960s and 1970s, there was an intense interest in the problems posed by big tench. During the late 1970s and very recently many have fished for tench, with success, but it has been part of a widely based angling success, to whit specimen hunting for carp, bream, chub, barbel, catfish and other species. But during this period specialist clubs and groups interested in tench as *the* quarry seem to have declined. Has the challenge lessened? Is it the problems posed, not the catching, that really matters? Or has serious winterkill held off so long that big bream and carp are a counterattraction? Sometimes, on a summer's morning, I can envisage no challenge to the magnetic draw of tench: I do hope that the future remains as rosy as the present.

# References

Bartles, B. 1973 Chapter 9 in *Coarse Fishing*. A. & C. Black. London.
BB 1955 (= Denys Watkins-Pitchford). *The Fisherman's Bedside Book* 2nd Ed. Eyre & Spottiswoode.
Berg, L. S. 1964 Freshwater Fishes of the U.S.S.R. and Adjacent Countries. 2, 4th ed. *Guide to the fauna of the U.S.S.R.* no. 29. Jerusalem: Israel Program for Scientific Translations.
Church, B. 1974 *Catch More Tench.* Wolfe Publishing Ltd. London.
Ellis, J. 1957. Chapter 16 in *Coarse Fishing with the Experts.* Norman, J., (ed.). Allen & Unwin Ltd. London.
Ellis, J. 1970 Tench Fishing. *Proc. 1st Brit. Angling Conf.* 11-21.
Guttfield, F. 1964. *In Search of Big Fish.* Angling Times, E.M.Art & Publishing. Peterborough.
Guttfield, F. 1967. Days after Tench in *Fishing as we find it;* Wheat, P., (ed.), Warne & Co Ltd. London, New York.
Holčik, J., Mihalik, J., & Maly, J. 1968 *Freshwater Fishes.* Spring Books.
Inland Fisheries Trust Inc. undated *Irish Sport Fishes, a guide to their identification.*
Kennedy, M. & Fitzmaurice, P. 1970. The Biology of the tench *Tinca tinca* (L.) in Irish waters. *Proc. roy Irish Acad.,* B, 69, no. 3, 31-82.
Jones, H. W. & Tombleson, P. H. 1964. *Know your fish.* Angling Times.
Marshall-Hardy, E. 1973. Chapter 17, Tinca tinca the tench, in *Angling Ways,* revised ed., Cacutt, L. Barrie & Jenkins. London.
Mount, H. 1969 Tench in *Mr Crabtree's Guide to Good Fishing Tackle.* I.P.C. Newspapers Ltd.
Pye, D. 1964 Chapter 4, in *The Way I Fish.* Angling Times Kingfisher Book, E.M. Art & Publishing. Peterborough.

Rickards, B. 1970. Chapter 2, Irish Fishing: Pike and Tench in *The Angler's Year*, Wheat, P., (ed.). Pelham Books. London.

Taylor, F. J. 1961 Chapter 9 in *Favourite Swims and Still Water Pitches.* Macgibbon & Kee. London.

Taylor, F. J. 1962 Chapter 5 Tench *in Angling in Earnest.* Macgibbon & Kee. London.

Taylor, F. J. 1971. Tench in *The Richard Walker Angling Library*, Walker, R. S. (ed.). Macdonald. London.

Vostradovsky, J. 1965. Certain biological facts and experiences gained with the catching of tench in the Jesenice and Lipno Valley water reservoirs. *Bul. VUR Vodnany* 3, 3-11.

Walker, R. S. 1955. *Stillwater Angling.* Macgibbon & Kee. London.

Walker, R. S. 1959. Chapter 3, Tench and the 'Lift' method, in *Walker's Pitch.* Allen & Unwin Ltd. London.

Watkins-Pitchford, see BB.

Weatherley, A. H. 1959. Some features of the biology of the tench *Tinca tinca* (Linnaeus) in Tasmania. *J. Anim: Ecol.,* 28, 73-87.

Weatheriey, A. H. 1961. Notes on distribution, taxonomy, and behaviour of *Tinca tinca* (L.) in Tasmania. *Ann. mag. nat. hist.* 13, 713-719.

Wells, A. L. The Tench in *The Observer's Book of Freshwater Fishes of the British Isles.* Warne & Co. Ltd. London, New York.

Wheat, P. 1971. Tench Fishing Days in *The Angler's Year No. 2*, Wheat, P., (ed.). Pelham Books. London.

Wheeler, A. 1969. *The Fishes of the British Isles and North West Europe.* Macmillan.

Went, A. E. J. 1966. The status of various species of coarse fish in Irish Waters. *Proc. 2nd Brit. Coarse Fish Conf.* 102-108.